A
Harmony
of the
Four Gospels

PALESTINE
IN THE TIME OF CHRIST

English Miles
0 5 10   20   30

SYRIA

PHŒNICIA

MEDITERRANEAN SEA

•Damascus

•Mt. Hermon

Sidon•

Tyre•

•Cæsarea Philippi

TETRARCHY

ITURÆA

OF PHILIP

TRACHONITIS

GALILEE

Chorazin•
Capernaum•
Bethsaida•   •Bethsaida
Tiberias•   Sea
           of
         Galilee

Cana•
Nazareth•

•Gerasenes

TETRARCHY

•Naln

DECAPOLIS

•Gadara

SAMARIA

•Ænon

River Jordan

OF HEROD ANTIPAS

•Sychar

PERÆA

Joppa•

TETRARCHY OF ARCHELAUS AFTERWARDS THE ROMAN PROVINCE OF JUDÆA

•Ephraim

Jericho•

Emmaus•   •Mt. of
JERUSALEM■   Olives
Bethlehem•   •Bethany

JUDÆA

The Dead Sea

•Machærus

ARABIA

•Hebron

•Kerioth

A
Harmony
of the
Four Gospels

The New International Version

Orville E. Daniel

BAKER BOOK HOUSE
Grand Rapids, Michigan 49516

ISBN: 0-8010-2974-0

Reprinted 1987 by
Baker Book House
with permission of copyright owner

Printed in the United States of America

To

BLANCHE

who has been my priceless
companion for more than fifty years

FOREWORD

This book is a harmony of the Gospels as opposed to a Synopsis or a Gospel Parallel.

A Gospel Parallel arranges Matthew, Mark and Luke and sometimes John in parallel columns, to show the student where the Gospels agree and disagree. Sometimes noncanonical parallels also are included. Gospel Parallels have become prerequisite research tools for scholars using modern methods of historical criticism.

A Synopsis is not designed to show where the Gospels agree or disagree. It is intended to enable the reader to follow the words and deeds of Jesus' life recorded in the four Gospels without the distraction of having to turn back and forth in the pages of the New Testament. A Synopsis is a connected record of the life of Christ that unites passages from the four Gospels into one in the probable chronological order. The life of Christ is thus presented in a connected and orderly sequence.

Harmonies of the Gospels that have been published look more like Gospel Parallels. The accounts are arranged in parallel columns, and the reader must scan each column to follow the story line.

The great advantage of Dr. Daniel's "Interwoven Harmony of the Gospels" is that the story line is in bold print. In this way he has provided us with a real harmony of the Gospels. The Gospel passages are still printed in a parallel arrangement so that the student who so desires may study them; but the bold face text presents a smooth, connected account through the four Gospels.

Devoted Bible students are indebted to Dr. Daniel for providing them with this helpful aid for studying and understanding the life of our Lord.

After graduating in Arts and Theology from McMaster University in Ontario, Canada, the author took further studies (Ph. D. in New Testament Interpretation) at the Southern Baptist Theological Seminary in Louisville, Kentucky. He then served for nineteen years as a missionary in India; subsequently he became General Secretary of the Canadian Baptist Overseas Mission Board, from which executive office he retired in 1970.

During his career, Dr. Daniel has written a number of books, some in English and several in the Telugu language of India.

In the Preface to this book he has provided more adequate explanatory information.

> David E. Garland,
> Associate Professor of New Testament,
> The Southern Baptist Theological Seminary

PREFACE

Bible students must face the fact that the dates and the order of events pertaining to Christ's earthly ministry cannot be entirely determined with indisputable accuracy. For this reason some New Testament scholars decry any attempt to put together in historical sequence the occurrences recorded in the Gospels. Others would limit any such arrangement to happenings described in the Synoptic Gospels (Matthew, Mark and Luke), because John's Gospel is so unlike the other three.

This Harmony bespeaks the author's conviction that there is real value in arranging the records of the New Testament writers so as to produce a combined account of the life of Christ, however historically tentative in detail it may be. Moreover, John's Gospel is included because the compiler of this Harmony agrees with the opinion expressed by a considerable number of Biblical scholars that the narrative in the fourth Gospel does not contradict but rather supplements the Synoptic accounts.

So-called Harmonies of the Gospels, however, which have appeared hitherto in various New Testament translations have presented the Gospels paralleled, but not really harmonized. This book is an attempt not merely to parallel but actually to harmonize the Gospels, by drawing out from the paralleled narratives a complete connected account of the life of Christ, free from repetition and yet comprising every detail given to us by the inspired writers. For this purpose two sizes and styles of type have been used, and **the complete connected story is obtained by simply following the bold face type back and forth from column to column down the page.**

At the same time, the use of two styles of type enables the reader to see at a glance which of the Gospels presents items of information not included in other Gospels. In the few instances where two or more Gospels present parallel material differing not merely in quantity but in substance, this fact has been pointed out; and explanations have been suggested in foot-notes for some of the seeming contradictions.

Care has also been taken in this Harmony so that the important benefits to be derived from the special arrangement of material may be obtained with a minimum of conscious effort on the part of the reader; thus one's mind is left free to concentrate upon the developing story itself. For example, even when a section of the story is recorded by only one Gospel writer, the section begins in single column, so that one may be instantly aware of which Gospel is being read. Again, parallel passages have been placed in exact juxtaposition as far as possible, to facilitate comparison. Furthermore, the Logia sections (as they are called) have been specially indicated by the use of double columns.

In 1937, while serving as a missionary in India, the author published a book of this sort, entitled "A Combined Harmony of the Gospels". It was enthusiastically received and speedily circulated among pastors and others in that country; a few copies found their way to Great Britain, Canada and the U.S.A. But it has long since been out of print.

At last, in response to promptings from various sources, this modified reproduction has been undertaken. Modifications include a slightly different title and a number of improvements in the wording of section headings and the rearrangement of a few scripture passages.

It would be impossible to mention the names of all persons to whom I am indebted. I have made full use of the invaluable work done by many New Testament scholars. Special mention, however, should be made of the late Dr. A. T. Robertson, one of my revered mentors, whose numerous books, including more than a dozen related to the life of Christ, are still widely read. My particular gratitude should be expressed to several contemporary seminary professors and pastors, in Canada and the U.S.A., who have encouraged me to proceed with the production of this Harmony. Among them I am especially thankful to Dr. David Garland, Dr. Roy Bell, Rev. Robert Muse and Dr. Allison Trites, whose written comments appear, in whole or in part, inside this book or elsewhere.

Sincere thanks are due also to the Zondervan Publishing House, by whose kind permission I have used the text of their New International Version of the Gospels, a popular modern translation of the early Greek New Testament manuscripts.

Orville E. Daniel

TABLE OF CONTENTS

Table of Contents

Table of Contents

PART IX — CHRIST'S PEREAN MINISTRY

A. THE FIRST PEREAN TOUR

Table of Contents

Table of Contents

Table of Contents

TABLE FOR FINDING VERSES OF SCRIPTURE IN THE HARMONY

MATTHEW

MARK

LUKE

JOHN

A
Harmony
of the
Four Gospels

PART I

INTRODUCTION

1. THE DEDICATION OF LUKE'S GOSPEL

Luke 1:1-4

> 1 Many have un-
> dertaken to draw
> up an account of

the things that have been fulfilled^a among us, 2 just as they were handed down to us by those who from the first were eyewitnesses and servants of the word. 3 Therefore, since I myself have carefully investigated everything from the beginning, it seemed good also to me to write an orderly account for you, most excellent Theophilus, 4 so that you may know the certainty of the things you have been taught.

^aOr "surely believed".

2. THE PRE-INCARNATE EXISTENCE OF CHRIST
HIS DIVINE NATURE AND MISSION

John 1:1-5,9-13

> 1 In the begin-
> ning was the
> Word, and the

Word was with God, and the Word was God. 2 He was with God in the beginning.
3 Through him all things were made; without him nothing was made that has been made. 4 In him was life, and that life was the light of men. 5 The light shines in the darkness, and the darkness has not extinguished it.*
9 The true light that gives light to every man was coming into the

---

*The NIV reads: "but the darkness has not *understood* it", and a footnote suggests "overcome" as an alternative translation. The Greek verb has more than one meaning. Many translators concur with the opinion of Thayer and other authorities that "overcome" or a synonym is preferable in John 1:5.

1

John 1

| | | world.[a] 10 He was in the world, and
though the world was made through him, the world did not recognize him.
11 He came to that which was his own, but his own did not receive him.
12 Yet to all who received him, to those who believed in his name, he gave
the right to become children of God — 13 children born not of natural
descent,[b] nor of human decision or a husband's will, but born of God.

[a]Or "This was the true light that gives light to every man who comes
into the world". [b]Greek, "of bloods".

3. THE HUMAN ANCESTRY OF JESUS

Matt. 1:1-17   Luke 3:23b-38

1 A record of
the genealogy of
Jesus Christ the
son of David, the son of Abraham: 2 Abraham was the father of Isaac,
Isaac the father of Jacob,   Jacob the father of Judah and his brothers,
3 Judah the father of Perez and Zerah, whose mother was Tamar, Perez
the father of Hezron, Hezron the father of Ram, 4 Ram the father of
Amminadab, Amminadab the father of Nahshon, Nahshon the father of
Salmon, 5 Salmon the father of Boaz, whose mother was Rahab, Boaz
the father of Obed, whose mother was Ruth, Obed the father of Jesse,
6 and Jesse the father of King David.

David was the father of Solomon, whose mother had been Uriah's wife,
7 Solomon the father of Rehoboam, Rehoboam the father of Abijah,
Abijah the father of Asa, 8 Asa the father of Jehoshaphat, Jehoshaphat
the father of Joram, Joram the father of Uzziah, 9 Uzziah the father of
Jotham, Jotham the father of Ahaz, Ahaz the father of Hezekiah,
10 Hezekiah the father of Manasseh, Manasseh the father of Amon,
Amon the father of Josiah, 11 and Josiah the father of Jeconiah[a] and
his brothers at the time of the exile to Babylon.

12 After the exile to Babylon: Jeconiah was the father of Shealtiel,
Shealtiel the father of Zerubbabel, 13 Zerubbabel the father of Abiud,
Abiud the father of Eliakim, Eliakim the father of Azor, 14 Azor the
father of Zadok, Zadok the father of Akim, Akim the father of Eliud,
15 Eliud the father of Eleazar, Eleazar the father of Matthan, Matthan
the father of Jacob, 16 and Jacob the father of Joseph, the husband of
Mary, of whom was born Jesus, who is called Christ.

17 Thus there were fourteen generations in all from Abraham to David,
fourteen from David to the exile to Babylon, and fourteen from the exile to the Christ.[b]

23b He was the
son, so it was
thought, of Jo-

2

Luke 3

| seph, the son of |
| Heli,* 24 the son |

of Matthat, the son of Levi, the son of Melki, the son of Jannai, the son of Joseph, 25 the son of Mattathias, the son of Amos, the son of Nahum, the son of Esli, the son of Naggai, 26 the son of Maath, the son of Mattathias, the son of Semein, the son of Josech, the son of Joda, 27 the son of Joanan, the son of Rhesa, the son of Zerubbabel, the son of Shealtiel, the son of Neri, 28 the son of Melki, the son of Addi, the son of Cosam, the son of Elmadam, the son of Er, 29 the son of Joshua, the son of Eliezer, the son of Jorim, the son of Matthat, the son of Levi, 30 the son of Simeon, the son of Judah, the son of Joseph, the son of Jonam, the son of Eliakim, 31 the son of Melea, the son of Menna, the son of Mattatha, the son of Nathan, the son of David, 32 the son of Jesse, the son of Obed, the son of Boaz, the son of Salmon,[c] the son of Nahshon, 33 the son of Amminadab, the son of Ram,[d] the son of Hezron, the son of Perez, the son of Judah, 34 the son of Jacob, the son of Isaac, the son of Abraham, the son of Terah, the son of Nahor, 35 the son of Serug, the son of Reu, the son of Peleg, the son of Eber, the son of Shelah, 36 the son of Cainan, the son of Arphaxad, the son of Shem, the son of Noah, the son of Lamech, 37 the son of Methuselah, the son of Enoch, the son of Jared, the son of Mahalaleel, the son of Cainan, 38 the son of Enos, the son of Seth, the son of Adam, the son of God.

[a]That is, Jehoiachin; also in verse 12. [b]Or, "Messiah". "The Christ" (Greek) and "the Messiah" (Hebrew) both mean "the Anointed One". [c]In some early manuscripts, "Sala". [d]In some manuscripts, "Amminadab, the son of Admin, the son of Arni"; other manuscripts vary widely.

---

*We are told in Matthew 1:16 that Joseph was the son of Jacob. Various suggestions have been offered to explain the differences between the two genealogies. Many scholars are of the opinion that Matthew records the legal ancestry of Jesus through Joseph, while Luke records the actual ancestry through Mary. If so, Joseph was the *son-in-law* of Heli.

PART II

JOHN THE BAPTIST AND JESUS
FROM BIRTH TO MANHOOD

B.C. 6 TO A.D. 8*

4. THE ANGEL'S INTIMATION TO ZECHARIAH
OF JOHN THE BAPTIST'S BIRTH

The temple, Jerusalem; B.C. 6

Luke 1:5-25

5 In the time of Herod king of Judea there was a priest named Zechariah, who belonged to the priestly division of Abijah; his wife Elizabeth was also a descendant of Aaron. 6 Both of them were upright in the sight of God, observing all the Lord's commandments and regulations blamelessly. 7 But they had no children, because Elizabeth was barren; and they were both well along in years.

8 Once when Zechariah's division was on duty and he was serving as priest before God, 9 he was chosen by lot, according to the custom of the priesthood, to go into the temple of the Lord and burn incense. 10 And when the time for the burning of incense came, all the assembled worshipers were praying outside.

11 Then an angel of the Lord appeared to him, standing at the right side of the altar of incense. 12 When Zechariah saw him, he was startled and was gripped with fear. 13 But the angel said to him: "Do not be afraid, Zechariah; your prayer has been heard. Your wife Elizabeth will bear you a son, and you are to give him the name John. 14 He will be a joy and delight to you, and many will rejoice because of his birth, 15 for he will be great in the sight of the Lord. He is never to take wine or other fermented drink, and he will be filled with the Holy Spirit even from birth.[a] 16 Many of the people of Israel will he bring back to the Lord their God. 17 And he will go on before the Lord, in the spirit and power of Elijah, to turn the hearts of the fathers to their children and the disobedient to the

---

*Dates in this book are only probable dates, derived from references such as Matt. 2:19 (Herod died in B.C. 4), Luke 3:23, etc.

4

Luke 1

| wisdom of the |
| righteous — to |

make ready a people prepared for the Lord."

18 Zechariah asked the angel, "How can I be sure of this? I am an old man and my wife is well along in years."

19 The angel answered, "I am Gabriel. I stand in the presence of God, and I have been sent to speak to you and to tell you this good news. 20 And now you will be silent and not able to speak until the day this happens, because you did not believe my words, which will come true at their proper time."

21 Meanwhile, the people were waiting for Zechariah and wondering why he stayed so long in the temple. 22 When he came out, he could not speak to them. They realized he had seen a vision in the temple, for he kept making signs to them but remained unable to speak.

23 When his time of service was completed, he returned home. 24 After this his wife Elizabeth became pregnant and for five months remained in seclusion. 25 "The Lord has done this for me," she said. "In these days he has shown his favor and taken away my disgrace among the people."

a Or "from his mother's womb".

5. THE ANGEL'S REASSURING MESSAGE TO MARY CONCERNING THE BIRTH OF JESUS

Nazareth; the end of B.C. 6 or beginning of B.C. 5

Luke 1:26-38

| 26 In the sixth |
| month, God sent |
| the angel Gabriel |

to Nazareth, a town in Galilee, 27 to a virgin pledged to be married to a man named Joseph, a descendant of David. The virgin's name was Mary. 28 The angel went to her and said, "Greetings, you who are highly favored! The Lord is with you."

29 Mary was greatly troubled at his words and wondered what kind of greeting this might be. 30 But the angel said to her, "Do not be afraid, Mary, you have found favor with God. 31 You will be with child and give birth to a son, and you are to give him the name Jesus. 32 He will be great and will be called the Son of the Most High. The Lord God will give him the throne of his father David, 33 and he will reign over the house of Jacob forever; his kingdom will never end."

34 "How will this be," Mary asked the angel, "since I am a virgin?"

35 The angel answered, "The Holy Spirit will come upon you, and the power of the Most High will overshadow you. So the holy one to be born will be called a the Son of God. 36 Even Elizabeth your relative is going to have a child in her old age, and she who was said to be barren is in her sixth month. 37 For nothing is impossible with God."

5

Luke 1

| | 38 "I am the |
| | Lord's servant," |

Mary answered. "May it be to me as you have said." Then the angel left her.

aOr, "So the child to be born will be called holy."

6. MARY'S VISIT TO ELIZABETH

Judea; the beginning of B.C. 5

Luke 1:39-56

	39 At that time
	Mary got ready
	and hurried to a

town in the hill country of Judah, 40 where she entered Zechariah's home and greeted Elizabeth. 41 When Elizabeth heard Mary's greeting, the baby leaped in her womb, and Elizabeth was filled with the Holy Spirit. 42 In a loud voice she exclaimed: "Blessed are you among women, and blessed is the child you will bear! 43 But why am I so favored, that the mother of my Lord should come to me? 44 As soon as the sound of your greeting reached my ears, the baby in my womb leaped for joy. 45 Blessed is she who has believed that what the Lord has said to her will be accomplished!"
46 And Mary said:
  "My soul praises the Lord
  47 and my spirit rejoices in God my Savior,
  48 for he has been mindful of the humble state of his servant.
    From now on all generations will call me blessed,
  49 for the Mighty One has done great things for me —
    holy is his name.
  50 His mercy extends to those who fear him,
    from generation to generation.
  51 He has performed mighty deeds with his arm;
    he has scattered those who are proud in their inmost thoughts.
  52 He has brought down rulers from their thrones
    but has lifted up the humble.
  53 He has filled the hungry with good things
    but has sent the rich away empty.
  54 He has helped his servant Israel,
    remembering to be merciful
  55 to Abraham and his descendants forever,
    even as he said to our fathers."
56 Mary stayed with Elizabeth for about three months and then returned home.

7. THE BIRTH OF JOHN THE BAPTIST

Judea; the spring of B.C. 5

Luke 1:57-79

| 57 When it was
| time for Eliza-
| beth to have her

baby, she gave birth to a son. 58 Her neighbors and relatives heard that the Lord had shown her great mercy, and they shared her joy.

59 On the eighth day they came to circumcise the child, and they were going to name him after his father Zechariah, 60 but his mother spoke up and said, "No! He is to be called John."

61 They said to her, "There is no one among your relatives who has that name."

62 Then they made signs to his father, to find out what he would like to name the child. 63 He asked for a writing tablet, and to everyone's astonishment he wrote, "His name is John." 64 Immediately his mouth was opened and his tongue was loosed, and he began to speak, praising God. 65 The neighbors were all filled with awe, and throughout the hill country of Judea people were talking about all these things. 66 Everyone who heard this wondered about it, asking, "What then is this child going to be?" For the Lord's hand was with him.

67 His father Zechariah was filled with the Holy Spirit and prophesied:

68 "Praise be to the Lord, the God of Israel,
   because he has come and has redeemed his people.
69 He has raised up a horn [a] of salvation for us
   in the house of his servant David
70 (as he said through his holy prophets of long ago),
71 salvation from our enemies and from the hand of all who hate us —
72 to show mercy to our fathers
   and to remember his holy covenant,
73 the oath he swore to our father Abraham:
74 to rescue us from the hand of our enemies,
   and to enable us to serve him without fear
75 in holiness and righteousness before him all our days.
76 And you, my child, will be called a prophet of the Most High;
   for you will go on before the Lord to prepare the way for him,
77 to give his people the knowledge of salvation
   through the forgiveness of their sins,
78 because of the tender mercy of our God,
   by which the rising sun will come to us from heaven
79 to shine on those living in darkness and in the shadow of death,
   to guide our feet into the path of peace."

[a] "Horn" here symbolizes strength.

8. THE ANGEL'S EXPLANATORY ADVICE TO JOSEPH ABOUT THE SAVIOR'S APPROACHING BIRTH

Nazareth; B.C. 5

Matt. 1:18-25a

18 This is how the birth of Jesus Christ came about. His mother Mary was pledged to be married to Joseph, but before they came together, she was found to be with child through the Holy Spirit. 19 Because Joseph her husband was a righteous man and did not want to expose her to public disgrace, he had in mind to divorce her quietly.

20 But after he had considered this, an angel of the Lord appeared to him in a dream and said, "Joseph son of David, do not be afraid to take Mary home as your wife, because what is conceived in her is from the Holy Spirit. 21 She will give birth to a son, and you are to give him the name Jesus,[a] because he will save his people from their sins."

22 All this took place to fulfill what the Lord had said through the prophet: 23 "The virgin will be with child and will give birth to a son, and they will call him Immanuel" — which means, "God with us."

24 When Joseph woke up, he did what the angel of the Lord had commanded him and took Mary home as his wife. 25 But he had no union with her until she gave birth to a son.

[a] "Jesus" is the Greek form of "Joshua", which means "the Lord saves".

9. THE BIRTH OF JESUS

Bethlehem; the autumn of B.C. 5

Luke 2:1-7   John 1:14a

1 In those days Caesar Augustus issued a decree that a census should be taken of the entire Roman world. 2 (This was the first census that took place while Quirinius was governor of Syria.)* 3 And everyone went to his own town to register.

---

*Augustus inaugurated a periodical census, to be taken every fourteen years from B.C. 8 on. The second census occurred in A.D. 6 (Acts 5:37). Quirinius was twice governor of Syria; the first time was during B.C. 10-7. But such an early date for the birth of Jesus is impossible in the light of other chronological references in the Gospels. So we must assume that there was some delay in carrying out the first census in Palestine.

Luke 2   John 1

| | 4 So Joseph also |
| | went up from the |

town of Nazareth in Galilee to Judea, to Bethlehem the town of David, because he belonged to the house and line of David. 5 He went there to register with Mary, who was pledged to be married to him and was expecting a child. 6 While they were there, the time came for the baby to be born, 7 and she gave birth to her firstborn, a son. She wrapped him in

cloths and placed
him in a manger,
because there
was no room for
them in the inn.

14 So* the Word
became flesh and
lived for a while
among us.

10. THE ANGELIC ANNOUNCEMENT TO THE SHEPHERDS AND THEIR RESPONSE

Near Bethlehem

Luke 2:8-20

8 And there
were shepherds
living out in the

fields nearby, keeping watch over their flocks at night. 9 An angel of the Lord appeared to them, and the glory of the Lord shone around them, and they were terrified. 10 But the angel said to them, "Do not be afraid. I bring you good news of great joy that will be for all the people. 11 Today in the town of David a Savior has been born to you; he is Christ the Lord. 12 This will be a sign to you: You will find a baby wrapped in cloths and lying in a manger."

13 Suddenly a great company of the heavenly host appeared with the angel, praising God and saying,

14 "Glory to God in the highest,
and on earth peace to men on whom his favor rests."

15 When the angels had left them and gone into heaven, the shepherds said to one another, "Let's go to Bethlehem and see this thing that has happened, which the Lord has told us about."

16 So they hurried off and found Mary and Joseph, and the baby, who

---

*In the original Greek the conjunction is "And"; the NIV omits it. "So" is inserted here to make the connected narrative run more smoothly.

9

Luke 2

| was lying in the |
| manger. 17 When |

they had seen him, they spread the word concerning what had been told them about this child, 18 and all who heard it were amazed at what the shepherds said to them. 19 But Mary treasured up all these things and pondered them in her heart. 20 The shepherds returned, glorifying and praising God for all the things they had heard and seen, which were just as they had been told.

11. THE CIRCUMCISION AND NAMING OF JESUS

Eight days after birth

Matt. 1:25b   Luke 2:21

25b And he gave him the name Jesus.

21 On the eighth day, when it was time to circumcise him, he was named Jesus, the name the angel had given him before he had been conceived.

12. THE PRESENTATION OF THE BABY JESUS IN THE TEMPLE

Jerusalem; forty days after birth

Luke 2:22-39a

22 When the time of their purification ac-

cording to the Law of Moses had been completed, Joseph and Mary took him to Jerusalem to present him to the Lord 23 (as it is written in the Law of the Lord, "Every firstborn male is to be consecrated to the Lord"), 24 and to offer a sacrifice in keeping with what is said in the Law of the Lord: "a pair of doves or two young pigeons."

25 Now there was a man in Jerusalem called Simeon, who was righteous and devout. He was waiting for the consolation of Israel, and the Holy Spirit was upon him. 26 It had been revealed to him by the Holy Spirit that he would not die before he had seen the Lord's Christ. 27 Moved by the Spirit, he went into the temple courts. When the parents brought in the child Jesus to do for him what the custom of the Law required,

10

Luke 2

| 28 Simeon took |
| him in his arms |

and praised God, saying:

29 "Sovereign Lord, as you have promised,
    you now dismiss [a] your servant in peace.
30 For my eyes have seen your salvation,
31 which you have prepared in the sight of all people,
32 a light for revelation to the Gentiles
    and for glory to your people Israel."

33 The child's father and mother marveled at what was said about him. 34 Then Simeon blessed them and said to Mary, his mother: "This child is destined to cause the falling and rising of many in Israel, and to be a sign that will be spoken against, 35 so that the thoughts of many hearts will be revealed. And a sword will pierce your own soul too."

36 There was also a prophetess, Anna, the daughter of Phanuel, of the tribe of Asher. She was very old; she had lived with her husband seven years after her marriage, 37 and then was a widow until she was eighty-four.[b] She never left the temple but worshiped night and day, fasting and praying. 38 Coming up to them at that very moment, she gave thanks to God and spoke about the child to all who were looking forward to the redemption of Jerusalem.

39 When Joseph and Mary had done everything required by the Law of the Lord, they returned...

[a]Or "promised, now dismiss".   [b]Or "widow for eighty-four years".

13. THE VISIT OF THE WISE MEN

Matt. 2:1-12

| 1 After Jesus |
| was born in Beth- |
| lehem in Judea, |

during the time of King Herod, Magi [a] from the east came to Jerusalem 2 and asked, "Where is the one who has been born king of the Jews? We saw his star in the east [b] and have come to worship him."

3 When King Herod heard this he was disturbed, and all Jerusalem with him. 4 When he had called together all the people's chief priests and teachers of the law, he asked them where the Christ [c] was to be born. 5 "In Bethlehem in Judea," they replied, "for this is what the prophet has written:

6 " 'But you, Bethlehem, in the land of Judah,
    are by no means least among the rulers of Judah;
    for out of you will come a ruler
    who will be the shepherd of my people Israel.' "

7 Then Herod called the Magi secretly and found out from them the

Matt. 2

exact time the |
star had ap- |
peared. 8 He sent them to Bethlehem and said, "Go and make a careful search for the child. As soon as you find him, report to me, so that I too may go and worship him."

9 After they had heard the king, they went on their way, and the star they had seen in the east[d] went ahead of them until it stopped over the place where the child was. 10 When they saw the star, they were overjoyed. 11 On coming to the house, they saw the child with his mother Mary, and they bowed down and worshiped him. Then they opened their treasures and presented him with gifts of gold and of incense and of myrrh. 12 And having been warned in a dream not to go back to Herod, they returned to their country by another route.

[a]Traditionally "Wise Men".   [b]Or "star when it rose".   [c]Or "Messiah".   [d]Or "seen when it rose".

14. THE FLIGHT OF JOSEPH AND HIS FAMILY INTO EGYPT
THE SLAUGHTER OF THE BETHLEHEM CHILDREN

Matt. 2:13-18

13 When they |
had gone, an an- |
gel of the Lord |
appeared to Joseph in a dream. "Get up," he said, "take the child and his mother and escape to Egypt. Stay there until I tell you, for Herod is going to search for the child to kill him."

14 So he got up, took the child and his mother during the night and left for Egypt, 15 where he stayed until the death of Herod. And so was fulfilled what the Lord had said through the prophet: "Out of Egypt I called my son."

16 When Herod realized that he had been outwitted by the Magi, he was furious, and he gave orders to kill all the boys in Bethlehem and its vicinity who were two years old and under, in accordance with the time he had learned from the Magi. 17 Then what was said through the prophet Jeremiah was fulfilled:

18 "A voice is heard in Ramah,
    weeping and great mourning,
    Rachel weeping for her children
    and refusing to be comforted,
    because they are no more."

15. THE RETURN OF JOSEPH AND HIS FAMILY
FROM EGYPT TO NAZARETH

B.C. 4

Matt. 2:19-23   Luke 2:39b

19 After Herod died, an angel of the Lord appeared in a dream to Joseph in Egypt 20 and said, "Get up, take the child and his mother and go to the land of Israel, for those who were trying to take the child's life are dead."

21 So he got up, took the child and his mother and went to the land of Israel. 22 But when he heard that Archelaus was reigning in Judea in place of his father Herod, he was afraid to go there. Having been warned in a dream,

he withdrew to the district of Galilee, 23 and* went and lived in a town called Nazareth. So was fulfilled what was said through the prophets: "He will be called a Nazarene."

39b they returned to Galilee to their own town of Nazareth.

16. THE CHILDHOOD OF JOHN THE BAPTIST IN JUDEA

Luke 1:80a

80 And the child grew and became strong in spirit;

---

*The NIV inserts "he" although Matthew's Gospel reads just as well without the repeated pronoun; it is omitted in this Harmony because the connected narrative reads "they" (Luke 2:39).

13

17. THE CHILDHOOD OF JESUS AT NAZARETH

B.C. 4 to A.D. 8

Luke 2:40

40 And the child grew and became strong; he was filled with wisdom, and the grace of God was upon him.

18. THE VISIT OF JESUS TO JERUSALEM AT AGE TWELVE

A.D. 8

Luke 2:41-51

41 Every year his parents went to Jerusalem for the Feast of the Passover. **42** When he was twelve years old, they went up to the Feast, according to the custom. **43** After the Feast was over, while his parents were returning home, the boy Jesus stayed behind in Jerusalem, but they were unaware of it. **44** Thinking he was in their company, they traveled on for a day. Then they began looking for him among their relatives and friends. **45** When they did not find him, they went back to Jerusalem to look for him. **46** After three days they found him in the temple courts, sitting among the teachers, listening to them and asking them questions. **47** Everyone who heard him was amazed at his understanding and his answers. **48** When his parents saw him, they were astonished. His mother said to him, "Son, why have you treated us like this? Your father and I have been anxiously searching for you."

49 "Why were you searching for me?" he asked. "Didn't you know I had to be in my Father's house?" **50** But they did not understand what he was saying to them.

51 Then he went down to Nazareth with them and was obedient to them. But his mother treasured all these things in her heart.

14

19. JESUS FROM YOUTH TO MANHOOD AT NAZARETH

A.D. 8 to 26

Luke 2:52

52 And Jesus grew in wisdom and stature, and in favor with God and men.

20. JOHN THE BAPTIST'S SECLUDED LIFE IN THE JUDEAN WILDERNESS

Luke 1:80b

80b and he lived in the desert until he appeared publicly to Israel.

PART III

THE PREPARATORY MINISTRY OF JOHN THE BAPTIST

FROM SPRING TO AUTUMN, A.D. 26

21. THE FIRST PUBLIC APPEARANCE OF JOHN THE BAPTIST

Judea; spring of A.D. 26

Matt. 3:1-6	Mark 1:1-6	Luke 3:1-6	John 1:6-8

1 The beginning of the gospel about Jesus Christ, the Son of God.[a]

1 In the fifteenth year of the reign of Tiberius Caesar — when Pontius Pilate was governor of Judea, Herod tetrarch of Galilee, his brother Philip tetrarch of Iturea and Trachonitis, and Lysanias tetrarch of Abilene — 2 during the high priesthood of Annas and Caiaphas, the word of God came to John son of Zechariah in the desert.

1 In those days John the Baptist came, preaching in the Desert of Judea 2 and saying, "Repent, for the kingdom of heaven is near." 3 This is he who was spoken of through the prophet Isaiah:

2 It is written in Isaiah the prophet:

4 As is written in the book of the words of Isaiah the prophet:

16

Matt. 3	Mark 1	Luke 3	John 1
	"I will send my messenger ahead of you, who will prepare your way"		
"A voice of one calling in the desert, 'Prepare the way for the Lord, make straight paths for him.'"	3 "a voice of one calling in the desert, 'Prepare the way for the Lord, make straight paths for him.'"	**"A voice of one calling in the desert, 'Prepare the way for the Lord, make straight paths for him.** 5 **Every valley shall be filled in, every mountain and hill made low. The crooked roads shall become straight, the rough ways smooth.** 6 **And all mankind will see God's salvation.'"**	
	4 **And so John came,**		6 There came a man who was sent from God;
		3 **He went into all the country around the Jordan,**	his name was John.
	baptizing in the desert region and		
	preaching a baptism of repentance for the forgiveness of sins.	**preaching a baptism of repentance for the forgiveness of sins.**	
			7 He came as a witness to testify concern-

Matt. 3	Mark 1	John 1
		ing the light,* so that through him all men might believe. 8 He himself was not the light; he came only as a witness to the light.
4 John's clothes were made of camel's hair, and he had a leather belt around his waist. His food was locusts and wild honey.	6 John wore clothing made of camel's hair, with a leather belt around his waist, and he ate locusts and wild honey.	
5 People went out to him from Jerusalem and all Judea and the whole region of the Jordan. 6 Confessing their sins, they were baptized by him in the Jordan River.	5 The whole Judean countryside and all the people of Jerusalem went out to him. Confessing their sins, they were baptized by him in the Jordan River.	

aSome manuscripts do not have "the Son of God".

22. JOHN THE BAPTIST'S FORCEFUL PREACHING

Matt. 3:7-10	Luke 3:7-14
7 But when he saw many of the Pharisees and Sadducees coming to where he was baptizing, he said to them: "You brood of vipers! Who warned you to flee from the coming wrath? 8 Produce fruit in keeping with repentance. 9 And do not think you can	7 John said to the crowds coming out to be baptized by him, "You brood of vipers! Who warned you to flee from the coming wrath? 8 Produce fruit in keeping with repentance. And do not begin to say

*The NIV reads "*that* light", in the context of John 1:1-5.

Matt. 3

Luke 3

say to yourselves, |
'We have Abra- |
ham as our father.' I tell you that
out of these stones God can raise up
children for Abraham. 10 The ax is
already at the root of the trees, and
every tree that does not produce
good fruit will be cut down and
thrown into the fire." *

to yourselves, |
'We have Abraham |
as our father.' For I tell you
that out of these stones God can
raise up children for Abraham.
9 The ax is already at the root
of the trees, and every tree that
does not produce good fruit will
be cut down and thrown into the
fire."

10 "What should we do then?" the
crowd asked.

11 John answered, "The man with
two tunics should share with him
who has none, and the one who has
food should do the same."

12 Tax collectors also came to be
baptized. "Teacher," they asked,
"what should we do?"

13 "Don't collect any more than
you are required to," he told them.

14 Then some soldiers asked him,
"And what should we do?"

He replied, "Don't extort money
and don't accuse people falsely —
be content with your pay."

23. JOHN THE BAPTIST'S MESSIANIC PROCLAMATION

Matt. 3:11-12   Mark 1:7-8   Luke 3:15-18

15 The people |
were waiting ex- |
pectantly and |
were all wonder- |
ing in their hearts |
if John might |
possibly be the |
Christ.[a] 16 John |

---

*This is the first of several sections (called the Logia passages) in which Matthew and Luke present similar material apart from Mark. New Testament scholars assume that in these passages the two writers drew upon an unknown common source, presumably a manuscript that recorded some sayings (Greek, "logia") of Jesus; it is labelled "Q" for purposes of academic reference.

Matt. 3	Mark 1	Luke 3
		answered them all,
	7 And this was his message:	
11 "I baptize you with [b] water for repentance. But after me will come one who is more powerful		"I baptize you with [b] water. But one more powerful than I will come, the
	"After me will come one more powerful	
	than I, the thongs of whose sandals	thongs of whose sandals I am not worthy to untie.
than I, whose sandals I am not fit to carry. He will baptize you with the Holy Spirit and with fire. 12 His	I am not worthy to stoop down and untie.* 8 I baptize you with [b] water, but he	He
winnowing fork is in his hand, and he will clear his threshing floor, gathering the wheat into his barn and burning up the chaff with unquenchable fire."	will baptize you with the Holy Spirit."	will baptize you with the Holy Spirit and with fire. 17 His winnowing fork is in his hand to clear his threshing floor and to gather the wheat into his barn, but he will burn up the chaff with unquenchable fire." 18 And with many other words John exhorted the people and preached the good news to them.

[a] Or "Messiah".   [b] Or "in".

---

*Note that the wording in Mark 1:7 and Luke 3:16 differs from Matt. 3:11 ("whose sandals I am unfit to carry").

PART IV

THE FIRST PUBLIC APPEARANCE
OF THE MESSIAH

THE AUTUMN OF A.D. 26

24. THE BAPTISM OF JESUS

The Jordan River

Matt. 3:13-17	Mark 1:9-11	Luke 3:21-23a
	9 At that time	
		21 When all the people were being baptized,
13 Then Jesus came from Galilee	**Jesus came from Nazareth in Galilee**	
to the Jordan to be baptized by		

John. 14 But John tried to deter him, saying, "I need to be baptized by you, and do you come to me?"

15 Jesus replied, "Let it be so now; it is proper for us to do this to fulfill all righteousness." Then John consented.

	and	
	was baptized	**Jesus was baptized**
	by	
	John in the Jordan.	too.
		And
16 As soon as Jesus was baptized, he went up out of the water. At that moment heaven was opened, and	**10 As Jesus was coming up out of the water, he saw heaven being torn open and**	**as he was praying,**
		heaven was opened 22 and

21

Matt. 3	Mark 1	Luke 3
he saw the Spirit of God des- cending like a dove **and light- ing on him.**	the Spirit **descending** on him **like a** **dove.** **11 And a** **voice came from** **heaven: "You are** **my Son, whom I** **love; with you I** **am well pleased."**	the Holy Spirit descended on him **in bodily form** l i k e a d o v e . And a voice came f r o m heaven: "You are my Son, w h o m I l o v e; with you I a m well pleased."
17 And a voice from heaven said, "This is my Son, w h o m I l o v e; with him I a m well pleased."		**23 Now Jesus** **himself was about** **thirty years old** **when he began** **his ministry.**

25. THE TEMPTATION OF JESUS

The wilderness of Judea

Matt. 4:1-11	Mark 1:12-13	Luke 4:1-13
		1 Jesus, full of **the Holy Spirit,** **returned from** **the Jordan and**
1 Then Jesus was led by the Spirit into the d e s e r t to be tempted by the devil. 2 After fasting f o r t y days and forty nights, he was hungry.	**12 At once the** **Spirit sent him** **out into the des-** **ert, 13 and he** **was in the desert** **forty days, being** **tempted by Sa-** **tan. He was with** **the wild animals,**	was led by the Spirit in the desert, 2 where for forty days he was tempted by the devil. **He ate nothing** **during those days,** **and at the end** **of them he was** **hungry.**
3 The **tempter came to** **him and said, "If**		**3 The d e v i l** said to him, "If

22

Matt. 4   Mark 1   Luke 4

you are the Son
of God, tell these
stones to become bread."

4 Jesus answered, "It is written:
'Man does not live on bread alone,
but on every word that comes from
the mouth of God.' "

5 Then the devil took him to the
holy city and had him stand on
the highest point of the temple.

6 "If you are the Son of God,"
he said, "throw yourself down.
For it is written:
" 'He will command his angels
    concerning you,
  and they will lift you up
    in their hands,
  so that you will not strike
    your foot against a
    stone.' "

7 Jesus answered him, "It is also
written: 'Do not put the Lord your
God to the test.' "

8 Again, the devil took him to a
very high mountain and showed him

all the kingdoms of the
                       world
and their splendor. 9 "All this I
will give you," he said, "if you will
bow down and worship me."

10 Jesus said to him, "Away from
me, Satan! For it is written: 'Wor-
ship the Lord your God, and serve
him only.' "

11 Then the dev-
il left him,

             and
angels came and
attended him.

13b and angels
attended him.

---

you are the Son
of God, tell
this stone to become bread."
4 Jesus answered, "It is written: 'Man does not live on bread
alone.' "

9 The devil led him to Jerusalem and had him stand on the
highest point of the temple.

"If you are the Son of God," he said,
"throw yourself down from here.
10 For it is written:
    " 'He will command his angels
      concerning you
      to guard you carefully;
  11 they will lift you up in their
      hands,
    so that you will not strike your
      foot against a stone.' "

12 Jesus answered, "It says: 'Do
not put the Lord your God to the
test.' "
5 The devil led him up to a
high p l a c e and showed him

in an instant all the kingdoms of
the

world. 6 And he said to him,

"I will give you all their authority
and splendor, for it has been given
to me, and I can give it to anyone I
want to. 7 So if you worship me, it
will all be yours."

8 Jesus answered, "It is written: 'Worship the Lord your God
and serve him only.' "

13 When the devil had finished all
this tempting, he
left him until an
opportune time.

26. JOHN THE BAPTIST'S TESTIMONY TO A
SANHEDRIN DELEGATION

Bethany, beyond the Jordan

John 1:15,19-28

19 Now this was John's testimony when the Jews of Jerusalem sent priests and Levites to ask him who he was. **20 He did not fail to confess, but confessed freely, "I am not the Christ.ᵃ"**

21 They asked him, "Then who are you? Are you Elijah?"

He said, "I am not."

"Are you the Prophet?"

He answered, "No."

22 Finally they said, "Who are you? Give us an answer to take back to those who sent us. What do you say about yourself?"

23 John replied in the words of Isaiah the prophet, "I am the voice of one calling in the desert, 'Make straight the way for the Lord.'"

24 Now some Pharisees who had been sent 25 questioned him, "Why then do you baptize if you are not the Christ, nor Elijah, nor the Prophet?"

26 "I baptize withᵇ water," John replied, "but among you stands one you do not know. 27 He is the one who comes after me, the thongs of whose sandals I am not worthy to untie."

15 John testified concerning him. He cried out,* saying, "This was he of whom I said, 'He who comes after me has surpassed me because he was before me.'"

28 This all happened at Bethany on the other side of the Jordan, where John was baptizing.

ᵃOr "Messiah". "The Christ" (Greek) and "the Messiah" (Hebrew) both mean "the Anointed One"; also in verse 25.   ᵇOr, "in".

27. JOHN THE BAPTIST'S INTRODUCTION OF JESUS
AS THE PROMISED MESSIAH

John 1:29-34

29 The next day John saw Jesus coming toward him and said, "Look, the Lamb of God, who takes away the sin of the world! 30 This is the one I meant when I said, 'A man who comes after me has surpassed me because he was before me.' 31 I myself did not know him,

---

*The NIV reads "John *testifies* concerning him. He *cries* out".

John 1

		but the reason I came baptizing

with^a water was that he might be revealed to Israel."

32 Then John gave this testimony: "I saw the Spirit come down from heaven as a dove and remain on him. 33 I would not have known him, except that the one who sent me to baptize with water told me, 'The man on whom you see the Spirit come down and remain is he who will baptize with the Holy Spirit.' 34 I have seen and I testify that this is the Son of God."

^aOr "in"; also in verse 33.

28. CHRIST'S FIRST CONTACT WITH SOME OF THE TWELVE

John 1:35-51

		35 The next day John was there again with two of

his disciples. 36 When he saw Jesus passing by, he said, "Look, the Lamb of God!"

37 When the two disciples heard him say this, they followed Jesus. 38 Turning around, Jesus saw them following and asked, "What do you want?"

They said, "Rabbi" (which means Teacher), "where are you staying?"

39 "Come," he replied, "and you will see."

So they went and saw where he was staying, and spent that day with him. It was about the tenth hour.*

40 Andrew, Simon Peter's brother, was one of the two who heard what John had said and who had followed Jesus. 41 The first thing Andrew did was to find his brother Simon and tell him, "We have found the Messiah" (that is, the Christ).

42 Then he brought Simon to Jesus, who looked at him and said, "You are Simon son of John. You will be called Cephas" (which, when translated, is Peter^a).

43 The next day Jesus decided to leave for Galilee. Finding Philip, he said to him, "Follow me."

44 Philip, like Andrew and Peter, was from the town of Bethsaida. 45 Philip found Nathanael and told him, "We have found the one Moses wrote about in the Law, and about whom the prophets also wrote — Jesus of Nazareth, the son of Joseph."

---

*The time was about 10 a.m. according to the Roman system of counting the hours from midnight and noon (which in due course became universal practice). John evidently used this chronological system throughout his Gospel.

John 1

| | | 46 "Nazareth!
Can anything

good come from there?" Nathanael asked.

"Come and see," said Philip.

47 When Jesus saw Nathanael approaching, he said of him, "Here is a true Israelite, in whom there is nothing false."

48 "How do you know me?" Nathanael asked.

Jesus answered, "I saw you while you were still under the fig tree before Philip called you."

49 Then Nathanael declared, "Rabbi, you are the Son of God; you are the King of Israel."

50 Jesus said, "You believe[b] because I told you I saw you under the fig tree. You shall see greater things than that." 51 He then added, "I tell you[c] the truth, you[c] shall see heaven open, and the angels of God ascending and descending on the Son of Man."

[a]Both "Cephas" (Aramaic) and "Peter" (Greek) mean "rock".   [b]Or "Do you believe ...?"   [c]The Greek is plural.

PART V

THE BEGINNING OF CHRIST'S PUBLIC MINISTRY
IN GALILEE, JUDEA AND SAMARIA

FROM THE END OF A.D. 26 TO THE AUTUMN OF A.D. 27

29. THE FIRST MIRACLE OF JESUS — CHANGING WATER TO WINE AT A WEDDING FEAST

Cana, in Galilee

John 2:1-11

1 On the third day a wedding took place at Cana in Galilee. Jesus' mother was there, 2 and Jesus and his disciples had also been invited to the wedding. 3 When the wine was gone, Jesus' mother said to him, "They have no more wine."

4 "Dear woman, why do you involve me?" Jesus replied, "My time has not yet come."

5 His mother said to the servants, "Do whatever he tells you."

6 Nearby stood six stone water jars, the kind used by the Jews for ceremonial washing, each holding from twenty to thirty gallons.[a]

7 Jesus said to the servants, "Fill the jars with water"; so they filled them to the brim.

8 Then he told them, "Now draw some out and take it to the master of the banquet."

They did so, 9 and the master of the banquet tasted the water that had been turned into wine. He did not realize where it had come from, though the servants who had drawn the water knew. Then he called the bridegroom aside 10 and said, "Everyone brings out the choice wine first and then the cheaper wine after the guests have had too much to drink; but you have saved the best till now."

11 This, the first of his miraculous signs, Jesus performed in Cana of Galilee. He thus revealed his glory, and his disciples put their faith in him.

[a]Greek "two to three metretes" (probably about 75 to 115 liters).

30. JESUS AND HIS FAMILY VISIT CAPERNAUM

John 2:12

12 After this he went down to Capernaum with his mother and brothers and his disciples. There they stayed for a few days.

31. CHRIST'S FIRST* CLEANSING OF THE TEMPLE

The Passover Festival at Jerusalem; spring of A.D. 27

John 2:13-22

13 When it was almost time for the Jewish Passover, Jesus went up to Jerusalem. 14 In the temple courts he found men selling cattle, sheep and doves, and others sitting at tables exchanging money. 15 So he made a whip out of cords, and drove all from the temple area, both sheep and cattle; he scattered the coins of the money changers and overturned their tables. 16 To those who sold doves he said, "Get these out of here! How dare you turn my Father's house into a market!"

17 His disciples remembered that it is written: "Zeal for your house will consume me."

18 Then the Jews demanded of him, "What miraculous sign can you show us to prove your authority to do all this?"

19 Jesus answered them, "Destroy this temple, and I will raise it again in three days."

20 The Jews replied, "It has taken forty-six years to build this temple, and you are going to raise it in three days?" 21 But the temple he had spoken of was his body. 22 After he was raised from the dead, his disciples recalled what he had said. Then they believed the Scripture and the words that Jesus had spoken.

---

*Some New Testament scholars consider this incident to be identical with that recorded in the Synoptic Gospels as taking place three years later (see Sec. 136). Other scholars, however, support the assumption that Jesus felt impelled on two occasions to express His indignation at the habitual desecration of the temple, and that John recorded what happened the first time.

32. SHALLOW BELIEF AT JERUSALEM

John 2:23-25

23 Now while he was in Jerusalem at the Passover Feast, many people saw the miraculous signs he was doing and believed in his name.[a] 24 But Jesus would not entrust himself to them, for he knew all men. 25 He did not need man's testimony about man, for he knew what was in a man.

[a]Or "and believed in him".

33. THE INTERVIEW OF NICODEMUS WITH JESUS

Jerusalem; during the Passover Festival, A.D. 27

John 3:1-21

1 Now there was a man of the Pharisees named Nicodemus, a member of the Jewish ruling council. 2 He came to Jesus at night and said, "Rabbi, we know you are a teacher who has come from God. For no one could perform the miraculous signs you are doing if God were not with him."

3 In reply Jesus declared, "I tell you the truth, unless a man is born again,[a] he cannot see the kingdom of God."

4 "How can a man be born when he is old?" Nicodemus asked. "Surely he cannot enter a second time into his mother's womb to be born!"

5 Jesus answered, "I tell you the truth, unless a man is born of water and the Spirit, he cannot enter the kingdom of God. 6 Flesh gives birth to flesh, but the Spirit[b] gives birth to spirit. 7 You should not be surprised at my saying, 'You[c] must be born again.' 8 The wind blows wherever it pleases. You hear its sound, but you cannot tell where it comes from or where it is going. So it is with everyone born of the Spirit."

9 "How can this be?" Nicodemus asked.

10 "You are Israel's teacher," said Jesus, "and do you not understand these things? 11 I tell you the truth, we speak of what we know, and we testify to what we have seen, but still you people do not accept our testimony. 12 I have spoken to you of earthly things and you do not believe; how then will you believe if I speak of heavenly things? 13 No one has ever gone into heaven except the one who came from heaven — the Son of Man.[d] 14 Just as Moses lifted up the snake in the desert, so the Son of Man must be lifted up, 15 that everyone who believes in him may have eternal life.[e]

16 "For God so loved the world that he gave his one and only Son,[f] that whoever believes in him shall not perish but have eternal life. 17 For God

29

John 3

| | | did not send his
| | | Son into the world

to condemn the world, but to save the world through him. 18 Whoever believes in him is not condemned, but whoever does not believe stands condemned already because he has not believed in the name of God's one and only Son.g 19 This is the verdict: Light has come into the world, but men loved darkness instead of light because their deeds were evil. 20 Everyone who does evil hates the light, and will not come into the light for fear that his deeds will be exposed. 21 But whoever lives by the truth comes into the light, so that it may be seen plainly that what he has done has been done through God."h

aOr "born from above"; also in verse 7.   bOr "but spirit".
cThe Greek is plural.   dSome manuscripts read "Man, who is in heaven".
eOr "believes may have eternal life in him".   fOr "his only begotten Son".   gOr "God's only begotten Son".   hSome interpreters end the quotation after verse 15.

34. A TEST OF LOYALTY DURING THE PARALLEL MINISTRY OF JESUS IN JUDEA AND OF JOHN THE BAPTIST IN SAMARIA

Spring to autumn of A.D. 27

John 3:22-36

| | | 22 After this,
| | | Jesus and his dis-
| | | ciples went out

into the Judean countryside, where he spent some time with them, and baptized. 23 Now John also was baptizing at Aenon near Salim, because there was plenty of water, and people were constantly coming to be baptized. 24 (This was before John was put in prison.) 25 An argument developed between some of John's disciples and a certain Jew over the matter of ceremonial washing. 26 They came to John and said to him, "Rabbi, that man who was with you on the other side of the Jordan — the one you testified about — well, he is baptizing, and everyone is going to him."

27 To this John replied, "A man can receive only what is given him from heaven. 28 You yourselves can testify that I said, 'I am not the Christa but am sent ahead of him.' 29 The bride belongs to the bridegroom. The friend who attends the bridegroom waits and listens for him, and is full of joy when he hears the bridegroom's voice. That joy is mine, and it is now complete. 30 He must become greater; I must become less.

31 "The one who comes from above is above all; the one who is from the earth belongs to the earth, and speaks as one from the earth. The one who comes from heaven is above all. 32 He testifies to what he has seen and heard, but no one accepts his testimony. 33 The man who has accepted it

John 3

| | | has certified that
God is truthful. |

34 For the one whom God has sent speaks the words of God; to him God gives the Spirit without limit. 35 The Father loves the Son and has placed everything in his hands. 36 Whoever believes in the Son has eternal life, but whoever rejects the Son will not see life, for God's wrath remains on him."[b]

[a]Or "Messiah".   [b]Some interpreters end the quotation after verse 30.

35. THE IMPRISONMENT OF JOHN THE BAPTIST

At Machaerus; autumn of A.D. 27

Matt. 14:3-5	Mark 6:17-20	Luke 3:19-20
		19 But when John rebuked Herod the tetrarch because of Herodias, his brother's wife, and all the other evil things he had
	17 For Herod himself	done, 20 Herod added this to them all: He
	had given orders to have John arrested, and he	
3 Now Herod had arrested John and bound him and put him in prison because of Herodias, his brother Philip's wife, 4 for John had been saying to him: "It is not lawful for you to have her."	had him bound and put in prison. He did this because of Herodias, his brother Philip's wife, whom he had married. 18 For John had been saying to Herod, "It is not lawful for you to have your brother's wife."	locked John up in prison.
5 Herod wanted to kill John, but he was		

31

Matt. 14	Mark 6	
afraid of the people, because they considered him a prophet.	19 So Herodias nursed a grudge against	

John and wanted to kill him. But she was not able to, 20 because Herod feared John and protected him, knowing him to be a righteous and holy man. When Herod heard John, he was greatly puzzled[a]; yet he liked to listen to him.

[a]Some early manuscripts read "he did many things".

36. CHRIST'S REASONS FOR LEAVING JUDEA

Matt. 4:12	Mark 1:14a	John 4:1-3,44
12 When **Jesus heard that John** had been put in prison,	**14 After** John **had been* put in prison,**	
		1 The Pharisees heard that Jesus was gaining and baptizing more disciples than John, 2 although in fact it was not Jesus who baptized, but his disciples. 3 When the Lord learned of this, he left Judea and went back once more to Galilee. 44 (Now Jesus himself had pointed out that a prophet has no honor in his own country.)
he returned to Galilee.	Jesus went into Galilee,	

*The NIV reads "was".

37. JESUS AND THE SAMARITAN WOMAN AT JACOB'S WELL

Sychar, in Samaria; autumn of A.D. 27

John 4:4-43

4 Now he had to go through Sa- maria. 5 So he came to a town in Samaria called Sychar, near the plot of ground Jacob had given to his son Joseph. 6 Jacob's well was there, and Jesus, tired as he was from the journey, sat down by the well. It was about the sixth hour.*

7 When a Samaritan woman came to draw water, Jesus said to her, "Will you give me a drink?" 8 (His disciples had gone into the town to buy food.)

9 The Samaritan woman said to him, "You are a Jew and I am a Samaritan woman. How can you ask me for a drink?" (For Jews do not associate with Samaritans.ᵃ)

10 Jesus answered her, "If you knew the gift of God and who it is that asks you for a drink, you would have asked him and he would have given you living water."

11 "Sir," the woman said, "you have nothing to draw with and the well is deep. Where can you get this living water? 12 Are you greater than our father Jacob, who gave us the well and drank from it himself, as did also his sons and his flocks and herds?"

13 Jesus answered, "Everyone who drinks this water will be thirsty again, 14 but whoever drinks the water I give him will never thirst. Indeed, the water I give him will become in him a spring of water welling up to eternal life."

15 The woman said to him, "Sir, give me this water so that I won't get thirsty and have to keep coming here to draw water."

16 He told her, "Go, call your husband and come back."

17 "I have no husband," she replied.

Jesus said to her, "You are right when you say you have no husband. 18 The fact is, you have had five husbands, and the man you now have is not your husband. What you have just said is quite true."

19 "Sir," the woman said, "I can see that you are a prophet. 20 Our fathers worshiped on this mountain, but you Jews claim that the place where we must worship is in Jerusalem."

21 Jesus declared, "Believe me, woman, a time is coming when you will worship the Father neither on this mountain nor in Jerusalem. 22 You Samaritans worship what you do not know; we worship what we do know, for salvation is from the Jews. 23 Yet a time is coming and has now come when the true worshipers will worship the Father in spirit and truth, for

---

*The time was about 6 p.m. (See the footnote on page 25).

they are the kind
of worshipers
the Father seeks. 24 God is spirit, and his worshipers must worship in spirit and in truth."

25 The woman said, "I know that Messiah" (called Christ) "is coming. When he comes, he will explain everything to us."

26 Then Jesus declared, "I who speak to you am he."

27 Just then his disciples returned and were surprised to find him talking with a woman. But no one asked, "What do you want?" or "Why are you talking with her?"

28 Then, leaving her water jar, the woman went back to the town and said to the people, 29 "Come, see a man who told me everything I ever did. Could this be the Christ[b]?" 30 They came out of the town and made their way toward him.

31 Meanwhile his disciples urged him, "Rabbi, eat something."

32 But he said to them, "I have food to eat that you know nothing about."

33 Then his disciples said to each other, "Could someone have brought him food?"

34 "My food," said Jesus, "is to do the will of him who sent me and to finish his work. 35 Do you not say, 'Four months more and then the harvest'? I tell you, open your eyes and look at the fields! They are ripe for harvest. 36 Even now the reaper draws his wages, even now he harvests the crop for eternal life, so that the sower and the reaper may be glad together. 37 Thus the saying 'One sows and another reaps' is true. 38 I sent you to reap what you have not worked for. Others have done the hard work, and you have reaped the benefits of their labor."

39 Many of the Samaritans from that town believed in him because of the woman's testimony, "He told me everything I ever did." 40 So when the Samaritans came to him, they urged him to stay with them, and he stayed two days. 41 And because of his words many more became believers.

42 They said to the woman, "We no longer believe just because of what you said; now we have heard for ourselves, and we know that this man really is the Savior of the world."

43 After the two days he left for Galilee.

[a]Or "do not use dishes Samaritans have used".   [b]Or "Messiah".

PART VI

CHRIST'S GREAT GALILEAN MINISTRY

FROM THE AUTUMN OF A.D. 27 TO THE SPRING OF A.D. 29

38. THE ARRIVAL AND RECEPTION OF JESUS IN GALILEE
A BRIEF SUMMARY OF HIS TEACHING

Matt. 4:17	Mark 1:14b-15	Luke 4:14-15	John 4:45
			45 When
	14b Jesus went into Galilee,	14 Jesus returned to Galilee in the power of the Spirit,	he arrived in Galilee,
			the Galileans welcomed him. They had seen all that he had done in Jerusalem at the Passover Feast, for they also had been there.
17 From that time on Jesus began			
	proclaiming the good news of God.		
		and news about him spread through the whole countryside.	
to preach, "Repent, for the kingdom of heaven is near."	15 "The time has come," he said. "The kingdom of God is near. Repent and believe the good news!"		
		15 He	

35

Luke 4

taught in their
synagogues, and
everyone praised
him.

39. THE HEALING OF A CAPERNAUM OFFICIAL'S SON

At Cana, in Galilee

John 4:46-54

46 Once more he
visited Cana in
Galilee, where he
had turned the water into wine. And there was a certain royal official
whose son lay sick at Capernaum. 47 When this man heard that Jesus had
arrived in Galilee from Judea, he went to him and begged him to come
and heal his son, who was close to death.

48 "Unless you people see miraculous signs and wonders," Jesus told
him, "you will never believe."

49 The royal official said, "Sir, come down before my child dies."

50 Jesus replied, "You may go. Your son will live."

The man took Jesus at his word and departed. 51 While he was still on
the way, his servants met him with the news that his boy was living.
52 When he inquired as to the time when his son got better, they said to
him, "The fever left him yesterday at the seventh hour."

53 Then the father realized that this was the exact time at which Jesus
had said to him, "Your son will live." So he and all his household believed.

54 This was the second miraculous sign that Jesus performed, having
come from Judea to Galilee.

40. THE FIRST REJECTION OF JESUS AT NAZARETH

Luke 4:16-30

16 He went to
Nazareth, where
he had been
brought up, and on the Sabbath day he went into the synagogue, as was
his custom. And he stood up to read. 17 The scroll of the prophet Isaiah
was handed to him. Unrolling it, he found the place where it is written:

18 "The Spirit of the Lord is on me,
because he has anointed me to preach good news to the poor.
He has sent me to proclaim freedom for the prisoners
and recovery of sight for the blind,
to release the oppressed,
19 to proclaim the year of the Lord's favor."

Luke 4

| 20 Then he rolled up the scroll,

gave it back to the attendant and sat down. The eyes of everyone in the synagogue were fastened on him, 21 and he began by saying to them, "Today this scripture is fulfilled in your hearing."

22 All spoke well of him and were amazed at the gracious words that came from his lips. "Isn't this Joseph's son?" they asked.

23 Jesus said to them, "Surely you will quote this proverb to me: 'Physician, heal yourself! Do here in your home town what we have heard that you did in Capernaum.'"

24 "I tell you the truth," he continued, "no prophet is accepted in his home town. 25 I assure you that there were many widows in Israel in Elijah's time, when the sky was shut for three and a half years and there was a severe famine throughout the land. 26 Yet Elijah was not sent to any of them, but to a widow in Zarephath in the region of Sidon. 27 And there were many in Israel with leprosy[a] in the time of Elisha the prophet, yet not one of them was cleansed — only Naaman the Syrian."

28 All the people in the synagogue were furious when they heard this. 29 They got up, drove him out of the town, and took him to the brow of the hill on which the town was built, in order to throw him down the cliff. 30 But he walked right through the crowd and went on his way.

[a]The Greek word was used for various diseases affecting the skin — not necessarily leprosy.

41. CHRIST'S NEW HOME IN CAPERNAUM

Matt. 4:13-16   Luke 4:31a

13 Leaving Nazareth, he went and lived in Capernaum,

31 Then he went down to Capernaum,

a town in Galilee,

which was by the lake in the area of Zebulun and Naphtali — 14 to fulfill what was said through the prophet Isaiah:
15 "Land of Zebulun and land of Naphtali,
    the way to the sea, along the Jordan,
    Galilee of the Gentiles —
16 the people living in darkness
    have seen a great light;
    on those living in the land of the shadow of death
    a light has dawned."

42. A REMARKABLE CATCH OF FISH — CHRIST'S ENLISTMENT OF FOUR FISHERMEN

The Lake of Galilee

Matt. 4:18-22   Mark 1:16-20   Luke 5:1-11

1 One day as Jesus was standing by the Lake of Gennesaret,[a] with the people crowding around him and listening to the word of God, 2 he saw at the water's edge two boats, left there by the fishermen, who were washing their nets. 3 He got into one of the boats, the one belonging to Simon, and asked him to put out a little from shore. Then he sat down and taught the people from the boat.

4 When he had finished speaking, he said to Simon, "Put out into deep water, and let down[b] the nets for a catch."

5 Simon answered, "Master, we've worked hard all night and haven't caught anything. But because you say so, I will let down the nets."

6 When they had done so, they caught such a large number of fish that their nets began to break. 7 So they signaled their partners in the other boat to come and help them, and they came and filled both boats so full that they began to sink.

8 When Simon Peter saw this, he fell at Jesus' knees and said, "Go away from me, Lord; I am a sinful man!" 9 For he and all his companions were astonished at the catch of fish they had taken, 10 and so were James and John, the sons of Zebedee, Simon's partners. Then

Matt. 4:18-22	Mark 1:16-20	Luke 5:1-11
18 As Jesus was walking beside the Sea of Galilee, he saw two brothers, Simon called Peter and his brother Andrew. They were casting a net into the lake, for they were fishermen. 19 "Come, follow me," Jesus said, "and I will make you fishers of men." 20 At once they left their nets and followed him.	16 As Jesus walked beside the Sea of Galilee, he saw Simon and his brother Andrew casting a net into the lake, for they were fishermen. 17 "Come, follow me," Jesus said, "and I will make you fishers of men." 18 At once they left their nets and followed him.	Jesus said to Simon, "Don't be afraid; from now on you will catch men."

38

Matt. 4	Mark 1	Luke 5
21 Going on from there, he saw two other brothers, James son of Zebedee and his **brother John. They were in a boat with their father Zebedee, preparing their nets. Jesus called them, 22 and immediately they** left the boat and their father and followed him.	**19 When he had gone a little farther, he saw James son of Zebedee and his** brother John in a boat, preparing their nets. 20 Without delay he called them, and they **left their father Zebedee in the boat with the hired men and followed him.**	11 So they pulled their boats up on shore, left everything and followed him.

aThat is, "Sea of Galilee". bThe Greek verb is plural.

43. A BUSY SABBATH IN CAPERNAUM — MANY HEALED INCLUDING PETER'S MOTHER-IN-LAW

Matt. 8:14-17	Mark 1:21-34	Luke 4:31b-41
	21 They went to Capernaum, and when the Sabbath came, Jesus went into the synagogue and began to teach. 22 The people were amazed at his teaching, because he taught them as one who had authority, not as the teachers of the law.	31b and on the Sabbath (he) began to teach the people. 32 They were amazed at his teaching, because his message had authority.
	23 Just then a man in their synagogue who was possessed by an evil spirit cried out,	**33 In the synagogue there was a man possessed by a demon, an evil**a **spirit. He cried out at the**

39

Mark 1	Luke 4
	top of his voice, 34 "Ha! What do
24 "What do you want with us, Jesus of Nazareth? Have you come to destroy us? I know who you are — the Holy One of God!" 25 "Be quiet!" said Jesus sternly. "Come out of him!" 26 The evil spirit	you want with us, Jesus of Nazareth? Have you come to destroy us? I know who you are — the Holy One of God!" 35 "Be quiet!" Jesus said sternly. "Come out of him!" Then the demon
shook the man violently and	
	threw the man down before them all and came
came out	out
of him with a shriek.	
	without injuring him.
27 The people were all so amazed that they asked each other, "What is this? A new teaching —	36 All the people were amazed and said to each other, "What is this teaching?
and with authority! He even gives orders to evil spirits	With authority and power he gives orders to evil spirits
and they obey him."	
	and they come out!" 37 And the news
28 News	
about him spread quickly over the whole region of Galilee. 29 As soon as they left the synagogue, they went with James and	about him spread throughout the surrounding area. 38 Jesus left the synagogue and went

Matt. 8	Mark 1	Luke 4
	John to the home of Simon and Andrew. 30 Simon's mother-in-law was in bed	to the home of Simon. Now Simon's mother-in-law was
	with a fever,	suffering from a high fever,
	and they told Jesus about her.	
	31 So he	and they asked him* to help her. 39 So he
14 When Jesus came into Peter's house, he saw Peter's mother-in-law lying in bed with a fever.	went to her,	bent over her and
15 He touched her hand and the fever left her, and she got up and began to wait on him.	took her hand and helped her up. The fever left her and she began to wait on them.	rebuked the fever, and it left her. She got up at once and began to wait on them.
16 When evening came, many who were demon-possessed were brought to him,	32 That evening after sunset the people brought to Jesus all the sick and demon-possessed. 33 The whole town gathered at the door, 34 and Jesus	40 When the sun was setting, the people brought to Jesus all who had various kinds of sickness, and
	healed many who had various diseases.	laying his hands on each one, he healed them.
		41 Moreover, de–

*For the sake of clarity, the NIV reads "Jesus"; but adherence to the pronoun "him" (which is an exact translation of the Greek) improves the wording of the connected narrative.

Matt. 8	Mark 1	Luke 4

and he drove out the spirits

with a word and

healed all the sick.

He also drove out many demons, but he would not let the demons speak because they knew who he was.

mons came out of many people,

shouting, "You are the Son of God!" But he rebuked them and would not allow them to speak, because they knew he was the Christ.[b]

17 This was to fulfill what was spoken through the prophet Isaiah:
"He took up our infirmities and carried our diseases."

[a]Greek "unclean"; also in vs. 36, and in Mark 1:23,26,27. [b]Or, "Messiah".

44. CHRIST'S FIRST TOUR OF GALILEE, WITH THE FOUR FISHERMEN

Matt. 4:23-25	Mark 1:35-39	Luke 4:42-44

35 Very early in the morning, while it was still dark, Jesus got up, left the house and went off to a solitary place, where he prayed. 36 Simon and his companions went

42 At daybreak Jesus went out to a solitary place.

to look for him, 37 and when they found him, they exclaimed: "Everyone is looking for you!"

38 Jesus replied, "Let us go somewhere else — to the nearby villages —

so I can preach there also. That is why I have come."

The people were looking for him and when

they came to where he was, they tried to keep him from leaving them.
43 But he said, "I must preach the good news of the kingdom of God to

Matt. 4	Mark 1	Luke 4
		the other towns also, because that is why I was sent."
23 Jesus went throughout	**39 So he traveled through-out**	
Gal-ilee, teaching in their synagogues, preaching the good news of the kingdom, and healing every disease and sickness among the people.	Galilee, preaching in their synagogues	44 And he kept on preach-ing in the syn-agogues of Ju-dea.[a]
	and driving out demons.	
24 News about him spread all		

over Syria, and people brought to him all who were ill with various dis-eases, those suffering severe pain, the demon-possessed, the epileptics and the paralytics, and he healed them. 25 Large crowds from Galilee, the Decapolis,[b] Jerusalem, Judea and the region across the Jordan fol-lowed him.

[a]Or "the land of the Jews"; some manuscripts "Galilee".   [b]That is, the Ten Cities.

45. THE HEALING OF A LEPER

A town in Galilee

Matt. 8:2-4	Mark 1:40-45	Luke 5:12-16
		12 While Jesus was in one of the towns, a man
2 A man with lep-rosy[a] came and knelt before him and said,	40 A man with leprosy[a] came to him and begged him	came along who was covered with leprosy.[a] When he saw Jesus, he fell
	on his knees,	
		with his face to the ground and

43

Matt. 8	Mark 1	Luke 5
"Lord, if you are willing, you can make me clean."	"If you are willing, you can make me clean."	begged him, "Lord, if you are willing, you can make me clean."
3 Jesus reached out his hand and touched the man. "I am willing," he said. "Be clean!" Immediately he was cured[b] of his leprosy.	**41 Filled with compassion, Jesus reached out his hand and touched the man. "I am willing," he said. "Be clean!" 42 Immediately the leprosy left him and he was cured.**	13 Jesus reached out his hand and touched the man. "I am willing," he said. "Be clean!" And immediately the leprosy left him.
4 Then Jesus said to him, "See that you don't tell anyone. But go, show yourself to the priest and offer the gift Moses commanded, as a testimony to them."	**43 Jesus sent him away at once with a strong warning: 44 "See that you don't tell this to anyone. But go, show yourself to the priest and offer the sacrifices that Moses commanded for your cleansing, as a testimony to them." 45 Instead he went out and began to talk freely, spreading the news. As a result, Jesus could no longer enter a town openly but stayed outside in lonely places.**	14 Then Jesus ordered him, "Don't tell anyone, but go, show yourself to the priest and offer the sacrifices that Moses commanded for your cleansing, as a testimony to them."
	Yet the people still came to him from everywhere.	**15 Yet the news about him spread all the more, so that crowds of people came**

44

Luke 5

to
hear him and to
be healed of their
sicknesses. 16 But
Jesus often with-
drew to lonely
places and prayed.

aThe Greek word was used for various diseases affecting the skin — not
necessarily leprosy.   bGreek "made clean".

46. THE HEALING OF A PARALYTIC LOWERED THROUGH A ROOF

Capernaum

Matt. 9:2-8	Mark 2:1-12	Luke 5:17-26
	1 A few days later, when Jesus again entered Capernaum,	17 One day
		as he was teaching,
	the people heard that he had come home. 2 So many gathered that there was no room left, not even outside the door, and he preached the word to them.	
		Pharisees and teachers of the law, who had come from every village of Galilee and from Judea and Jerusalem, were sitting there. And the power of the Lord was present for him to heal the sick.
2 Some men	3 Some men came, bring-	18 Some men came

45

Matt. 9	Mark 2	Luke 5
brought to him a paralytic, lying on a mat.	ing to him a paralytic,	carrying a paralytic
		on a mat
	carried by four of them.	
		and they* tried to take him into the house to lay him before Jesus.
	4 Since they could not get him to Jesus because of the crowd, they	19 When they could not find a way to do this because of the crowd, they went up on the roof and
	made an opening in the roof above Jesus and, after digging through it, they*	
	lowered the mat the paralyzed man was lying on.	lowered him on his mat through the tiles into the middle of the crowd, right in front of Jesus.
When Jesus saw their faith,	5 When Jesus saw their faith,	20 When Jesus saw their faith,
he said to the paralytic, "Take heart, son; your sins are forgiven."	he said to the paralytic, "Son, your sins are forgiven."	he said, "Friend, your sins are forgiven."
3 At this, some of the teachers of the law said to themselves,	6 Now some teachers of the law were sitting there, thinking to themselves, 7 "Why	21 The Pharisees and the teachers of the law began thinking to themselves, "Who

---

*To make the connected narrative run smoothly, "they" (omitted in the NIV) has been inserted; the pronoun is embodied in the Greek verb.

Matt. 9	Mark 2	Luke 5
"This fellow is blaspheming!"	**does this fellow talk like that? He's blaspheming! Who can forgive sins but God alone?"** 8 **Immediately Jesus knew in his spirit that this was what they were thinking in their hearts, and he said to them,**	is this fellow who speaks blasphemy? Who can forgive sins but God alone?" 22 Jesus knew what they were thinking
4 Knowing their thoughts, Jesus said,		
"Why do you entertain evil thoughts in your hearts? 5 Which	"Why are you thinking these things? 9 Which **is easier: to say to the paralytic, 'Your sins are forgiven,' or to say, 'Get up, take your mat and walk'? 10 But that you may know that the Son of Man has authority on earth to forgive sins...." He said to the paralytic, 11 "I tell you, get up, take your mat and go home."**	and asked, "Why are you thinking these things in your hearts? 23 Which is easier:
is easier: to say, 'Your sins are forgiven,' or to say, 'Get up and walk'? 6 But so that you may know that the Son of Man has authority on earth to forgive sins...." Then he said to the paralytic, "Get up, take your mat and go home." 7 And the man got up and went home.		to say, 'Your sins are forgiven,' or to say, 'Get up and walk'? 24 But that you may know that the Son of Man has authority on earth to forgive sins..." He said to the paralyzed man, "I tell you, get up, take your mat and go home."
	12 He got up, took his mat **and walked out in full view of them all.**	25 **Immediately he stood up in front of them, took what he had been lying on**
		and went home praising God.
8 When the crowd saw this, they		

47

Matt. 9	Mark 2	Luke 5
were filled with awe; and they praised God, who had given such authority to men.	This amazed everyone and they praised God, saying,	26 Everyone was amazed and gave praise to God. They were filled with awe
		and said, "We have seen remarkable things today."
	"We have never seen anything like this!"	

47. CHRIST'S ENLISTMENT OF MATTHEW LEVI

Capernaum

Matt. 9:9	Mark 2:13-14	Luke 5:27-28
	13 Once again Jesus went out beside the lake. A large crowd came to him, and he began to teach them.	
		27 After this,
9 As Jesus went on from there, he saw a man	14 As he walked along, he saw	Jesus went out and saw
		a tax collector
named Matthew		
sitting at the tax collector's booth. "Follow me," he told him, and	Levi son of Alphaeus sitting at the tax collector's booth. "Follow me," Jesus told him, and	by the name of Levi sitting at his tax booth. "Follow me," Jesus said to him, 28 and Levi got
Matthew	Levi got	
got up and followed him.	up and followed him.	up, left everything and followed him.

48

48. AT MATTHEW'S BANQUET JESUS ANSWERS
A QUESTION ABOUT FASTING

Capernaum

Matt. 9:10-17	Mark 2:15-22	Luke 5:29-39
10 While Jesus was having dinner at Matthew's house, many tax collectors and "sinners" came and ate with him and his disciples. 11 When the Pharisees saw this, they asked his disciples,	15 While Jesus was having dinner at Levi's house, many tax collectors and "sinners" were eating with him and his disciples, for there were many who followed him. 16 When the teachers of the law who were Pharisees saw him eating with the "sinners" and tax collectors, they asked	29 Then Levi held a great banquet for Jesus at his house, and a large crowd of tax collectors and others were eating with them. 30 But the Pharisees and the teachers of the law who belonged to their sect com- plained to
"Why does your teacher eat with tax collectors, and 'sinners'?" 12 On hearing this, Jesus said, "It is not the healthy who need a doctor, but the sick.	his disciples: "Why does he eat with tax collectors and 'sinners'?" 17 On hearing this, Jesus said to them, "It is not the healthy who need a doctor, but the sick.	his disciples, "Why do you eat and drink with tax collectors and 'sinners'?" 31 Jesus answered them, "It is not the healthy who need a doctor, but the sick. 32 I have not come
13 But go and learn what this means: 'I desire mercy, not sacrifice.' For		

49

Matt. 9	Mark 2	Luke 5
I have not come to call the righteous, but sinners."	I have not come to call the righteous, but sinners.	to call the righteous, but sinners to repentance."
	18 Now John's disciples and the Pharisees were fasting.	
14 Then John's disciples came and asked him, "How is it that we and	Some people came and **asked Jesus,** "How is it that John's disciples and	33 They said to him, "John's disciples
the Pharisees fast,	**the disciples of the Pharisees**	**often fast and pray,**
but **your disciples do not fast?"** **15 Jesus answered, "How can the guests of the bridegroom mourn while he is with them?**	are fasting, but yours are not?" 19 Jesus answered, "How can the guests of the bridegroom fast while he is with them?	**and** so do the disciples of the Pharisees, but yours go on eating and drinking." 34 Jesus answered, "Can you make the guests of the bridegroom fast while he is with them?
The time will come when the bridegroom will be taken from them; then they will fast.	**They cannot, so long as they have him with them. 20 But the time will come when the bridegroom** will be taken from them, and on that day they will fast.	35 But the time will come when the bridegroom **will be taken from them; in those days they will fast."**
16 "No one sews a patch of unshrunk cloth on an old garment,	21 "No one sews a patch **of unshrunk cloth** on an old garment. If he does,	**36 He told them this parable: "No one tears a patch** from a new garment and sews it **on an old one. If he does, he will have torn the new**

Matt. 9	Mark 2	Luke 5
		garment, and
for the patch will pull away from the garment, making the tear worse.	the new piece will pull away from the old, making the tear worse. 22 And	
		the patch from the new will not match the old. 37 And
17 Neither do men pour new wine into old wine-skins. If they do, the skins will burst, the wine will run out and the wineskins will be ruined. No, they pour	no one pours new wine into old wineskins. If he does, the wine will burst the skins, and	no one pours new wine into old wine-skins. If he does, the new wine will burst the skins, the wine will run out and
	both the wine and the wineskins will be ruined. No, he pours	the wine-skins will be ruined. 38 No, new wine must be poured into new wineskins.
new wine into new wineskins, and both are pre-served."	new wine into new wine-skins."	
		39 And no one after drinking old wine wants the new, for he says, 'The old is bet-ter.'"

49. JESUS HEALS A MAN AT A POOL IN JERUSALEM A CONSEQUENT SABBATH CONTROVERSY

Probably during the Passover Festival,
in the spring of A.D. 28

John 5

1 Some time later, Jesus went up to Jerusalem

for a feast* of the Jews. 2 Now there is in Jeru-salem near the Sheep Gate a pool, which in Aramaic is called Bethesda[a] and which is surrounded by five covered colonnades. 3 Here a great number of disabled people used to lie — the blind, the lame, the para-lyzed.[b] 5 One who was there had been an invalid for thirty-eight years. 6 When Jesus saw him lying there and learned that he had been in this condition for a long time, he asked him, "Do you want to get well?"

7 "Sir," the invalid replied, "I have no one to help me into the pool when the water is stirred. While I am trying to get in, someone else goes down ahead of me."

8 Then Jesus said to him, "Get up! Pick up your mat and walk." 9 At once the man was cured; he picked up his mat and walked.

The day on which this took place was a Sabbath, 10 and so the Jews said to the man who had been healed, "It is the Sabbath; the law forbids you to carry your mat."

11 But he replied, "The man who made me well said to me, 'Pick up your mat and walk.'"

12 So they asked him, "Who is this fellow who told you to pick it up and walk?"

13 The man who was healed had no idea who it was, for Jesus had slipped away into the crowd that was there.

14 Later Jesus found him at the temple and said to him, "See, you are well again. Stop sinning or something worse may happen to you." 15 The man went away and told the Jews that it was Jesus who had made him well.

16 So, because Jesus was doing these things on the Sabbath, the Jews persecuted him. 17 Jesus said to them, "My Father is always at his work to this very day, and I, too, am working." 18 For this reason the Jews tried all the harder to kill him; not only was he breaking the Sabbath, but he was even calling God his own Father, making himself equal with God.

19 Jesus gave them this answer: "I tell you the truth, the Son can do nothing by himself; he can do only what he sees his Father doing, because whatever the Father does the Son also does. 20 For the Father loves the Son and shows him all he does. Yes, to your amazement he will show him even greater things than these. 21 For just as the Father raises the dead and gives them life, even so the Son gives life to whom he is pleased to give it. 22 Moreover, the Father judges no one, but has entrusted all judgment to the Son, 23 that all may honor the Son just as they honor the Father. He who does not honor the Son does not honor the Father, who

---

*New Testament scholars differ in their opinions about the identity of this unnamed religious festival. The strongest ar-guments seem to be those which support the probability that it was the Passover Festival.

sent him.
24 "I tell you the
truth, whoever

hears my word and believes him who sent me has eternal life and will not
be condemned; he has crossed over from death to life. 25 I tell you the
truth, a time is coming and has now come when the dead will hear the
voice of the Son of God and those who hear will live. 26 For as the Father has life in himself, so he has granted the Son to have life in himself.
27 And he has given him authority to judge because he is the Son of Man.

28 "Do not be amazed at this, for a time is coming when all who are in
their graves will hear his voice 29 and come out — those who have done
good will rise to live, and those who have done evil will rise to be condemned. 30 By myself I can do nothing; I judge only as I hear, and my
judgment is just, for I seek not to please myself but him who sent me.

31 "If I testify about myself, my testimony is not valid. 32 There is
another who testifies in my favor, and I know that his testimony about
me is valid.

33 "You have sent to John and he has testified to the truth. 34 Not that
I accept human testimony; but I mention it that you may be saved. 35 John
was a lamp that burned and gave light, and you chose for a time to enjoy
his light.

36 "I have testimony weightier than that of John. For the very work
that the Father has given me to finish, and which I am doing, testifies
that the Father has sent me. 37 And the Father who sent me has himself
testified concerning me. You have never heard his voice nor seen his
form, 38 nor does his word dwell in you, for you do not believe the one
he sent. 39 You diligently study[c] the Scriptures because you think that by
them you possess eternal life. These are the Scriptures that testify about
me, 40 yet you refuse to come to me to have life.

41 "I do not accept praise from men, 42 but I know you. I know that you
do not have the love of God in your hearts. 43 I have come in my Father's
name, and you do not accept me; but if someone else comes in his own
name, you will accept him. 44 How can you believe if you accept praise
from one another, yet make no effort to obtain the praise that comes
from the only God[d]?

45 "But do not think I will accuse you before the Father. Your accuser
is Moses, on whom your hopes are set. 46 If you believed Moses, you
would believe me, for he wrote about me. 47 But since you do not believe
what he wrote, how are you going to believe what I say?"

[a]Some manuscripts "Bethzatha"; other manuscripts "Bethsaida".   [b]Some
manuscripts "paralyzed — and they waited for the moving of the waters";
some less important manuscripts continue "4 From time to time an angel of
the Lord would come down and stir up the waters. The first one into the
pool after each such disturbance would be cured of whatever disease he
had".   [c]Or "Study diligently" (the imperative).   [d]Some early manuscripts "the Only One".

50. THE DISCIPLES OF JESUS PLUCKING GRAIN
ANOTHER SABBATH CONTROVERSY

Toward the end of April or in early May, A.D. 28

Matt. 12:1-8	Mark 2:23-28	Luke 6:1-5
1 At that time Jesus went through the grainfields on the Sabbath. His disciples **were hungry and began** to pick some heads of grain and eat them.	**23 One Sabbath Jesus was going through the grainfields, and as his disciples walked along, they** began **to pick some** heads of grain.	1 One Sabbath Jesus was going through the grainfields, and his disciples began to pick some heads of **grain, rub them in their hands and eat the kernels.**
2 When the Pharisees saw this, they said to him,* **"Look! Your disciples are doing what is unlawful on the Sabbath."**	24 The Pharisees said to him, "Look, why are they doing what is unlawful on the Sabbath?"	2 Some of the Pharisees asked, "Why are you doing what is unlawful on the Sabbath?"
3 He answered, "Haven't you read what David did when he and his companions were hungry?	**25 He answered, "Have you never read what David did when he and his companions were hungry and in need? 26 In the days of Abiathar the high priest, he entered the house of God and ate the consecrated bread, which is lawful only for priests to eat. And he also gave some to**	3 Jesus answered them, "Have you never read what David did when he and his companions were hungry? 4 He entered the house of God, and taking the consecrated bread, he ate what is lawful only for priests to eat. And he also gave some to his companions."
4 He entered the house of God, and he and his companions ate the consecrated bread — which was not lawful for them to do, but only for the priests.		

---

*Note that according to Luke's account (6:2), some of the Pharisees also addressed the disciples directly.

Matt. 12	Mark 2	Luke 6
	his companions."	

5 Or haven't you read in the Law that on the Sabbath the priests in the temple desecrate the day and yet are innocent? **6** I tell you that one[a] greater than the temple is here. **7** If you had known what these words mean, 'I desire mercy, not sacrifice,' you would not have condemned the innocent.

Matt. 12	Mark 2	Luke 6
8 For the Son of Man is Lord of the Sabbath."	**27** Then he said to them, "The Sabbath was made for man, not man for the Sabbath. **28** So the Son of Man is Lord even of the Sabbath."	**5** Then Jesus said to them, "The Son of Man is Lord of the Sabbath."

[a]Or "something".

51. THE HEALING OF A MAN WITH A SHRIVELED HAND
ANOTHER SABBATH CONTROVERSY

A synagogue in Galilee

Matt. 12:9-15a	Mark 3:1-6	Luke 6:6-11
9 Going on from that place, he went into their synagogue, **10** and a man with a shriveled hand was there. Looking for a reason to accuse Jesus, they asked him, "Is it lawful to heal on the Sabbath?"	**1** Another time he went into the synagogue, and a man with a shriveled hand was there. **2** Some of them were looking for a reason to accuse Jesus, so they watched him closely to see if he would heal him on the Sabbath.	**6** On another Sabbath he went into the synagogue and was teaching, and a man was there whose right hand was shriveled. **7** The Pharisees and the teachers of the law were looking for a reason to accuse Jesus, so they watched him closely to see if he would heal on the Sabbath. **8** But Jesus knew

Matt. 12	Mark 3	Luke 6
11 He said		what they were thinking and said
to them, "If any of you has a sheep		

and it falls into a pit on the Sabbath, will you not take hold of it and lift it out? 12 How much more valuable is a man than a sheep! Therefore it

Matt. 12	Mark 3	Luke 6
is lawful to do good on the Sabbath."		
13 Then he said	3 Jesus said	to the man with the shriveled
to the man,	to the man with the shriveled hand, "Stand up	hand, "Get up and stand
		in front of everyone." So he got up and stood there.
	in front of everyone."	
	4 Then Jesus asked them, "Which is lawful on the Sabbath: to do good or to do evil, to save life or to kill?"	9 Then Jesus said to them, "I ask you, which is lawful on the Sabbath: to do good or to do evil, to save life or to destroy it?"
	But they remained silent.	
	5 He looked around at them in anger and, deeply distressed at their stubborn hearts, said to	10 He looked around at them all, and then said to the man,
"Stretch out your hand." So he stretched it out and it was completely restored,	the man, "Stretch out your hand." He stretched it out, and his hand was completely restored.	"Stretch out your hand." He did so, and his hand was completely restored.
just as sound as the other.		
		11 But they were furious and began to discuss with one

Matt. 12	Mark 3	Luke 6
		another what they might do to Je-sus.
14 But the Phari-sees went out and plotted how they might kill Jesus.	6 Then the Pharisees went out and be-gan to plot with the Herodians how they might kill Jesus.	
15 Aware of this, Jesus withdrew from that place.		

52. MULTITUDES HEALED BY THE LAKE OF GALILEE

Matt. 12:15b-21   Mark 3:7-12

	7 Jesus withdrew with his disciples to the lake, and a large crowd from Galilee fol-lowed. 8 When they heard all he	
15b Many fol-lowed him,		

was doing, many people came to him from Judea, Jerusalem, Idumea, and the regions across the Jordan and around Tyre and Sidon. 9 Because of the crowd he told his disciples to have a small boat ready for him, to keep

	the people from crowding him.	
and he healed all their sick,	10 For he had healed many, so that those with diseases were pushing forward to touch him. 11 Whenever the evil[a] spirits saw him, they fell down before him and cried out, "You are the Son of God." 12 But he gave them strict orders	

57

Matt. 12	Mark 3
16 warning them not to tell who he was. 17 This was to fulfill what was spoken	not to tell who he was.

through the prophet Isaiah:

> 18 "Here is my servant whom I have chosen,
>   the one I love, in whom I delight;
>   I will put my Spirit on him,
>   and he will proclaim justice to the nations.
> 19 He will not quarrel or cry out;
>   no one will hear his voice in the streets.
> 20 A bruised reed he will not break,
>   and a smoldering wick he will not snuff out,
>   till he leads justice to victory.
> 21 In his name the nations will put their hope."

[a]Greek "unclean".

53. CHRIST'S SELECTION OF TWELVE APOSTLES

Matt. 10:2-4	Mark 3:13-19	Luke 6:12-16
	13 Jesus went up into the hills and called to him those he wanted, and they came to him. 14 He appointed twelve — designating them apostles[a] —	12 One of those days Jesus went out into the hills to pray, and spent the night praying to God. 13 When morning came, he called his disciples to him and chose twelve of them, whom he also designated apostles:
	that they might be with him and that he might send them out to preach 15 and to have authority to drive out demons. 16 These are	
2 These are the names of the		

58

Matt. 10	Mark 3	Luke 6
twelve apostles: first,	the twelve	
Simon (who is called Peter)	he appointed: Simon (to whom he gave the name Peter);	14 Simon (whom he named Peter),
and his brother Andrew; James son of Zebedee, and his brother John;	17 James son of Zebedee, and his brother John (to them he gave the name Boanerges, which means Sons of Thunder);	his brother Andrew, James, John, Philip, Bartholomew,
3 Philip and Bartholomew; Thomas and Matthew the tax collector; James	18 Andrew, Philip, Bartholomew, Matthew, Thomas, James son of Alphaeus,	15 Matthew, Thomas, James son of Alphaeus,
son of Alphaeus, and Thaddaeus; 4 Simon the Zealot and Judas Iscariot, who betrayed him.	Thaddaeus, Simon the Zealot 19 and Judas Iscariot, who betrayed him.	Simon who was called the Zealot, 16 Judas* son of James, and Judas Iscariot, who became a traitor.

aSome manuscripts do not have "designating them apostles".

54. CHRIST'S MOMENTOUS SERMON ON A GALILEAN MOUNTAINSIDE

Matt. 5:1—8:1	Luke 6:17-49
	17 He went down with them and stood on a level place. A large crowd of his disciples was there and a great number of people from all over Judea, from Jerusalem, and from the seacoast of Tyre and Sidon, 18 who had come

*In Matt. 10:3 and Mark 3:18 this Judas is called Thaddaeus, which was probably his surname.

Matt. 5   Luke 6

to hear him and|
to be healed of|
their diseases. Those troubled by
evil[a] spirits were cured, 19 and the
people all tried to touch him, because power was coming from him
and healing them all.

1 Now when he
saw the crowds,
he went up on
a mountainside and sat down.
His disciples came to him, 2 and

                   he   20 Looking at his disciples,
began to teach them, saying: he
   3 "Blessed are the poor in spirit,   said:
     for theirs is the kingdom of
      heaven.   "Blessed are you who are
   4 Blessed are those who mourn,   poor,
     for they will be comforted.   for yours is the kingdom
   5 Blessed are the meek,   of God.
     for they will inherit the earth. 21 Blessed are you who hunger
   6 Blessed are those who hunger   now,
     and thirst for righteousness,   for you will be satisfied.
     for they will be filled.   Blessed are you who weep
   7 Blessed are the merciful,   now,
     for they will be shown mercy.   for you will laugh.
   8 Blessed are the pure in heart,
     for they will see God.
   9 Blessed are the peacemakers,
     for they will be called sons
      of God.
   10 Blessed are those who are per-
     secuted because of righteous-
     ness,
     for theirs is the kingdom of
     heaven.

                          22 Blessed are you when men
                           hate you,
11 "Blessed are you when people   when they exclude you and
insult you,   insult you

             persecute you and false-
ly say all kinds of evil against you   and reject your name as evil,
                        because of the Son of Man.
because of me. 12 Rejoice and   23 "Rejoice in that day and leap for
be glad, because great is your   joy, because great is your reward in
reward in heaven,

60

Matt. 5	Luke 6
for in the same way they	heaven. For that is how their fa-thers
perse-cuted the prophets who were before you.	treated the prophets.

13 "You are the salt of the earth. But if the salt loses its saltiness, how can it be made salty again? It is no longer good for anything, except to be thrown out and trampled by men.

14 "You are the light of the world. A city on a hill cannot be hidden. 15 Neither do people light a lamp and put it under a bowl. Instead they put it on its stand, and it gives light to everyone in the house. 16 In the same way, let your light shine before men, that they may see your good deeds and praise your Father in heaven.

17 "Do not think that I have come to abolish the Law or the Prophets; I have not come to abolish them but to fulfill them. 18 I tell you the truth, until heaven and earth disappear, not the smallest letter, not the least stroke of a pen, will by any means disappear from the Law until every-thing is accomplished. 19 Anyone who breaks one of the least of these commandments and teaches others to do the same will be called least in the kingdom of heaven, but whoever practices and teaches these commands will be called great in the kingdom of heaven. 20 For I tell you that unless your righteousness surpasses that of the Pharisees and the teachers of the law, you will certainly not enter the kingdom of heaven.

21 "You have heard that it was said to the people long ago, 'Do not mur-der, and anyone who murders will be subject to judgment.' 22 But I tell you that anyone who is angry with his brother[b] will be subject to judgment. Again, anyone who says to his brother, 'Raca,[c]' is answerable to the San-hedrin. But anyone who says, 'You fool!' will be in danger of the fire of hell.

23 "Therefore, if you are offering your gift at the altar and there re-member that your brother has something against you, 24 leave your gift there in front of the altar. First go and be reconciled to your brother; then come and offer your gift.

25 "Settle matters quickly with your adversary who is taking you to court. Do it while you are still with him on the way, or he may hand you over to the judge, and the judge may hand you over to the officer, and you may be thrown into prison. 26 I tell you the truth, you will not get out until you have paid the last penny.[d]

27 "You have heard that it was said, 'Do not commit adultery.' 28 But I tell you that anyone who looks at a woman lustfully has already committed adultery with her in his heart. 29 If your right eye causes you to sin, gouge it out and throw it away. It is better for you to lose one part of your body than for your whole body to be thrown into hell. 30 And if your right hand causes you to sin, cut it off and throw it away. It is better for you to lose one part of your body than for your whole body to go into hell.

Matt. 5   Luke 6

31 "It has been said, 'Anyone who divorces his wife must give her a certificate of divorce.' 32 But I tell you that anyone who divorces his wife, except for marital unfaithfulness, causes her to commit adultery, and anyone who marries a woman so divorced commits adultery.

33 "Again, you have heard that it was said to the people long ago, 'Do not break your oath, but keep the oaths you have made to the Lord.' 34 But I tell you, Do not swear at all: either by heaven, for it is God's throne; 35 or by the earth, for it is his footstool; or by Jerusalem, for it is the city of the Great King. 36 And do not swear by your head, for you cannot make even one hair white or black. 37 Simply let your 'Yes' be 'Yes,' and your 'No,' 'No'; anything beyond this comes from the evil one.

38 "You have heard that it was said, 'Eye for eye, and tooth for tooth.' 39 But I tell you, Do not resist an evil person. If someone strikes you on the right cheek, turn to him the other also. 40 And if someone wants to sue you and take your tunic, let him have your cloak as well. 41 If someone forces you to go one mile, go with him two miles. 42 Give to the one who asks you, and do not turn away from the one who wants to borrow from you.

29 If someone strikes you on one cheek, turn to him the other also. If someone takes your cloak, do not stop him from taking your tunic. 30 Give to everyone who asks you, and if anyone takes what belongs to you, do not demand it back.

43 "You have heard that it was said, 'Love your neighbor and hate your enemy.' 44 But I tell you: Love your enemies[e] and pray for those who persecute you, 45 that you may be sons of your Father in heaven. He causes his sun to rise on the evil and the good, and sends rain on the righteous and the unrighteous. 46 If you love those who love you, what reward will you get? Are not even the tax collectors doing that?

27 "But I tell you who hear me: Love your enemies, do good to those who hate you, 28 bless those who curse you, pray for those who mistreat you. 32 "If you love those who love you, what credit is that to you?

Matt. 5-6   Luke 6

Even 'sinners' love
those who love
them. 33 And if you do good to those
who are good to you, what credit is
that to you? Even 'sinners' do that.
34 And if you lend to those from
whom you expect repayment, what
credit is that to you? Even 'sinners'
lend to 'sinners', expecting to be repaid in full.

47 And if you greet
only your brothers,
what are you doing more than others? Do not even pagans do that?

35 But love your ene-
mies, do good to them, and lend to
them without expecting to get anything back. Then your reward will be
great, and you will be sons of the
Most High, because he is kind to the
ungrateful and wicked.

48 Be perfect, therefore, as your
heavenly Father is perfect.

26 Woe to you when all men speak
well of you,
for that is how their fathers
treated the false prophets.

1 "Be careful not to do your 'acts
of righteousness' before men, to be
seen by them. If you do, you will have no reward from your Father in
heaven.
2 "So when you give to the needy, do not announce it with trumpets, as
the hypocrites do in the synagogues and on the streets, to be honored by
men. I tell you the truth, they have received their reward in full. 3 But
when you give to the needy, do not let your left hand know what your
right hand is doing, 4 so that your giving may be in secret. Then your
Father, who sees what is done in secret, will reward you.
5 "But when you pray, do not be like the hypocrites, for they love to
pray standing in the synagogues and on the street corners to be seen by
men. I tell you the truth, they have received their reward in full. 6 When
you pray, go into your room, close the door and pray to your Father, who
is unseen. Then your Father, who sees what is done in secret, will reward
you. 7 And when you pray, do not keep on babbling like pagans, for they
think they will be heard because of their many words. 8 Do not be like
them, for your Father knows what you need before you ask him.
9 "This is how you should pray:
     " 'Our Father in heaven,

Matt. 6   Luke 6

hallowed be |
your name, |
10 your kingdom come,
your will be done
on earth as it is in heaven.
11 Give us today our daily bread.
12 Forgive us our debts,
as we also have forgiven our
debtors.
13 And lead us not into temptation,
but deliver us from the evil one.[f1] |

14 For if you forgive men when they sin against you, your heavenly Father will also forgive you. 15 But if you do not forgive men their sins, your Father will not forgive your sins.

16 "When you fast, do not look somber as the hypocrites do, for they disfigure their faces to show men they are fasting. I tell you the truth, they have received their reward in full. 17 But when you fast, put oil on your head and wash your face, 18 so that it will not be obvious to men that you are fasting, but only to your Father, who is unseen; and your Father, who sees what is done in |
secret, will reward you.

24 "But woe to you
who are rich, |
for you have already received
your comfort.
25 Woe to you who are well fed now,
for you will go hungry.
Woe to you who laugh now,
for you will mourn and weep.

19 "Do not store up for yourselves |
treasures on earth, where moth and |
rust destroy, and where thieves break in and steal. 20 But store up for yourselves treasures in heaven, where moth and rust do not destroy, and where thieves do not break in and steal. 21 For where your treasure is, there your heart will be also.

22 "The eye is the lamp of the body. If your eyes are good, your whole body will be full of light. 23 But if your eyes are bad, your whole body will be full of darkness. If then the light within you is darkness, how great is that darkness!

24 "No one can serve two masters. Either he will hate the one and love the other, or he will be devoted to the one and despise the other. You cannot serve both God and Money.

25 "Therefore I tell you, do not worry about your life, what you will eat or drink; or about your body, what you will wear. Is not life more important than food, and the body more important than clothes? 26 Look at the birds of the air; they do not sow or reap or store away in barns, and yet your heavenly Father feeds them. Are you not much more valuable than

Matt. 6-7   Luke 6

they? 27 Who of
you by worrying
can add a single hour to his life[9]?

28 "And why do you worry about clothes? See how the lilies of the field grow. They do not labor or spin. 29 Yet I tell you that not even Solomon in all his splendor was dressed like one of these. 30 If that is how God clothes the grass of the field, which is here today and tomorrow is thrown into the fire, will he not much more clothe you, O you of little faith? 31 So do not worry, saying, 'What shall we eat?' or 'What shall we drink?' or 'What shall we wear?' 32 For the pagans run after all these things, and your heavenly Father knows that you need them. 33 But seek first his kingdom and his righteousness, and all these things will be given to you as well. 34 Therefore do not worry about tomorrow, for tomorrow will worry about itself. Each day has enough trouble of its own.

36 Be merciful, just as your Father is merciful.

1 "Do not judge, or you too will be judged.

37 "Do not judge, and you will not be judged. Do not condemn, and you will not be condemned. Forgive, and you will be forgiven. 38 Give, and it will be given to you. A good measure, pressed down, shaken together and running over, will be poured into your lap.

2 For in the same way you judge others, you will be judged, and with the measure you use, it will be measured to you.

For with the measure you use, it will be measured to you."

39 He also told them this parable: "Can a blind man lead a blind man? Will they not both fall into a pit? 40 A student is not above his teacher, but everyone who is fully trained will be like his teacher.

3 "Why do you look at the speck of sawdust in your brother's eye and pay no attention to the plank in your own eye? 4 How can you say to your brother, 'Let me take the speck out of your eye,' when all the time there is a plank in your own eye? 5 You hypocrite, first take the plank out of your own eye, and then you will see clearly to remove the speck from your brother's eye.

41 "Why do you look at the speck of sawdust in your brother's eye and pay no attention to the plank in your own eye? 42 How can you say to your brother, 'Brother, let me take the speck out of your eye,' when you yourself fail to see the plank in your own eye? You hypocrite, first take the plank out of your eye, and then you will see clearly to remove the speck from your brother's eye.

6 "Do not give dogs what is sacred;

Matt. 7   Luke 6

do not throw your pearls to pigs. If you do, they may trample them under their feet, and then turn and tear you to pieces.

7 "Ask and it will be given to you; seek and you will find; knock and the door will be opened to you. 8 For everyone who asks receives; he who seeks finds; and to him who knocks, the door will be opened.

9 "Which of you, if his son asks for bread, will give him a stone? 10 Or if he asks for a fish, will give him a snake? 11 If you, then, though you are evil, know how to give good gifts to your children, how much more will your Father in heaven give good gifts to those who ask him! 12 In everything, do to others what you would have them do to you, for this sums up the Law and the Prophets.

31 Do to others as you would have them do to you.

13 "Enter through the narrow gate. For wide is the gate and broad is the road that leads to destruction, and many enter through it. 14 But small is the gate and narrow the road that leads to life, and only a few find it.

15 "Watch out for false prophets. They come to you in sheep's clothing, but inwardly they are ferocious wolves. 16 By their fruit you will recognize them.

44 Each tree is recognized by its own fruit.

Do people pick grapes from thornbushes, or figs from thistles? 17 Likewise every good tree bears good fruit, but a bad tree bears bad fruit. 18 A good tree cannot bear bad fruit, and a bad tree cannot bear good fruit. 19 Every tree that does not bear good fruit is cut down and thrown into the fire. 20 Thus, by their fruit you will recognize them.

People do not pick figs from thornbushes, or grapes from briers.

43 "No good tree bears bad fruit, nor does a bad tree bear good fruit.

45 The good man brings good things out of the good stored up in his heart, and the evil man brings evil things out of the evil stored up in his heart. For out of the overflow of his heart his mouth speaks.

46 "Why do you call me, 'Lord, Lord,' and do not do what I say?

21 "Not everyone who says to me, 'Lord, Lord,' will enter the kingdom of heaven, but only he who does the will of my Father who is in heaven. 22 Many will say to me on that day, 'Lord, Lord, did we not prophesy in

Matt. 7-8   Luke 6

your name, and in
your name drive
out demons and perform many miracles?' 23 Then I will tell them
plainly, 'I never knew you. Away
from me, you evildoers!'

24 "Therefore everyone
who hears these words of
mine and puts them into
practice is like

            a wise man

who built his house on the rock.

47 I will show
you what he is
like who comes to me and hears
my words and puts them into
practice. 48 He is like

            a man
building a house, who dug down deep
and laid the foundation on rock.
When a flood came, the torrent struck
that house but could not shake it,
because it was well built.

25 The rain came down, the streams
rose, and the winds blew and beat
against that house; yet it did not
fall, because it had its foundation
on the rock. 26 But everyone who
hears these words of mine and does
not put them into practice is like a
foolish man who built his house
on sand.

        27 The rain came down,
the streams rose, and the winds
blew and beat against that house,
and it fell with a great crash."

49 But
the one who hears my words and
does not put them into practice
is like a man who built a house

on the ground without a foundation.

    The moment the torrent
struck that house, it collapsed

and its destruction was complete."

28 When Jesus had finished saying
these things, the crowds were amazed
at his teaching, 29 because he taught
as one who had authority, and not
as their teachers of the law.
1 When he came down from the
mountainside, large crowds followed
him.

---

aGreek "unclean".   bSome manuscripts "brother without cause".   cAn
Aramaic term of contempt.   dGreek "kodrantes".   eSome later manuscripts "enemies, bless those who curse you, do good to those who hate
you".   fOr "from evil"; some late manuscripts "one, for yours is the
kingdom and the power and the glory forever. Amen."   gOr "single cubit
to his height".

55. A CENTURION'S SERVANT HEALED

Capernaum

Matt. 8:5-13	Luke 7:1-10

5 When Jesus had entered Capernaum, a centurion came to him, asking for help. 6 "Lord," he said, "my servant lies at home paralyzed and in terrible suffering."

1 When Jesus had finished saying all this in the hearing of the people, he entered Capernaum. 2 There a centurion's servant, whom his master valued highly, was sick and about to die. 3 The centurion heard of Jesus and sent some elders of the Jews to him, asking him to come and heal his servant.* 4 When they came to Jesus, they pleaded earnestly with him, "This man deserves to have you do this, 5 because he loves our nation and has built our synagogue."

7 Jesus said,** "I will go and heal him.."

6 So Jesus went with them. He was not far from the house when the centurion sent friends to say to him: "Lord, don't trouble yourself, for I do not deserve to have you come under my roof. 7 That is why I did not even consider myself worthy to come to you.

8 The centurion replied, "Lord, I do not deserve to have you come under my roof.

But just say the word, and my servant will be healed. 9 For I myself am a man under authority, with soldiers under me. I tell this one, 'Go,' and he goes; and that one, 'Come,' and he comes. I say to my servant, 'Do this,' and he does it."

But say the word, and my servant will be healed. 8 For I myself am a man under authority, with soldiers under me. I tell this one, 'Go,' and he goes; and that one, 'Come,' and he comes. I say to my servant, 'Do this,' and he does it."

10 When Jesus heard this, he was astonished and said to those following him,

9 When Jesus heard this, he was amazed at him, and turning to the crowd following him, he said,

---

*Matthew's Gospel reads as though the centurion came personally to Jesus, whereas Luke's account is more specific. Matthew, however, with reference to the servant's illness, provides information which Luke does not record, namely, that the servant was "paralyzed and in terrible suffering".

**Two words, "to him", have been omitted from Matthew's account in order to avoid ambiguity in the composite narrative.

Matt. 8	Luke 7
"I tell you the truth, I have not found anyone in Israel with such great faith. 11 I say to you that many will come from the east and the west, and will take their places at the feast with Abraham, Isaac and Jacob in the kingdom of heaven. 12 But the subjects of the kingdom will be thrown outside, into the darkness, where there will be weeping and gnashing of teeth." 13 Then, to reassure the centurion, Jesus said,* "It will be done just as you believed it would." And his servant was healed at that very hour.	"I tell you, I have not found such great faith even in Israel."
	10 Then the men who had been sent returned to the house and found the servant well.

56. A WIDOW'S SON RESTORED TO LIFE

Nain

Luke 7:11-17

11 Soon afterward, Jesus went to a town called Nain, and his disciples and a large crowd went along with him. 12 As he approached the town gate, a dead person was being carried out — the only son of his mother, and she was a widow. And a large crowd from the town was with her. 13 When the Lord saw her, his heart went out to her and he said, "Don't cry."

14 Then he went up and touched the coffin, and those carrying it stood still. He said, "Young man, I say to you, get up!" 15 The dead man sat up and began to talk, and Jesus gave him back to his mother.

16 They were all filled with awe and praised God. "A great prophet has appeared among us," they said. "God has come to help his people." 17 This news about Jesus spread throughout Judea[a] and the surrounding country.

[a]Or "the land of the Jews".

---

*Matthew's Gospel reads "Then Jesus said to the centurion, 'Go!'". The wording has been changed, without violating Matthew's account, in order to minimize ambiguity in the composite narrative.

69

57. AN INQUIRY FROM JOHN THE BAPTIST IN PRISON AND THE REPLY OF JESUS

Matt. 11:2-30   Luke 7:18-35

2 When John heard

in prison what Christ was doing,

he sent his disciples 3 to ask him, "Are you the one who was to come, or should we expect someone else?"

4 Jesus replied, "Go back and report to John what you hear and see: 5 The blind receive sight, the lame walk, those who have leprosy[a] are cured, the deaf hear, the dead are raised, and the good news is preached to the poor. 6 Blessed is the man who does not fall away on account of me."

7 As John's disciples were leaving, Jesus began to speak to the crowd about John: "What did you go out into the desert to see? A reed swayed by the wind? 8 If not, what did you go out to see? A man dressed in fine clothes? No, those who wear fine clothes are in kings' palaces. 9 Then what did you go out to see? A prophet? Yes, I tell you, and more than a prophet. 10 This is the one about whom it is written:

" 'I will send my messenger ahead of you,

18 John's disciples told him

about all these things.

Calling two of them, 19 he sent them to the Lord to ask, "Are you the one who was to come, or should we expect someone else?"
20 When the men came to Jesus, they said, "John the Baptist sent us to you to ask, 'Are you the one who was to come, or should we expect someone else?'"
21 At that very time Jesus cured many who had diseases, sicknesses and evil spirits, and gave sight to many who were blind. 22 So he replied to the messengers, "Go back and report to John what you have seen and heard: The blind receive sight, the lame walk, those who have leprosy[a] are cured, the deaf hear, the dead are raised, and the good news is preached to the poor. 23 Blessed is the man who does not fall away on account of me."
24 After John's messengers left, Jesus began to speak to the crowd about John: "What did you go out into the desert to see? A reed swayed by the wind? 25 If not, what did you go out to see? A man dressed in fine clothes? No, those who wear expensive clothes and indulge in luxury are in palaces. 26 But what did you go out to see? A prophet? Yes, I tell you, and more than a prophet. 27 This is the one about whom it is written:

" 'I will send my messenger ahead of you,

Matt. 11

Luke 7

who will pre-
pare your
way before you.'
11 I tell you the truth: Among
those born of women there has not
risen anyone greater than John the
Baptist; yet he who is least in the
kingdom of heaven is greater than
he. 12 From the days of John the
Baptist until now, the kingdom of

who will
prepare
your way before you.'
28 I tell you, among those born
of women there is no one greater
than John; yet the one who is
least in the kingdom of God is
greater than he."

heaven has been forcefully advancing, and forceful men lay hold of it.
13 For all the Prophets and the Law prophesied until John. 14 And
if you are willing to accept it,
he is the Elijah who was to come.

29 (All the peo-
ple, even the tax

collectors, when they heard Jesus' words, acknowledged that God's way
was right, because they had been baptized by John. 30 But the Pharisees
and experts in the law rejected God's purpose for themselves, because they
had not been bap-
tized by John.)

15 He who has ears, let him hear.

31 "To what, then, can I compare the
people of this generation? What are
they like? 32 They are like children
sitting in the marketplace and calling out to each other:

16 "To what can I compare this
generation? They are like children sitting in the marketplaces
and calling out to others:
17 "'We played the flute for you,
    and you did not dance;
we sang a dirge,
    and you did not mourn.'

" 'We played the flute for you,
    and you did not dance;
we sang a dirge,
    and you did not cry.'

18 For John came neither eating
nor drinking, and they say, 'He
has a demon.' 19 The Son of Man
came eating and drinking, and
they say, 'Here is a glutton and
a drunkard, a friend of tax collectors and "sinners."' But wisdom is proved right by her
actions."

33 For John the Baptist came neither
eating bread nor drinking wine, and
you say, 'He has a demon.' 34 The
Son of Man came eating and drinking, and you say, 'Here is a glutton
and a drunkard, a friend of tax collectors and "sinners."' 35 But wisdom
is proved right by all her children."*

20 Then Jesus began to denounce
the cities in which most of his mir-
acles had been performed, because they did not repent. 21 "Woe to you,

---

*Matthew's Gospel (vs. 19) reads "by her actions". The mean-
ing in both Gospels is the same, namely, that the worth of
Christ's teaching is attested by the demonstrated results.

Matt. 11

Korazin! Woe to
you, Bethsaida!
If the miracles that were performed in you had been performed in Tyre
and Sidon, they would have repented long ago in sackcloth and ashes.
22 But I tell you, it will be more bearable for Tyre and Sidon on the day of
judgment than for you. 23 And you, Capernaum, will you be lifted up to
the skies? No, you will go down to the depths.[b] If the miracles that were
performed in you had been performed in Sodom, it would have remained
to this day. 24 But I tell you that it will be more bearable for Sodom on
the day of judgment than for you."

25 At that time Jesus said, "I praise you, Father, Lord of heaven and
earth, because you have hidden these things from the wise and learned,
and revealed them to little children. 26 Yes, Father, for this was your
good pleasure.

27 "All things have been committed to me by my Father. No one knows
the Son except the Father, and no one knows the Father except the Son
and those to whom the Son chooses to reveal him.

28 "Come to me, all you who are weary and burdened, and I will give you
rest. 29 Take my yoke upon you and learn from me, for I am gentle and
humble in heart, and you will find rest for your souls. 30 For my yoke is
easy and my burden is light."

[a]The Greek word was used for various diseases affecting the skin — not
necessarily leprosy.   [b]Greek "Hades".

58. A PENITENT WOMAN EXPRESSES DEVOTION TO CHRIST IN A PHARISEE'S HOUSE

Luke 7:36-50

36 Now one of the
Pharisees invited
Jesus to have dinner with him, so he went to the Pharisee's house and
reclined at the table. 37 When a woman who had lived a sinful life in that
town learned that Jesus was eating at the Pharisee's house, she brought
an alabaster jar of perfume, 38 and as she stood behind him at his feet
weeping, she began to wet his feet with her tears. Then she wiped them
with her hair, kissed them and poured perfume on them.

39 When the Pharisee who had invited him saw this, he said to himself,
"If this man were a prophet, he would know who is touching him and what
kind of woman she is — that she is a sinner."

40 Jesus answered him, "Simon, I have something to tell you."

"Tell me, teacher," he said.

41 "Two men owed money to a certain moneylender. One owed him five
hundred denarii,[a] and the other fifty. 42 Neither of them had the money
to pay him back, so he canceled the debts of both. Now which of them
will love him more?"

72

Luke 7

| 43 Simon replied, |
| "I suppose the one |

who had the bigger debt canceled."

"You have judged correctly," Jesus said.

44 Then he turned toward the woman and said to Simon, "Do you see this woman? I came into your house. You did not give me any water for my feet, but she wet my feet with her tears and wiped them with her hair. 45 You did not give me a kiss, but this woman, from the time I entered, has not stopped kissing my feet. 46 You did not put oil on my head, but she has poured perfume on my feet. 47 Therefore, I tell you, her many sins have been forgiven — for she loved much. But he who has been forgiven little loves little."

48 Then Jesus said to her, "Your sins are forgiven."

49 The other guests began to say among themselves, "Who is this who even forgives sins?"

50 Jesus said to the woman, "Your faith has saved you; go in peace."

aA denarius was a coin worth about a day's wages.

59. CHRIST'S SECOND TOUR OF GALILEE, WITH THE TWELVE AND SOME WOMEN

Luke 8:1-3

| 1 After this, Je- |
| sus traveled about |
| from one town |

and village to another, proclaiming the good news of the kingdom of God. The Twelve were with him, 2 and also some women who had been cured of evil spirits and diseases: Mary (called Magdalene) from whom seven demons had come out; 3 Joanna the wife of Cuza, the manager of Herod's household; Susanna; and many others. These women were helping to support them out of their own means.

60. THE DEATH OF JOHN THE BAPTIST

Matt. 14:6-13a   Mark 6:21-29

6 On Herod's birthday	21 Finally the opportune time came. On his birthday Herod gave a banquet for his high officials and military commanders and the leading

Matt. 14	Mark 6
the	men of Galilee. 22 When the daughter of Herodias came in and danced, she pleased Herod and his dinner guests.
daughter of Herodias danced for them and pleased Herod so much 7 that he promised with an oath to give her whatever she asked. 8 Prompted by her mother, she said, "Give me here on a platter the head of John the Baptist." 9 The king was distressed, but because of his oaths and his dinner guests, he ordered that her request be granted 10 and had John beheaded in the prison.	The king said to the girl, "Ask me for anything you want, and I'll give it to you." 23 And he promised her with an oath, "Whatever you ask I will give you, up to half my kingdom." 24 She went out and said to her mother, "What shall I ask for?" "The head of John the Baptist," she answered. 25 At once the girl hurried in to the king with the request: "I want you to give me right now the head of John the Baptist on a platter." 26 The king was greatly distressed, but because of his oaths and his dinner guests, he did not want to refuse her. 27 So he immediately sent an executioner with orders to bring John's head. The man went, beheaded John in the prison, 28 and

Matt. 14	Mark 6	
11 His head was brought in on a platter and given to the girl, who carried it to her mother. 12 John's disciples came and took his body and buried it. Then they went and told Jesus.	brought back his head on a platter. He presented it to the girl, and she gave it to her mother. 29 On hearing of this, John's disciples came and took his body and laid it in a tomb.	

13 When Jesus heard what had happened, he withdrew . . . . . .

61. CHRIST'S INTENSIVE AND TROUBLED MINISTRY AROUSES FAMILY CONCERN

Probably Capernaum

Matt. 12:22-50	Mark 3:20-35	Luke 8:19-21
	20 Then Jesus entered a house, and again a crowd	

gathered, so that he and his disciples were not even able to eat. 21 When his family heard about this, they went to take charge of him, for they

	said, "He is out of his mind."	
22 Then they brought him a		

demon-possessed man who was blind and mute, and Jesus healed him, so that he could both talk and see. 23 All the people were astonished and said, "Could this be the Son of David?"
24 But when the Pharisees

	22 And the teachers of the law who came down from Jerusalem	
heard this, they said,	said,	
	"He is possessed by Beelzebub[a]!	

75

Matt. 12	Mark 3
"It is only by Be-elzebub,[a] the prince of demons, that this fellow drives out de-mons."	By the prince of demons he is driving out de-mons."
25 Jesus knew their thoughts and	23 So Jesus
said to them,	called them and spoke to them in parables: "How can Satan drive out Satan? 24 If a kingdom is di-vided against it-self, that kingdom
"Every kingdom divided against itself	
will be ruined, and every city or household divided against itself will not	cannot stand. 25 If a house is divided against itself, that house cannot
stand. 26 If Satan	stand. 26 And if Satan opposes himself and
drives out Satan, he is divided against himself. How then can his kingdom stand?	is di-vided, he cannot stand;
	his end has come.
27 And if I drive out demons	

by Beelzebub, by whom do your people drive them out? So then, they will be your judges. 28 But if I drive out demons by the Spirit of God, then

the kingdom of God has come upon you.	
29 "Or again, how can anyone enter a strong man's house and carry off his possessions unless he first ties up the strong man? Then	27 In fact, no one can enter a strong man's house and carry off his possessions unless he first ties up the strong man. Then

Matt. 12	Mark 3
he can rob his house.	he can rob his house.
30 "He who is not with me is against me, and he who does not gather with me scatters.	
31 And so I tell you, every sin and blasphemy will be forgiven men, but	28 I tell you the truth, all the sins and blasphemies of men will be forgiven them. 29 But
the blasphemy against the Spirit will not be forgiven. 32 Anyone who speaks a word against the Son of Man will be forgiven, but anyone who speaks against the Holy Spirit will not be forgiven, either in this age or in the age to come.	whoever blasphemes against the Holy Spirit will never be forgiven;
	he is guilty of an eternal sin."
33 "Make a tree good and its fruit	

will be good, or make a tree bad and its fruit will be bad, for a tree is recognized by its fruit. 34 You brood of vipers, how can you who are evil say anything good? For out of the overflow of the heart the mouth speaks. 35 The good man brings good things out of the good stored up in him, and the evil man brings evil things out of the evil stored up in him. 36 But I tell you that men will have to give account on the day of judgment for every careless word they have spoken. 37 For by your words you will be

acquitted, and by your words you will be condemned."	
	30 He said this because they were saying, "He has an evilᵇ spirit."

77

Matt. 12	Mark 3	Luke 8

38 Then some of the Pharisees and teachers of the law said to him, "Teacher, we want to see a miraculous sign from you."

39 He answered, "A wicked and adulterous generation asks for a miraculous sign! But none will be given it except the sign of the prophet Jonah. **40** For as Jonah was three days and three nights in the belly of a huge fish, so the Son of Man will be three days and three nights in the heart of the earth. **41** The men of Nineveh will stand up at the judgment with this generation and condemn it; for they repented at the preaching of Jonah, and now one[c] greater than Jonah is here. **42** The Queen of the South will rise at the judgment with this generation and condemn it; for she came from the ends of the earth to listen to Solomon's wisdom, and now one greater than Solomon is here.

43 "When an evil[b] spirit comes out of a man, it goes through arid places seeking rest and does not find it. **44** Then it says, 'I will return to the house I left.' When it arrives, it finds the house unoccupied, swept clean and put in order. **45** Then it goes and takes with it seven other spirits more wicked than itself, and they go in and live there. And the final condition of that man is worse than the first. That is how it will be with this wicked generation."

Matt. 12	Mark 3	Luke 8
46 While Jesus was still talking to the crowd, his mother and brothers	**31** Then Jesus' mother and brothers **arrived.**	**19** Now Jesus' mother and brothers came to see him, **but they were not able to get near him because of the crowd.**
stood outside, wanting to speak to him. **47** Someone told	**Standing outside, they sent someone in to call him. 32** A crowd was sitting around him, and they told	
him, "Your mother and brothers are standing outside, wanting to speak to you."[d] **48** He replied, "Who is my mother, and who are my brothers?"	him, "Your mother and brothers are outside looking for you." **33** "Who are my mother and my brothers?" he asked.	**20** Someone told him, "Your mother and brothers are standing outside, wanting to see you."

78

Matt. 12	Mark 3	Luke 8
	34 Then he looked at those seated in a circle around him and	
49 Pointing to his disciples, he said, "Here are my mother and my brothers.	said, "Here are my mother and my brothers!	21 He replied,
	35 Whoever does God's will is my brother and sister and mother."	"My mother and brothers are those who hear God's word and put it into practice."
50 For whoever does the will of my Father in heaven is my brother and sister and mother."		

aGreek "Beezeboul" or "Beelzeboul"; also in Matt. 12:27.   bGreek "unclean".   cOr "something".   dSome manuscripts do not have verse 47.

62. PARABLES ABOUT THE KINGDOM OF GOD

Matt. 13:1-53	Mark 4:1-34	Luke 8:4-18
1 That same day Jesus went out of the house and sat by the lake. 2 Such large crowds gathered around him that he got into a boat and sat in it, while all the people stood on the shore. 3 Then he told them many things	1 On another occasion Jesus began to teach by the lake. The crowd that gathered around him was so large that he got into a boat and sat in it out on the lake, while all the people were along the shore at the water's edge. 2 He taught them many things by	4 While a large crowd was gathering and people were coming to Jesus from town after town,

Matt. 13	Mark 4	Luke 8
in parables, saying: "A farmer went out to sow his seed. 4 As he was scattering the seed, some fell along the path, and the birds came and ate it up. 5 Some fell on rocky places, where it did not have much soil. It sprang up quickly, because the soil was shallow. 6 But when the sun came up, the plants were scorched, and they withered because they had no root. 7 Other seed fell among thorns, which grew up and choked the plants. 8 Still other seed fell on good soil, where it produced a crop — a hundred, sixty or thirty times	parables, and in his teaching said: 3 "Listen! A farmer went out to sow his seed. 4 As he was scattering the seed, some fell along the path, and the birds came and ate it up. 5 Some fell on rocky places, where it did not have much soil. It sprang up quickly, because the soil was shallow. 6 But when the sun came up, the plants were scorched, and they withered because they had no root. 7 Other seed fell among thorns, which grew up and choked the plants, so that they did not bear grain. 8 Still other seed fell on good soil. It came up, grew and produced a crop, multiplying thirty, sixty, or even	he told this parable: 5 "A farmer went out to sow his seed. As he was scattering the seed, some fell along the path; it was trampled on, and the birds of the air ate it up. 6 Some fell on rock, and when it came up, the plants withered because they had no moisture. 7 Other seed fell among thorns, which grew up with it and choked the plants. 8 Still other seed fell on good soil. It came up and yielded a crop,

Matt. 13	Mark 4	Luke 8
what was sown.	a hundred times."	**a hundred times more than was sown."**
	9 Then Jesus said,	**When he said this, he called out,**
9 He who has ears, let him hear."	**"He who has ears to hear, let him hear."**	"He who has ears to hear, let him hear."
10 The disciples	**10 When he was alone, the Twelve and the others around him**	9 His disciples asked him what
came to him and asked, **"Why do you speak to the people in parables?"** **11 He replied, "The knowledge of the secrets of the kingdom of heaven has been given to you, but not to them. 12 Whoever has will be given more, and he will have an abundance. Whoever does not have, even what he has will be taken from him. 13 This is why**	asked him about the parables. **11 He** told them, "The secret of the kingdom of God has been given to you.	this parable meant. **10 He** said, "The knowledge of the secrets of the kingdom of God has been given to you,
I speak to them in parables: " Though seeing, they do not see; though hearing, they do not hear or understand.	But **to those on the outside everything is said in parables 12 so that,** **"'they may be ever seeing but never perceiving, and ever hearing but never understanding;**	but to others I speak in parables, so that, "'though seeing, they may not see; though hearing, they may not understand.'

81

Matt. 13	Mark 4	Luke 8
	otherwise they might turn and be for- given!'"	
14 In them is ful- filled the proph- ecy of Isaiah:		

" 'You will be ever hearing but never understanding;
   you will be ever seeing but never perceiving.
15 For this people's heart has become calloused;
      they hardly hear with their ears,
      and they have closed their eyes.
   Otherwise they might see with their eyes,
      hear with their ears,
      understand with their hearts
   and turn, and I would heal them.'

16 But blessed are your eyes because they see, and your ears because they hear. 17 For I tell you the truth, many prophets and righteous men longed

to see what you see but did not see it, and to hear what you hear but did not hear it.		
	13 Then Jesus said to them, "Don't you under- stand this para- ble? How then will you under- stand any para- ble?	
18 "Listen then to what the para- ble of the sower means:		11 "This is the meaning of the parable:
		The seed is the word of God.
	14 The farmer sows the word. 15 Some people are like seed along the path, where the word is sown. As soon as they hear	12 Those along the path are the ones who hear,
19 When anyone hears		

82

Matt. 13	Mark 4	Luke 8
the message about the kingdom, not understanding* it, the evil one comes and snatches away what was sown in his heart. This is the seed sown along the path.	it, Satan comes and takes away the word that was sown in them.	and then the devil comes and takes away the word from their hearts, so that they cannot believe and be saved.
20 What was sown on rocky places is the man who hears the word and at once receives it with joy.	16 Others, like seed sown on rocky places, hear the word and at once receive it with joy. 17 But since they have no root,	13 Those on the rock are the ones who receive the word with joy when they hear it, but they have no root. They believe for a while, but
21 But since he has no root, he lasts only a short time. When trouble or persecution comes because of the word, he quickly falls away.	they last only a short time. When trouble or persecution comes because of the word, they quickly fall away.	in the time of testing they fall away.
22 What was sown among the thorns is the man who hears the word, but the worries of this life and the deceitfulness of	18 Still others, like seed sown among thorns, hear the word; 19 but the worries of this life, the deceitfulness of	14 The seed that fell among thorns stands for those who hear, but as they go on their way

*The NIV reads "and does not understand". The wording has been slightly altered to avoid ambiguity in the composite narrative.

Matt. 13	Mark 4	Luke 8
wealth choke it,	**wealth and the desires for other things come in and choke the word,**	they are choked by life's worries, riches and pleasures,
making it unfruitful.	making it un-fruitful. 20	**and they do not mature. 15 But the seed on good**
23 But what was sown on good soil is the man who hears the word and under-stands it. He produces a crop, yielding a hun-dred, sixty or thirty times what was sown."	Others, l i k e seed sown on good soil, hear the word, accept it, and produce **a crop — thirty, sixty or even a hundred times what was sown."**	**soil stands for those with a noble and good heart, who hear the word, retain it, and by persevering pro-duce**
	21 He said to them, "Do you bring in a lamp to put it under a bowl or a bed?	a c r o p .
	Instead, don't you put it on its stand? 22 For whatever is hidden is meant to be disclosed, and whatever is concealed i s m e a n t t o b e brought out into the open.	**16 "No one lights a lamp and hides it in a jar or puts it under a bed. Instead, he puts it on a stand, so that those who come in can see the light. 17 For there is nothing hidden that will not be disclosed, and nothing con-cealed that will not be known or brought out in-to the open.**
	23 If anyone has ears to hear, let him hear." **24 "Consider carefully what you hear,"** he contin-	18 Therefore con-sider carefully how you listen.

Matt. 13	Mark 4	Luke 8

ued. "With the measure you use, it will be measured to you — and even more. 25 Whoever has will be given more; whoever does not have, even what he has will be taken from him."

Whoever has will be given more; whoever does not have, even what he thinks he has will be taken from him."

26 He also said, "This is what the kingdom of God is like. A man scatters seed on the ground. 27 Night and day, whether he sleeps or gets up, the seed sprouts and grows, though he does not know how. 28 All by itself the soil produces grain — first the stalk, then the head, then the full kernel in the head. 29 As soon as the grain is ripe, he puts the sickle to it, because the harvest has come."

24 Jesus told them another parable: "The kingdom of heaven is like a man who sowed good seed in his field. 25 But while everyone was sleeping, his enemy came and sowed weeds among the wheat, and went away. 26 When the wheat sprouted and formed heads, then the weeds also appeared.

27 "The owner's servants came to him and said, 'Sir, didn't you sow good seed in your field? Where then did the weeds come from?'

28 "'An enemy did this,' he replied.

"The servants asked him, 'Do you want us to go and pull them up?'

29 "'No,' he answered, 'because while you are pulling the weeds, you may root up the wheat with them. 30 Let both grow together until the harvest. At that time I will tell the harvesters: First collect the weeds and tie them in bundles to be burned, then gather the wheat and bring it into my barn.'"

30 Again he said, "What shall we say the kingdom of God is like, or what parable shall we use to describe it?

31 He told them another parable:

"The kingdom of heaven is like a mustard seed,

31 It is like a mustard seed,

85

Matt. 13	Mark 4	
which a man took and planted in his field. 32 Though it is the smallest of all your seeds, yet when it grows, it is the largest of garden plants and becomes a tree,	which is the smallest seed you plant in the ground. 32 Yet when planted, it grows and becomes the largest of all garden plants,	
so that the birds of the air come and perch in its branches."	with such big branches that the birds of the air can perch in its shade."	
33 He told them still another parable: "The kingdom of heaven is like yeast that a woman took and mixed into a large amount[a] of flour until it worked all through the dough."		
34 Jesus spoke all these things	33 With many similar parables Jesus spoke the word	
to the crowd	to them, as much as they could understand.	
in parables; he did not say anything to them without using a parable.	34 He did not say anything to them without using a parable.	
35 So was fulfilled what		

was spoken through the prophet:

"I will open my mouth in parables,
I will utter things hidden since the creation of the world."

| 36 Then he left the crowd and went into the house. His disciples came to him and said, "Explain to us the parable of the | But when he was alone with his own disciples, he explained everything. | |

Matt. 13

weeds in the field."
37 He answered,

"The one who sowed the good seed is the Son of Man. 38 The field is the world, and the good seed stands for the sons of the kingdom. The weeds are the sons of the evil one, 39 and the enemy who sows them is the devil. The harvest is the end of the age, and the harvesters are angels.

40 "As the weeds are pulled up and burned in the fire, so it will be at the end of the age. 41 The Son of Man will send out his angels, and they will weed out of his kingdom everything that causes sin and all who do evil. 42 They will throw them into the fiery furnace, where there will be weeping and gnashing of teeth. 43 Then the righteous will shine like the sun in the kingdom of their Father. He who has ears, let him hear.

44 "The kingdom of heaven is like treasure hidden in a field. When a man found it, he hid it again, and then in his joy went and sold all he had and bought that field.

45 "Again, the kingdom of heaven is like a merchant looking for fine pearls. 46 When he found one of great value, he went away and sold everything he had and bought it.

47 "Once again, the kingdom of heaven is like a net that was let down into the lake and caught all kinds of fish. 48 When it was full, the fishermen pulled it up on the shore. Then they sat down and collected the good fish in baskets, but threw the bad away. 49 This is how it will be at the end of the age. The angels will come and separate the wicked from the righteous 50 and throw them into the fiery furnace, where there will be weeping and gnashing of teeth."

51 "Have you understood all these things?" Jesus asked.

"Yes," they replied.

52 He said to them, "Therefore every teacher of the law who has been instructed about the kingdom of heaven is like the owner of a house who brings out of his storeroom new treasures as well as old."

53 When Jesus had finished these parables, he moved on from there.

aGreek "three satas" (probably about ½ bushel or 22 liters).

63. THE MIRACULOUS CALMING OF A VIOLENT STORM

The Lake of Galilee

Matt. 8:18,23–27	Mark 4:35–41	Luke 8:22–25
	35 That day when evening came,	22 One day Jesus said to
18 When Jesus saw the crowd around him, he gave orders to	he said to his disciples, "Let us go	his disciples, "Let's go over

87

Matt. 8	Mark 4	Luke 8
cross **to the other side of the lake.** **23 Then he got into the boat and his disciples followed him.**	**over** to the other side."	to the other side of the lake." So they got into a boat
	36 Leaving the crowd behind, they took him along, just as he was, in the boat. There were also other boats with him.	and set out.
		23 As they sailed, he fell asleep.
24 Without warning, a furious storm came up on the lake, so that the waves swept over the boat. But Jesus was sleeping. 25 The disciples went and woke him, saying,	**37 A furious squall came up, and the waves broke over** **the boat, so that it** was nearly swamped. **38 Jesus was in the stern, sleeping on a cushion.** The disciples woke him and said to him,	A squall came down on the lake, so that the boat **was being swamped, and they were in great danger.** **24 The disciples went and woke him, saying, "Master, Master, we're going to drown!"**
"Lord, save us! We're going to drown!" 26 He replied, "You of little faith, why are you so afraid?" Then he got up and rebuked the winds and the waves, and it	**"Teacher, don't you care if we drown?"** **39 He got up, rebuked the wind and said to the** waves, **"Quiet! Be still!"** Then the wind died down	He got up and rebuked the wind and the **raging** waters; the storm subsided,

88

Matt. 8	Mark 4	Luke 8
was completely calm.	and it was completely calm. **40 He said to his disciples, "Why are you so afraid? Do you still have no faith?" 41 They were terrified and**	and all was calm. 25 "Where is your faith?" he asked his disciples.
27 The men were amazed and asked,	asked each other, "Who is this?	In fear and amazement they asked one another, "Who is this?
"What kind of man is this?		
Even the winds and the waves obey him!"	Even the wind and the waves obey him!"	He commands even the winds and the water, and they obey him."

64. THE HEALING OF A GERASENE DEMONIAC

South-east of the Lake of Galilee

Matt. 8:28—9:1a	Mark 5:1-20	Luke 8:26-39
28 When he arrived at the other side in the region of the Gadarenes,[b] two demon-possessed men coming from the tombs met him. They were	1 They went across the lake to the region of the Gerasenes.[a] 2 When Jesus got out of the boat, a man with an evil[c] spirit came from the tombs to meet him. 3 This man lived	26 They sailed to the region of the Gerasenes,[a] which is across the lake from Galilee. 27 When Jesus stepped ashore, he was met by a demon-possessed man* from the town. For a long time this man had not worn clothes or lived in a house, but had lived

---

*Matthew mentions two demoniacs. As Mark and Luke describe only one, it is probable that he was the more prominent one.

89

Matt. 8	Mark 5	Luke 8
so violent that no one could pass that way.	in the tombs,	in the tombs.
	and	29b Many times the demon* had seized him, and
	no one could bind him any more, not even with a chain. 4 For he had often been chained hand and foot,	though he was chained hand and foot
		and kept under guard,
	but he tore the chains apart and broke the irons on his feet.	he had broken his chains
		and had been driven by the demon into solitary places.
	No one was strong enough to subdue him. 5 Night and day among the tombs and in the hills he would cry out and cut himself with stones.	
29 "What do you want with us, Son of God?" they shouted.	6 When he saw Jesus from a distance, he ran and fell on his knees in front of him. 7 He shouted at the top of his voice, "What do you want with me,	28 When he saw Jesus, he cried out and fell at his feet, shouting at the top of his voice, "What do you want with me,

*The NIV reads "it". The words "the demon" have been substituted for the sake of clarity.

Matt. 8	Mark 5	Luke 8
	Jesus, Son of the Most High God? Swear to God that you won't torture me!" 8 For Jesus was saying to him, "Come out of this man, you evil spirit!"	Jesus, Son of the Most High God? I beg you, don't torture me!" 29 For Jesus had commanded the evil spirit to come out of the man.
	9 Then Jesus asked him, "What is your name?"	30 Jesus asked him, "What is your name?"
	"My name is Legion," he replied, "for we are many."	"Legion," he replied,
		because many demons had gone into him.
"Have you come here to torture us before the appointed time?" they cried.*	10 And he	
	begged Jesus again and again not to send them **out** of the area.	**31 And they** begged him repeatedly not to **order them to go** into the Abyss.
30 Some distance from them a large herd of pigs was feeding. 31 The demons begged Jesus,	11 A large herd of pigs was feeding **on the nearby hillside. 12 The demons begged Jesus,**	**32 A large herd of pigs was feeding there** on the hillside. The demons begged Jesus to let them go into
"If you drive us out, send us into the herd of pigs."	**"Send us** among the pigs; **allow us to go into them." 13 He gave**	them, and he gave them per-

---

*To make the composite narrative read smoothly, the words "they cried" have been inserted; they are not in the NIV.

Matt. 8	Mark 5	Luke 8
32 He said to them, "Go!" So they came out and went into the pigs, and the **whole herd** rushed down the steep bank into the lake and died in the water. 33 Those tending the pigs **ran off, went into the town and reported all** this, including what had happened to the demon-possessed men. 34 Then the whole town went out to meet Jesus.	**them permission, and the evil spirits came out** **and went into the pigs. The** herd, **about two thousand in number, rushed down the steep bank into the lake and were drowned.** 14 Those tending the pigs ran off and reported **this in the town and countryside, and the people went out to see what had happened. 15 When they came to Jesus, they saw the man who had been possessed by the legion of demons,** sitting there, dressed and in his right mind; and they were afraid. 16 Those who had seen it told the people what had happened to the demon-possessed man — **and told about the pigs as well. 17 Then**	mission. 33 When the demons came out **of the man,** they went into the pigs, and the herd rushed down the steep bank into the lake and was drowned. **34 When those tending the pigs saw what had happened, they** ran off and reported this in the town and countryside, 35 and the people went out to see what had happened. When they came to Jesus, they found the man **from whom the demons had gone out, sitting at Jesus' feet, dressed and in his right mind; and they were afraid. 36 Those who had seen it told the people how the demon-possessed man had been cured.** 37 Then

Matt 8-9	Mark 5	Luke 8
And when they saw him, they pleaded with him to leave their region.	the people be-gan to plead with Jesus to leave their region.	all the people of the region of the Gerasenes asked Jesus to leave them, because they were over-come with fear.
1 Jesus stepped into a boat,	18 As Jesus was getting into the boat, the man who had been demon-possessed	So he got into the boat and left. 38 The man from whom the demons had gone out
	beg-ged to go with him. 19 Jesus did not let him, but said, "Go home to your family and tell them how much the Lord has done for you, and how he has had mercy on you." 20 So the man went away and began to tell in the Decapolis^d how much Jesus had done for him. And all the people were amazed.	beg-ged to go with him, but Jesus sent him away, saying, 39 "Return home and tell how much God has done for you." So the man went away and told all over town how much Jesus had done for him.

---

aSome manuscripts "Gadarenes"; other manuscripts "Gergesenes"; also in Luke 8:37.   bSome manuscripts "Gergesenes"; others "Gerasenes". cGreek "unclean"; also in Mark 5:8 and 13, and Luke 8:29.   dThat is, the Ten Cities.

65. THE HEALING OF A WOMAN WHO TOUCHED CHRIST'S CLOAK AND THE RESTORATION OF JAIRUS' DAUGHTER TO LIFE

Capernaum

Matt. 9:1b,18-26	Mark 5:21-43	Luke 8:40-56
[1a Jesus ...], 1b crossed over and came	**21 When Jesus had again crossed over by boat to the other side of the lake,**	40 N o w when Jesus returned, a crowd
to his own town.	a large crowd	
	gathered around him.	welcomed him, for they were all expecting him.
18 While he was	**While he was by the lake, 22 one of the synagogue rulers, named Jai-rus, came there. Seeing Jesus, he fell at his feet**	
saying this, a		41 Just then a man named Jai-
ruler came		rus, a ruler of the synagogue,
		came and fell
and knelt before him		at Jesus' feet,
	23 and pleaded earnestly with	pleading w i t h
	him, "My little	
		him to come to his house
and said, "My		
daughter h a s just died.[a] But come a n d p u t y o u r h a n d o n h e r, a n d s h e w i l l l i v e."	**daughter* is dy-ing. Please come and put your hands on her so that she will be healed and live."**	42 because his only daugh-ter, a girl of about twelve, was dying.
19 Jesus got up and went with him, and so did his disciples.	**24 So** Jesus went with him.	
		As Jesus was on his way,
	A large crowd	

---

*Luke, in 8:42, compassionately adds that the girl was Jairus' only daughter.

Matt. 9	Mark 5	Luke 8
	followed and pressed around him. **25 And a woman was there who had been subject to bleeding for twelve years. 26 She had suffered a great deal under the care of many doctors and had spent all she had, yet instead of getting better she grew worse.**	the crowds almost crushed him. 43 And a woman was there who had been subject to bleeding for twelve years,[b]
20 Just then a woman who had been subject to bleeding for twelve years		
		but no one could heal her.
came up behind him and	**27 When she heard about Jesus, she came up behind him in the crowd and**	44 She came up behind him and touched the edge of his cloak,
touched the edge of his cloak. 21 She said to herself, "If I only touch his cloak, I will be healed."	touched his cloak, 28 b e c a u s e she thought, "If I just touch his clothes, I will be healed."	and immediately her bleeding stopped.
	29 Immediately her bleeding stopped and she felt in her body that she was freed from her suffering.	
	30 At once Jesus realized that power had gone out from him. He turned around in the crowd and asked, "Who touched my clothes?"	45 "Who touched me?" Jesus asked.
	31 "You see the people crowding against you," his disciples answer-	

95

Matt. 9	Mark 5	Luke 8
	ed, "and yet you can ask, 'Who touched me?'" 32 But Jesus kept looking around to see who had done it.	
		When they all denied it, Peter said, "Master, the people are crowding and pressing against you." 46 But Jesus said, "Someone touched me; I know that power has gone out from me."
	33 Then the woman, knowing what had happened to her, came and fell at his feet and, trembling with fear, told him the whole truth.	47 Then the woman, seeing that she could not go unnoticed, came trembling and fell at his feet. In the presence of all the people, she told why she had touched him and how she had been instantly healed. 48 Then he said to her,
22 Jesus turned and saw her. "Take heart, daughter," he said, "your faith has healed you." And the woman was healed from that moment.	34 He said to her, "Daughter, your faith has healed you. Go in peace and be freed from your suffering." 35 While Jesus	"Daughter, your faith has healed you. Go in peace."

Matt. 9	Mark 5	Luke 8
	was still speaking, some men came from the house of Jairus, the synagogue ruler. "Your daughter is dead," they said. "Why bother the teacher any more?"	49 While Jesus was still speaking, someone came from the house of Jairus, the synagogue ruler. "Your daughter is dead," he said. "Don't bother the teacher any more."
	36 Ignoring what they said, Jesus told the synagogue ruler,	50 Hearing this, Jesus said to Jairus,
	"Don't be afraid; just believe."	"Don't be afraid; just believe, and she will be healed."
23 When Jesus entered the ruler's house and	37 He did not let anyone follow him except Peter, James and John the brother of James. 38 When they came to the home of the synagogue ruler, Jesus	51 When he arrived at the house of Jairus, he did not let anyone go in with him except Peter, John and James, and the child's father and mother. 52
saw the flute players and the noisy crowd,	saw a commotion, with people crying and wailing loudly. 39 He went in and said to them, "Why all this commotion and wailing?	Meanwhile, all the people were wailing and mourning for her.
24 he said,		
"Go away.		"Stop wailing," Jesus said. "She is
The girl is not dead but asleep." But they laughed at him. 25 After the crowd had been put outside,	The child is not dead but asleep." But they laughed at him. After he put them all out, he took the child's	not dead but asleep." 53 They laughed at him, knowing that she was dead.

Matt. 9	Mark 5	Luke 8
	father and mother and the disciples who were with	
he went	**him, and went in**	
in and took the	**where the child**	
girl by the	**was. 41 He took**	54 But he took
hand,	**her by the hand**	
	and said to her,	her by the hand
	"Talitha koum!"	
	(which means,	and said, "My
	"Little girl, I say	
	to you, get up!").	child, get up!"
	42 Immediately	
		55 Her spirit re-
	the girl	**turned, and at**
and she		**once she**
got up.	**stood up**	
	and walked around	stood up.
	(she was twelve	
	years old). At this	
	they were	**56 Her parents**
		were
	com-	astonished,
	pletely astonished.	but he ordered
	43 He gave strict	them not to tell
	orders not to let	anyone
	anyone know about	
		what had
	this, and told	**happened. 55b**
	them	**Then Jesus told**
		them
	to give her	to give her
	something to eat.	something to eat.
26 News		
of this spread		
through all that		
region.		

^aOr "daughter is now dying".   ^bMany manuscripts "years, and she had
spent all she had on doctors".

98

66. THE HEALING OF TWO BLIND MEN AND A DUMB DEMONIAC

Probably Capernaum

Matt. 9:27-34

27 As Jesus went on from there, two blind men followed him, calling out, "Have mercy on us, Son of David!"

28 When he had gone indoors, the blind men came to him, and he asked them, "Do you believe that I am able to do this?"

"Yes, Lord," they replied.

29 Then he touched their eyes and said, "According to your faith will it be done to you"; 30 and their sight was restored. Jesus warned them sternly, "See that no one knows about this." 31 But they went out and spread the news about him all over that region.

32 While they were going out, a man who was demon-possessed and could not talk was brought to Jesus. 33 And when the demon was driven out, the man who had been dumb spoke. The crowd was amazed and said, "Nothing like this has ever been seen in Israel."

34 But the Pharisees said, "It is by the prince of demons that he drives out demons."

67. THE FINAL* REJECTION OF JESUS AT NAZARETH

Matt. 13:54-58   Mark 6:1-6a

54 Coming to his home town, he began teaching the people in their synagogue, and they were amazed. "Where did this man	1 Jesus left there and went to his home town, accompanied by his disciples. 2 When the Sabbath came, he began to teach in the synagogue, and many who heard him were amazed. "Where did this man get these

---

*It is not necessary to identify this visit to Nazareth with that recorded by Luke (in sec. 40) as taking place at the beginning of Christ's great Galilean ministry. It is only natural that after a long interval Jesus should give His own townspeople another opportunity to accept Him and His message. Moreover, the recorded details of the two visits are different.

Matt. 13	Mark 6
get this wisdom and these miraculous powers?" they asked. 55 "Isn't this the carpenter's son? Isn't his mother's name Mary, and aren't his brothers James, Joseph, Simon and Judas? **56 Aren't all his** sisters with us? Where then did this man get all these things?" 57 And they took offense at him. But Jesus said to them, "Only in his home town and in his own house is a prophet without honor." 58 And he did not do many miracles there because of their lack of faith.	things?" they asked. "What's this wisdom that has been given him, that he even does miracles! 3 Isn't this the carpenter? Isn't this Mary's son and the brother of James, Joses, Judas and Simon? Aren't his sisters here with us?" And they took offense at him. 4 Jesus said to them, "Only in his home town, among his relatives and in his own house is a prophet without honor." 5 He could not do any miracles there, except lay his hands on a few sick people and heal them. 6 And he was amazed at their lack of faith.

68. CHRIST'S THIRD TOUR OF GALILEE, WITH HIS DISCIPLES

Matt. 9:35-38	Mark 6:6b
35 Jesus went **through all the towns and villages, teaching in their synagogues, preaching the**	6b Then Jesus went around teaching from village to village.

Matt. 9

good news of the
kingdom and
healing every disease and sickness. 36 When he saw the crowds, he had
compassion on them, because they were harassed and helpless, like sheep
without a shepherd. 37 Then he said to his disciples, "The harvest is
plentiful but the workers are few. 38 Ask the Lord of the harvest, therefore, to send out workers into his harvest field."

69. CHRIST'S INSTRUCTION OF THE TWELVE BEFORE SENDING THEM OUT ON A PREACHING MISSION

Matt. 10:1,5-11:1	Mark 6:7-13	Luke 9:1-6
1 He called his twelve	7 Calling the Twelve to him,	1 When Jesus had called the Twelve together,
dis-ciples to him		he gave them power and author-ity to drive out all demons and to cure diseases, 2 and he
and gave them authority to drive out evil[a] spirits and to heal every dis-ease and sick-ness.	he **sent them out two by two**	sent them out to preach the king-dom of God
5 These twelve Jesus sent out with the follow-ing instruc-tions:	and **gave them author-ity over evil[a] spirits.** 8 These were his instructions:	and to heal the sick. 3 He told them:

"Do not go among the Gentiles or enter any town of the Samaritans. 6 Go rather to the lost sheep of Israel. 7 As you go, preach this message: 'The kingdom of heaven is near.' 8 Heal the sick, raise the dead, cleanse those who have leprosy,[b] drive out demons. Freely you have received, freely give.

| | **"Take nothing for the journey** | "Take nothing for the journey |

101

Matt. 10	Mark 6	Luke 9
9 Do not take along any gold or silver or copper in your belts; 10 take no bag for the journey, or extra tunic, or sandals or a staff;*	except a staff—	— no staff, no bag, no bread, no money, no extra tunic.
for the worker is worth his keep.	**no bread,** no bag, no money in your belts. 9 Wear sandals but not an extra tunic. 10 Whenever you enter a house, stay there until you leave that town.	4
11 "Whatever town or village you enter, search for some worthy person there and stay at his house until you leave. 12 As you enter the home, give it your greeting. 13 If the home is deserving, let your peace rest on it; if it is not, let your peace return to you. 14 If anyone will not welcome you or listen to your words, shake the dust off your feet when you		Whatever house you enter, stay there until you leave that town. 5 If people do not welcome you, shake the dust off your feet when you leave their town, as a testimony
leave that home or town.	**leave, as a testimony against them."**	against them."

---

*It should be noticed that according to Mark the instructions included permission to carry staves and to wear sandals. This would seem to indicate that in this respect the instructions to all the disciples were not the same, and that Peter (who is believed to be the main source for Mark's Gospel) and his companion, at least, were permitted this additional equipment probably because they were being sent to a more rugged part of the country.

Matt. 10

15 I tell
you the truth, it
will be more bearable for Sodom and Gomorrah on the day of judgment
than for that town.

16 "I am sending you out like sheep among wolves. Therefore be as shrewd
as snakes and as innocent as doves. 17 But be on your guard against men;
they will hand you over to the local councils and flog you in their synagogues. 18 On my account you will be brought before governors and kings
as witnesses to them and to the Gentiles. 19 But when they arrest you, do
not worry about what to say or how to say it. At that time you will be
given what to say, 20 for it will not be you speaking, but the Spirit of
your Father speaking through you.

21 "Brother will betray brother to death, and a father his child; children
will rebel against their parents and have them put to death. 22 All men
will hate you because of me, but he who stands firm to the end will be
saved. 23 When you are persecuted in one place, flee to another. I tell
you the truth, you will not finish going through the cities of Israel before
the Son of Man comes.

24 "A student is not above his teacher, nor a servant above his master.
25 It is enough for the student to be like his teacher, and the servant like
his master. If the head of the house has been called Beelzebub,[c] how
much more the members of his household!

26 "So do not be afraid of them. There is nothing concealed that will not
be disclosed, or hidden that will not be made known. 27 What I tell you in
the dark, speak in the daylight; what is whispered in your ear, proclaim
from the housetops. 28 Do not be afraid of those who kill the body but
cannot kill the soul. Rather, be afraid of the one who can destroy both
soul and body in hell. 29 Are not two sparrows sold for a penny[d]? Yet not
one of them will fall to the ground apart from the will of your Father.
30 And even the very hairs of your head are all numbered. 31 So don't be
afraid; you are worth more than many sparrows.

32 "Whoever acknowledges me before men, I will also acknowledge him
before my Father in heaven. 33 But whoever disowns me before men, I will
disown him before my Father in heaven.

34 "Do not suppose that I have come to bring peace to the earth. I did
not come to bring peace, but a sword. 35 For I have come to turn

    " 'a man against his father,
       a daughter against her mother,
       a daughter-in-law against her mother-in-law —
   36   a man's enemies will be the members of his own household.'

37 "Anyone who loves his father or mother more than me is not worthy
of me; anyone who loves his son or daughter more than me is not worthy
of me; 38 and anyone who does not take his cross and follow me is not
worthy of me. 39 Whoever finds his life will lose it, and whoever loses his
life for my sake will find it.

40 "He who receives you receives me, and he who receives me receives
the one who sent me. 41 Anyone who receives a prophet because he is a

Matt. 10-11	Mark 6	Luke 9

prophet will re- | |
ceive a prophet's |

reward, and anyone who receives a righteous man because he is a righteous man will receive a righteous man's reward. 42 And if anyone gives a cup of cold water to one of these little ones because he is my disciple, I tell you the truth, he will certainly not lose his reward."

1 After Jesus had finished instructing his twelve disciples, he went on

from there to teach and preach in the towns of Galilee.[e]		
		6 So they set out and went from village to village, preaching the gospel
	12 They went out and preached	
	that people should repent. 13 They drove out many demons and anointed many sick people with oil and healed them.	and healing people everywhere.

[a]Greek "unclean". [b]The Greek word was used for various diseases affecting the skin — not necessarily leprosy. [c]Greek "Beezeboul" or "Beelzeboul". [d]Greek "an assarion". [e]Greek "in their towns".

70. HEROD ANTIPAS AGITATED BY A RUMOR

Probably Tiberias

Matt. 14:1-2	Mark 6:14-16	Luke 9:7-9
1 At that time Herod the tetrarch heard the reports about Jesus, 2 and	14 King Herod heard about this,	7 Now Herod the tetrarch heard
		about all that was going on.
	for Jesus' name had become well known.	
		And he was perplexed, be-
he said	Some were saying,[a]	cause some were saying
to his attendants, "This		

104

Matt. 14	Mark 6	Luke 9
is John the Baptist; he has risen from the dead! That is why miraculous powers are at work in him."	"John the Baptist has been raised from the dead, and that is why miraculous powers are at work in him."	that John had been raised from the dead,
	15 Others said,	8 others
	"He is Elijah." And still others	**that Elijah had appeared, and still others**
	claimed,	
	"He is a prophet, like one of the prophets of long ago."	**that one of the prophets of long ago had come back to life.**
	16 But when Herod heard this, he said,	9 But Herod said,
		"I beheaded John. Who, then, is this I hear such things about?"
	"John, the man I beheaded, has been raised from the dead!"	
		And he tried to see him.

ᵃSome early manuscripts "He was saying".

71. THE RETURN OF THE TWELVE FROM THEIR MISSION

Mark 6:30	Luke 9:10a
	10 When the apostles returned, they
30 The apostles **gathered around Jesus and reported to him all they had done and taught.**	reported to Jesus what they had done.

105

THE INTENSIVE TRAINING OF THE TWELVE
IN DISTRICTS BEYOND GALILEE

FROM SPRING TO AUTUMN, A.D. 29

A. THE FIRST BRIEF WITHDRAWAL FROM
GALILEE*, ACROSS THE LAKE

72. AN UNSUCCESSFUL ATTEMPT TO FIND PRIVACY — THE MIRACULOUS FEEDING OF MORE THAN FIVE THOUSAND PEOPLE

North-east shore of the Lake of Galilee

Matt. 14:13b-21	Mark 6:31-44	Luke 9:10b-17	John 6:1-13
	31 Then, because so many people were coming and going that they did not even have a chance to eat, he	10b Then	1 Some time after this,
	said to them, "Come with me by yourselves to a quiet place and get some rest." 32 So		Jesus
		he took them with him and	

---

*During this six months' period Jesus retired three times from Galilee to outlying districts, seeking privacy with the Twelve. Leaving the hot shores of the lake, He planned to spend the summer on the cooler plateaus for more intensive training of those whom He had chosen to become apostles.

Matt. 14	Mark 6	Luke 9	John 6
13b he withdrew by boat privately	**they went away by themselves in a boat**	they withdrew by themselves	crossed
			to the far shore of the Sea of Galilee (that is, the Sea of Tiberias),
		to a town called Bethsaida,*	
to a solitary place.	**to a solitary place. 33 But**	11 but	
Hearing of this,		**the crowds learned about it and**	
the crowds followed him on foot from the towns.	**many who saw them leaving recognized them and ran on foot from all the towns and got there ahead of them.**	followed him.	2 and a great crowd of people followed him
			because they saw the miraculous signs he had performed on the sick. 3 Then Jesus
14 When Jesus	34 When Jesus		**went up on the hillside and sat down with his disciples. 4 The Jewish Passover Feast was near.**
landed and	**landed and**		**5 When Jesus looked up and saw a great crowd coming toward him,**
saw a large crowd,	saw a large crowd,		
he	he	**He welcomed them and**	

*This was evidently Bethsaida Julias (so named by the tetrarch Philip), near the north-east shore of the Lake of Galilee.

Matt. 14	Mark 6	Luke 9	John 6
had compassion on them	had compassion on them, because they were like sheep without a shepherd. So he began teaching them many things.	spoke to them about the kingdom of God, and healed those who needed healing.	
and healed their sick.			
15 As evening approached, the disciples came to him and said, "This is a remote place, and it's already getting late. Send the crowds away, so they can go to the villages and buy themselves some food."	35 By this time it was late in the day, so his disciples came to him. "This is a remote place," they said, "and it's already very late. 36 Send the people away so they can go to the surrounding countryside and villages	12 Late in the afternoon the Twelve came to him and said, "Send the crowd away so they can go to the surrounding villages and countryside and find food and lodging,	
	and buy themselves something to eat."	because we are in a remote place here."	
16 Jesus replied,	37 But he answered,	13 He replied, "You	
"They do not need to go away. You give them something to eat."	"You give them something to eat."	give them something to eat."	
		And*	
			he said to Philip, "Where

Matt. 14	Mark 6	Luke 9	John 6
			shall we buy bread for these people to eat?" 6 He asked this only to test him, for he already had in mind what he was going to do.
	They said to him, "That would take eight months of a man's wages[a]!		7 Philip answered him, "Eight months' wages[a] would not buy enough bread for each one to have a bite!"
	Are we to go and spend that much on bread and give it to them to eat?" **38 "How many loaves do you have?" he asked.** "Go and see." **When they found out,**		8 Another of his disciples,
17 "We have here only five loaves of bread and two fish," they answered.	they said, "Five — and two fish."	they answered, "We have only five loaves of bread and two fish — unless we go and buy food for all this crowd." 14b But he	**Andrew, Simon Peter's brother,** spoke up, 9 "Here is a boy with five small barley loaves and two small fish, but how far will they go among so many?" 10 Jesus said,
18 "Bring them here to me," he said. 19 And he directed the people to sit down on the grass.	**39 Then Jesus** directed them to have **all the people sit down in groups on the green grass.**	said to his disciples, "Have them sit down in groups of about fifty each." 15 The disciples	"Have the people sit down."

Matt. 14	Mark 6	Luke 9	John 6
		did so,	
			There was plenty of grass in that place,
	40 So they	and everybody	and the
	sat down in groups of hundreds and fifties.	sat down.	men sat down,
		16 Taking	11 Jesus then took
Taking the five loaves and the two fish and looking up to heaven, he gave thanks and broke the loaves.	41 Taking the five loaves and the two fish and looking up to heaven, he gave thanks and broke the loaves.	the five loaves and the two fish and looking up to heaven, he gave thanks and broke	the loaves,
Then he gave them to the disciples, and the disciples gave them to the people.	Then he gave them to his disciples to set before the people.	them. Then he gave them to the disciples to set before the people.	gave thanks, and distributed to those who were seated
			as much as they wanted.
	He also divided the two fish among them all.		He did the same with the fish.
		17 They	12 When they had all had enough to eat,
20 They all ate and were satisfied,	42 They all ate and were satisfied,	all ate and were satisfied,	
			he said to his disciples, "Gather the pieces that are left over. Let nothing be wasted." 13 So
and the disciples picked up twelve basketfuls of broken pieces	43 and the disciples picked up twelve basketfuls of broken pieces of bread	and the disciples picked up twelve basketfuls of broken pieces	they gathered them and filled twelve baskets with the pieces of the five bar-

Matt. 14	Mark 6	Luke 9	John 6
	and fish.		ley loaves
that were left over.		**that were left** over.	left **over by those who had eaten.**
21 The number of	**44 The number of**		
those who ate was about five thousand men, besides women and children.	the men who had eaten was five thousand.	14 (About five thousand men were there.)	10b about five thousand of them.

aGreek "two hundred denarii".

73. CHRIST'S REJECTION OF POLITICAL KINGSHIP PRECIPITATES A DRAMATIC CRISIS

North-east shore of the Lake of Galilee

Matt. 14:22-23	Mark 6:45-46	John 6:14-17a
		14 After the people saw the miraculous sign that Jesus did, they began to say, "Surely this is the Prophet who is to come into the world." 15 Jesus, knowing that they in-**tended to come and make him king by force,**
22 Immediately Jesus **urged* the disciples to get into the boat and go on ahead of him to the other side,**	**45 Immediately** Jesus made his disciples get into the boat and go on ahead of him **to Bethsaida,****	with-drew again into the hills by himself.
		16 When evening came, his disciples

*The NIV reads "made". But "urged" provides for a logical understanding of the sequence of events in the composite narrative; the reluctant disciples apparently delayed their departure until after Jesus repeatedly entreated them to leave.

**This was evidently not Bethsaida Julias, but the other Bethsaida on the western shore of the Lake of Galilee, south of Capernaum, by the plain of Gennesaret (see sec. 75).

Matt. 14	Mark 6	John 6
		went down to the lake, 17 where they got into a boat and set off across the lake for Capernaum.
while he dismissed the crowd.	while he dismissed the crowd.	
23 After he had dismissed them, he went up into the hills by himself to pray. When evening came, he was there alone,	46 After leaving them, he went into the hills to pray.	

74. THE DISMAYED DISCIPLES ARE REASSURED BY A MIRACLE JESUS WALKING ON THE WATER

The Lake of Galilee

Matt. 14:24-33	Mark 6:47-52	John 6:17b-21a
	47 When evening came, the boat was in the middle of the lake, and he was alone on land.	17b By now it was dark, and Jesus
		had not yet joined them. 18 A strong wind was blowing and the waters grew rough. 19 When
24 but the boat was already a considerable distance [a] from land, buffeted by the waves		
	48 He saw the disciples straining at the oars, because the	
because the wind was against it.	wind was against	

112

Matt. 14	Mark 6	John 6
	them.	
25 During the fourth watch of the night Jesus went out to them, walking on the lake. 26 When the disciples	About the fourth watch of the night he went out to them,	they had rowed three or three and a half miles,[b] they saw Jesus approaching the boat,
saw him walking on the lake,	**walking on the lake. He was about to pass by them, 49 but when they saw him walking on the lake,**	walking on the water; and they were
they were terrified. "It's a ghost," they said, and cried out in fear. **27 But Jesus immediately said to them: "Take courage! It is I. Don't be afraid." 28 "Lord, if it's you," Peter replied, "tell me to come to you on the water." 29 "Come," he said.**	they thought he was a ghost. They cried out, 50 because they all saw him and were terrified. Immediately he spoke to them and said, "Take courage! It is I. Don't be afraid."	terrified. 20 But he said to them, "It is I; don't be afraid."

Then Peter got down out of the boat and walked on the water to Jesus. 30 But when he saw the wind, he was afraid and, beginning to sink, cried out, "Lord, save me!"

31 Immediately Jesus reached out his hand and caught him. "You of little

faith," he said, "why did you doubt?"	51 Then	
		21 Then they were willing to take him into the boat,
32 And when		

Matt. 14	Mark 6
they climbed into the boat,	he climbed into the boat with them,
the wind died down. 33 Then those who were in the boat worshiped him, saying, "Truly you are the Son of God."	and the wind died down.
	They were completely amazed,

52 for they had not understood about the loaves; their hearts were hardened.

[a]Greek "many stadia".   [b]Greek "rowed twenty-five or thirty stadia"
(about 5 or 6 kilometers).

75. JESUS AND THE TWELVE RETURN TEMPORARILY TO GALILEE CROWDS HEALED IN THE REGION OF GENNESARET

Western shore of the Lake of Galilee

Matt. 14:34-36	Mark 6:53-56	John 6:21b
34 When they had crossed over, they landed at Gennesaret.	53 When they had crossed over, they landed at Gennesaret and anchored there. 54 As soon as they got out of the boat, people	21b and immediately the boat reached the shore where they were heading.
35 And when the men		
of that place		
recognized Jesus, they	recognized Jesus. 55 They ran throughout that whole region and	
sent word to all the surrounding country. People brought all their sick	carried the sick	
to him	on mats to wherever they heard he was. 56 And everywhere he	

Matt. 14	Mark 6	
	went — into villages, towns or countryside — they placed the	
36 and begged him to let the sick just touch the edge of his cloak, and all who touched him were healed.	sick in the marketplaces. They begged him to let them touch even the edge of his cloak, and all who touched him were healed.	

76. CHRIST'S DISCOURSE ON THE BREAD OF LIFE
A TEST OF LOYALTY

The synagogue in Capernaum

John 6:22-71

		22 At that time* the crowd that had

stayed on the opposite shore of the lake realized that only one boat had been there, and that Jesus had not entered it with his disciples, but that they had gone away alone. 23 Then some boats from Tiberias landed near the place where the people had eaten the bread after the Lord had given thanks. 24 Once the crowd realized that neither Jesus nor his disciples were there, they got into the boats and went to Capernaum in search of Jesus.

25 When they found him on the other side of the lake, they asked him, "Rabbi, when did you get here?"

26 Jesus answered, "I tell you the truth, you are looking for me, not because you saw miraculous signs but because you ate the loaves and had your fill. 27 Do not work for food that spoils, but for food that endures to eternal life, which the Son of Man will give you. On him God the Father has placed his seal of approval."

28 Then they asked him, "What must we do to do the works God requires?"

29 Jesus answered, "The work of God is this: to believe in the one he has sent."

---

*The NIV reads "the next day", in accord with the original Greek. Substitution of the phrase "at that time" helps to connect the events recorded in John 6:22-71 with those described by Matthew and Mark in sec. 75. Christ's discourse in the Capernaum synagogue apparently occurred during the time of His healing ministry in the nearby Gennesaret region.

30 So they asked
him, "What mirac-
ulous sign then will you give that we may see it and believe you? What
will you do? 31 Our forefathers ate the manna in the desert; as it is
written: 'He gave them bread from heaven to eat.'"

32 Jesus said to them, "I tell you the truth, it is not Moses who has given
you the bread from heaven, but it is my Father who gives you the true
bread from heaven. 33 For the bread of God is he who comes down from
heaven and gives life to the world."

34 "Sir," they said, "from now on give us this bread."

35 Then Jesus declared, "I am the bread of life. He who comes to me
will never go hungry, and he who believes in me will never be thirsty.
36 But as I told you, you have seen me and still you do not believe. 37 All
that the Father gives me will come to me, and whoever comes to me I will
never drive away. 38 For I have come down from heaven not to do my will
but to do the will of him who sent me. 39 And this is the will of him who
sent me, that I shall lose none of all that he has given me, but raise them
up at the last day. 40 For my Father's will is that everyone who looks to
the Son and believes in him shall have eternal life, and I will raise him up
at the last day."

41 At this the Jews began to grumble about him because he said, "I am
the bread that came down from heaven." 42 They said, "Is this not Jesus,
the son of Joseph, whose father and mother we know? How can he now
say, 'I came down from heaven'?"

43 "Stop grumbling among yourselves," Jesus answered. 44 "No one can
come to me unless the Father who sent me draws him, and I will raise him
up at the last day. 45 It is written in the Prophets: 'They will all be taught
by God.' Everyone who listens to the Father and learns from him comes to
me. 46 No one has seen the Father except the one who is from God; only
he has seen the Father. 47 I tell you the truth, he who believes has ever-
lasting life. 48 I am the bread of life. 49 Your forefathers ate the manna
in the desert, yet they died. 50 But here is the bread that comes down
from heaven, which a man may eat and not die. 51 I am the living bread
that came down from heaven. If a man eats of this bread, he will live forever. This bread is my flesh, which I will give for the life of the world."

52 Then the Jews began to argue sharply among themselves, "How can
this man give us his flesh to eat?"

53 Jesus said to them, "I tell you the truth, unless you eat the flesh of
the Son of Man and drink his blood, you have no life in you. 54 Whoever
eats my flesh and drinks my blood has eternal life, and I will raise him up
at the last day. 55 For my flesh is real food and my blood is real drink.
56 Whoever eats my flesh and drinks my blood remains in me, and I in him.
57 Just as the living Father sent me and I live because of the Father, so
the one who feeds on me will live because of me. 58 This is the bread that
came down from heaven. Our forefathers ate manna and died, but he who
feeds on this bread will live forever." 59 He said this while teaching in
the synagogue in Capernaum.

John 6

60 On hearing it, many of his dis-
ciples said, "This is a hard teaching. Who can accept it?"

61 Aware that his disciples were grumbling about this, Jesus said to them,
"Does this offend you? 62 What if you see the Son of Man ascend to where
he was before! 63 The Spirit gives life; the flesh counts for nothing. The
words I have spoken to you are spirit[a] and they are life. 64 Yet there are
some of you who do not believe." For Jesus had known from the beginning
which of them did not believe and who would betray him. 65 He went on to
say, "This is why I told you that no one can come to me unless the Father
has enabled him."

66 From this time many of his disciples turned back and no longer followed him.

67 "You do not want to leave too, do you?" Jesus asked the Twelve.

68 Simon Peter answered him, "Lord, to whom shall we go? You have the
words of eternal life. 69 We believe and know that you are the Holy One
of God."

70 Then Jesus replied, "Have I not chosen you, the Twelve? Yet one of
you is a devil!" 71 (He meant Judas, the son of Simon Iscariot, who, though
one of the Twelve, was later to betray him.)

[a]Or "Spirit".

77. CONTROVERSY OCCASIONED BY PHARISAIC INSISTENCE ON CEREMONIAL HAND WASHING

Matt. 15:1-20   Mark 7:1-23

1 Then some Pharisees	1 The Pharisees
	and some of the
and	**teachers of the**
teachers of the law came to Je-	**law who had come**
sus from Jeru-	**from Jerusalem**
salem	**gathered around**
	Jesus and 2 saw
	some of his dis-
	ciples eating

food with "unclean" — that is, ceremonially unwashed — hands. 3 (The
Pharisees and all the Jews do not eat unless they give their hands a ceremonial washing, holding to the tradition of the elders. 4 When they come
from the marketplace they do not eat unless they wash. And they observe
many other traditions, such as the washing of cups, pitchers and kettles.[a])

	5 So the Phari-
	sees and teachers
and ask-	of the law asked
ed, 2 "Why do	Jesus, "Why don't

Matt. 15	Mark 7
your disciples break the tradition of the elders?	your disciples live according to the tradition of the elders instead of eating their food with 'unclean' hands?"
They don't wash their hands before they eat!"	
3Jesus replied, 7 You hypocrites! Isaiah was right when he prophesied about you: 8 "'These people honor me with their lips, but their hearts are far from me. 9 They worship me in vain; their teachings are but rules taught by men.' "	6 He replied, "Isaiah was right when he prophesied about you hypocrites; as it is written: "'These people honor me with their lips, but their hearts are far from me. 7 They worship me in vain; their teachings are but rules taught by men.'
3b "And why do you break the command of God for the sake of your tradition?	8 You have let go of the commands of God and are holding on to the traditions of men." 9 And he said to them: "You have a fine way of setting aside the commands of God in order to observe[b] your own traditions! 10 For Moses said, 'Honor your father and mother,' and, 'Anyone who curses his father or mother must be put to death.' 11 But you
4 For God said, 'Honor your father and mother' and 'Anyone who curses his father or mother must be put to death.' 5 But	

118

Matt. 15 | Mark 7

you say that if a man says to his father or mother, 'Whatever help you might otherwise have received from me is a gift devoted to God,' 6 he is not to 'honor his father[c]' with it. Thus you nullify the word of God for the sake of your tradition.

say that if a man says to his father or mother: 'Whatever help you might otherwise have received from me is Corban' (that is, a gift devoted to God), 12 then you no longer let him do anything for his father or mother. 13 Thus you nullify the word of God by your tradition that you have handed down. And you do many things like that."

10 Jesus called the crowd to him and said, "Listen and understand. 11 What goes into a man's mouth does not make him 'unclean,' but what comes out of his mouth, that is what makes him 'unclean.'"

14 Again Jesus called the crowd to him and said, "Listen to me, everyone, and understand this. 15 Nothing outside a man can make him 'unclean' by going into him. Rather, it is what comes out of a man that makes him 'unclean.'[d]"

12 Then

17 After he had left the crowd and entered the house,

the disciples came to him and asked, "Do you know that the Pharisees were offended when they heard this?"

13 He replied, "Every plant that my heavenly Father has not planted will be pulled up by the roots. 14 Leave them; they are blind guides.[e] If a blind man leads a blind man, both will fall into a pit."

Matt. 15 | Mark 7

15 Peter said, "Explain the parable to us."
16 "Are you still so dull?" Jesus asked them. 17 "Don't you see

that

whatever enters the mouth

goes into the stomach and then out of the body?

18 But the things that come out of the mouth come from the heart, and these make a man 'unclean.' 19 For

out of the heart come evil thoughts, murder, adultery, sexual immorality, theft,

false testimony,

slander. 20 These

are what make a man 'unclean'; but eating with un-

his disciples asked him about this parable. 18 "Are you so dull?" he asked. "Don't you see

that nothing that enters a man from the outside can make him 'unclean'?
19 For

it

doesn't go into his heart but into his stomach, and then out of his body." (In saying this, Jesus declared all foods "clean.")
20 He went on:

"What comes out of a man is what makes him 'unclean.' 21 For

from within, out of men's hearts, come evil thoughts, sexual immorality, theft, murder, adultery, 22 greed, malice, deceit, lewdness, envy, slander, arrogance and folly. 23 All these evils come from inside and make a man 'unclean.'"

120

Matt. 15

washed hands
does not make
him 'unclean.'"

aSome early manuscripts "pitchers, kettles and dining couches".
bSome manuscripts "set up".   cSome manuscripts "father or his mother".
dSome early manuscripts "'unclean.' 16 If anyone has ears to hear, let
him hear".   eSome manuscripts "guides of the blind".

B. THE SECOND WITHDRAWAL FROM GALILEE, NORTH-WESTWARD TO THE REGION OF TYRE AND SIDON, AND SOUTH-EASTWARD TO THE DECAPOLIS

78. A SYROPHOENICIAN WOMAN'S HUMBLE FAITH AND THE HEALING OF HER DAUGHTER

The region of Tyre and Sidon

Matt. 15:21-28   Mark 7:24-30

Matt. 15:21-28	Mark 7:24-30	
21 Leaving that place, Jesus withdrew to the region of Tyre and Sidon.	24 Jesus left that place and went to the vicinity of Tyre.a	
	He entered a house and did not want anyone to know it; yet he could not keep his presence secret. 25 In fact, as soon as she heard about him,	
22 A Canaanite woman from that vicinity	a woman	
	whose little daughter was possessed by an evilb spirit came and fell at his feet.	
came to him,		
crying out, "Lord, Son of David, have mercy on me! My daughter		

121

Matt. 15   **Mark 7**

is suffering ter-
ribly from demon-
possession."

　　　26 The wo-
man was a Greek,
born in Syrian
Phoenicia. She
begged Jesus to
drive the demon
out of her daugh-
ter.

23 Jesus did not
answer a word.
So his disciples came to him and urged him, "Send her away, for she keeps
crying out after us."
24 He answered, "I was sent only to the lost sheep of Israel."
25 The woman
came and knelt
before him. "Lord,
help me!" she said.

　　　27 "First let the
26 He replied, children eat all
"It is not right they want," he told
to take the her, "for it is not
children's bread right to take the
and toss it to children's bread
their dogs." and toss it to
27 "Yes, Lord," their dogs."
she said, "but 28 "Yes, Lord,"
even the dogs she replied, "but
eat the even the dogs un-
der the table eat
the children's
crumbs
that fall from crumbs."
their masters'
table."
28 Then Jesus 29 Then he told
answered, "Woman, her,
you have great
faith! Your re-
quest is granted."

　　　"For such a
reply, you may go;
the demon has left
your daughter."

And her daughter

Matt. 15	Mark 7

was healed from that very hour.

30 She went home and found her child lying on the bed, and the demon gone.

aMany early manuscripts "Tyre and Sidon".   bGreek "unclean".

79. JESUS HEALS A DEAF MAN WITH A SPEECH IMPEDIMENT AND MANY OTHERS IN THE DECAPOLIS

Matt. 15:29-31	Mark 7:31-37

29 Jesus left there and went along the Sea of Galilee.

31 Then Jesus left the vicinity of Tyre and went through Sidon, down to the Sea of Galilee and into the region of the Decapolis.a **32 There some people brought a man to him who was deaf and could hardly talk, and they begged him to place his hand on the man.**

33 After he took him aside, away from the crowd, Jesus put his fingers into the man's ears. Then he spit and touched the man's tongue. 34 He looked up to heaven and with a deep sigh said to him, *"Ephphatha!"* (which means, "Be opened!"). 35 At this, the man's ears were opened, his tongue was loosened and he began to speak plainly.

36 Jesus commanded them not to tell anyone. But the more he did so, the more they kept talking about it. 37 People were overwhelmed with amazement. "He has done everything well," they said. "He even makes the deaf hear and the dumb speak."

Then he went up into the hills and sat down. 30 Great crowds came to him, bringing the lame, the blind, the crippled, the dumb and many others, and laid them at his feet; and he healed them. 31 The people were amazed when they saw the dumb speaking, the crippled made well, the lame walking and the blind seeing. And they praised the God of Israel.

aThat is, the Ten Cities.

80. THE MIRACULOUS FEEDING OF FOUR THOUSAND PEOPLE
The Decapolis

Matt. 15:32-39a   Mark 8:1-9

	1 During those days another large crowd gathered. Since they had nothing to eat,
32 Jesus called his disciples to him and said, "I have compassion for these people; they have already been with me three days and have nothing to eat. I do not want to send them away hungry, or they may collapse on the way."	Jesus called his disciples to him and said, 2 "I have compassion for these people; they have already been with me three days and have nothing to eat. 3 If I send them home hungry, they will collapse on the way, because some of them have come a long distance."
33 His disciples answered, "Where could we get enough bread in this remote place to feed such a crowd?"	4 His disciples answered, "But where in this remote place can anyone get enough bread to feed them?"
34 "How many loaves do you have?" Jesus asked. "Seven," they replied, "and a few small fish." 35 He told the crowd to sit down on the ground. 36 Then he took the seven loaves and the fish, and when he had given thanks, he broke them and	5 "How many loaves do you have?" Jesus asked. "Seven," they replied. 6 He told the crowd to sit down on the ground. When he had taken the seven loaves and given thanks, he broke them and gave

124

Matt. 15	Mark 8	
gave them to the disciples, and they in turn	them to his disciples to set before the people, and they did so. 7 They had a few small fish as well; he gave thanks for them also and told the disciples to distribute them.	
to the people. 37 They all ate and were satisfied. Afterward the disciples picked up seven basketfuls of broken pieces that were left over. 38 The number of those who ate was four thousand, besides women and children. 39 After Jesus had sent the crowd away, [he got into the boat ...]	8 The people ate and were satisfied. Afterward the disciples picked up seven basketfuls of broken pieces that were left over. 9 About four thousand men were present. And having sent them away, [10 he got into the boat ...]	

81. A SECOND BRIEF RETURN TO GALILEE — SOME PHARISEES AND SADDUCEES DEMAND MIRACULOUS PROOF OF CHRIST'S MESSIAHSHIP

Dalmanutha or Magadan in Galilee

Matt.15:39b-16:4a	Mark 8:10-12	
39b he got into the boat and went to the vicinity of Magadan. 1 The Pharisees	10 he got into the boat with his disciples and went to the region of Dalmanutha. 11 The Pharisees	

125

Matt. 16	Mark 8	
and Sadducees		
came to Jesus and tested him by asking him	came and began to question Jesus. To test him, they asked him	
to show them a sign from heaven.	for a sign from heaven.	
2 He replied,[a] "When evening		

comes, you say, 'It will be fair weather, for the sky is red,' 3 and in the morning, 'Today it will be stormy, for the sky is red and overcast.' You know how to interpret the appearance of the sky, but you cannot interpret the signs of the times.

4 A	12 He sighed deeply and said, "Why does this	
wicked and adulterous generation	gener-ation	
looks for a miraculous sign, but none will be	ask for a miraculous sign? I tell you the truth, no sign will be	
given it except the sign of Jonah."	given to it."	

[a]Some early manuscripts do not have the rest of verse 2 and all of verse 3.

C. THE THIRD WITHDRAWAL FROM GALILEE, TO BETHSAIDA JULIAS AND CAESAREA PHILIPPI

82. AGAIN CROSSING THE LAKE, JESUS WARNS THE TWELVE AGAINST THE PHARISEES, SADDUCEES AND HEROD ANTIPAS — HE EXPRESSES SURPRISE AT HIS DISCIPLES' SLOW UNDERSTANDING

North-east shore of the Lake of Galilee

Matt. 16:4b-12	Mark 8:13-21	
4b Jesus then left	13 Then he left them, got back into the boat and	

Matt. 16	Mark 8
them and went away.	crossed to the other side.
5 When they went across the lake,	
the disciples forgot to take bread.	**14 The disciples had forgotten to bring bread, except for one loaf they had with them in the boat.**
6 "Be careful," Jesus said to them. "Be on your guard against the yeast of the Pharisees and Sadducees."	15 "Be careful," Jesus warned them. "Watch out for the yeast of the Pharisees
	and that of Herod."
7 They discussed this among themselves and said, "It is because we didn't bring any bread."	16 They discussed this with one another and said, "It is because we have no bread."
8 Aware of their discussion, Jesus asked, "You of little faith, why are you talking among yourselves about having no bread? 9 Do you still not	17 Aware of their discussion, Jesus asked them: "Why are you talking about having no bread? Do you still not
understand?	**see or understand? Are your hearts hardened? 18 Do you have eyes but fail to see, and ears but fail to**
Don't you remember the five loaves for the five thousand, and how many basketfuls you gathered?	hear? **And don't you remember? 19 When I broke the five loaves for the five thousand, how many basketfuls of pieces did you pick up?"**

127

Matt. 16	Mark 8	
	"Twelve," they replied.	
	20 "And when I	
10 Or the seven	broke the seven	
loaves for the	loaves for the four	
four thousand,	thousand, how	
and how many	many basketfuls	
basketfuls you	of pieces did you	
gathered?	pick up?"	
	They answered, "Seven."	
11 How	21 He said to	
is it you don't	them, "Do you still not	
understand that		
I was not talking	understand?"	
to you about		

bread? But be on your guard against the yeast of the Pharisees and Sadducees." 12 Then they understood that he was not telling them to guard
against the yeast used in bread, but against the teaching of the Pharisees
and Sadducees.

83. A BLIND MAN HEALED AT BETHSAIDA JULIAS

Mark 8:22-26

	22 They came to Bethsaida,* and	

some people brought a blind man and begged Jesus to touch him. 23 He
took the blind man by the hand and led him outside the village. When he
had spit on the man's eyes and put his hands on him, Jesus asked, "Do you
see anything?"

24 He looked up and said, "I see people; they look like trees walking
around."

25 Once more Jesus put his hands on the man's eyes. Then his eyes were
opened, his sight was restored, and he saw everything clearly. 26 Jesus
sent him home, saying, "Don't go into the village.[a]"

[a]Some manuscripts "Don't go and tell anyone in the village".

---

*This village, north-east of the Lake of Galilee, in the te-
trarchy of Philip, was named by him Bethsaida Julias. It was
near the place where Jesus miraculously fed more than five thousand people (see page 107). Another village called Bethsaida was
located on the western shore of the lake (see page 111).

84. JESUS TESTS THE TWELVE NEAR CAESAREA PHILIPPI
PETER'S FIRM DECLARATION OF FAITH

Matt. 16:13-20	Mark 8:27-30	Luke 9:18-21
13 When Jesus came to the region of Caesarea Philippi, he asked his disciples,	27 Jesus and his disciples went on to the villages around Caesarea Philippi. On the way he asked them,	18 Once when Jesus was praying in private and his disciples were with him, he asked them,
"Who do people say the Son of Man is?"	"Who do people say I am?"	"Who do the crowds say I am?"
14 They replied, "Some say John the Baptist; others say Elijah; and still others, **Jeremiah or one** of the prophets."	28 They replied, "Some say John the Baptist; others say Elijah; and still others, one of the prophets."	19 They replied, "Some say John the Baptist; others say Elijah; and still others, that one of the prophets of long ago has come back to life."
15 "But what about you?" he asked. "Who do you say I am?"	29 "But what about you?" he asked. "Who do you say I am?"	20 "But what about you?" he asked. "Who do you say I am?"
16 Simon Peter answered, "You are the Christ,[a] the Son of the living God."	Peter answered, "You are the Christ.[a]"	Peter answered, "The Christ[a] of God."

17 Jesus replied, "Blessed are you, Simon son of Jonah, for this was not revealed to you by man, but by my Father in heaven. 18 And I tell you that you are Peter,[b] and on this rock I will build my church, and the gates of Hades[c] will not overcome it.[d] 19 I will give you the keys of the kingdom of heaven; whatever you bind on earth will be bound in heaven, and what-

ever you loose on earth will be loosed in heaven." 20 Then he warned		21 Jesus strictly warned

Matt. 16	Mark 8	Luke 9
his disciples **not to tell anyone that he was the Christ.**	30 Jesus warned them not to tell anyone about him.	them not to tell this to anyone.

aOr "Messiah"; also in Matt. 16:20. "The Christ" (Greek) and "the Messiah" (Hebrew) both mean "the Anointed One". bPeter means "rock". cOr "hell". dOr "not prove stronger than it".

85. CHRIST'S BEWILDERING FORECAST ABOUT HIS DEATH AND RESURRECTION AND THE COMING OF HIS KINGDOM

Matt. 16:21-28	Mark 8:31-9:1	Luke 9:22-27
21 From that time on Jesus began to explain to his disciples that he must go to Jerusalem and suffer many things at the hands of the elders, chief priests and teachers of the law, and that he must be killed and on the third day be raised to life.	31 He then began to teach them that the Son of Man must **suffer many things and be rejected by the elders, chief priests and teachers of the law, and that he must be killed and** after three days rise again.	22 And he said, "The Son of Man must suffer many things and be rejected by the elders, chief priests and teachers of the law, and he must be killed and on the third day be raised to life."
22 Peter took him aside and began to rebuke him. "Never, Lord!" he said. "This shall never happen to you!"	**32 He spoke plainly about this, and Peter** took him aside and began to rebuke him.	
23 Jesus turned and said to Peter, "Out of my	**33 But when Jesus turned and looked at his disciples, he rebuked Peter. "Out of my**	

Matt. 16	Mark 8	Luke 9
sight, Satan! You **are a stumbling block to me; you do not have in mind the things** of God, but the things of men." 24 Then Jesus said to his disciples, "If anyone would come after me, he must deny himself and take up his cross and follow me. 25 For whoever wants to save his life[a] will lose it, but whoever loses his life for me will find it. 26 What good will it be for a man if he gains the whole world, yet forfeits his soul? Or what can a man give in exchange for his soul?	**sight, Satan!"** he **said. "You** do not have in mind the things **of God, but the things of men." 34 Then he called the crowd to him along with his disciples and** said: "If anyone would come after me, he must deny himself and take up his cross **and follow me. 35 For whoever wants to save his life[a] will lose it, but whoever loses his life for me and for the gospel will save it. 36 What good is it for a man to gain the** whole world, yet forfeit his soul? **37 Or what can a man give in exchange for his soul? 38 If anyone is ashamed of me and my words in this adulterous and sinful generation, the Son of Man will be ashamed of him** when he comes in his Father's glory	23 Then he said **to them all: "If anyone would come after me, he must deny himself and take up his cross daily** and follow me. 24 For whoever wants to save his life will lose it, but whoever loses his life for me will save it. 25 What good is it for a man to gain the **whole world, and yet lose or forfeit his very self?** 26 If anyone is ashamed of me and my words, the Son of Man will be ashamed of him **when he comes in his glory and in the glory of the**
27 For the Son of Man is going to come in his Father's glory		

Matt. 16	Mark 8-9	Luke 9
with his	**with the** holy	**Father**
angels, and then he will reward each person according to what he has done. 28 I tell you the truth, some who are standing here	angels." 1 And he said to them, "I tell you the truth, some who are standing here	and of the holy angels. 27 I tell you the truth, some who are standing here will not
will not taste death before they see the Son of Man coming in his kingdom."	**will not taste death before they see the kingdom of God come with power."***	taste death before they see the kingdom of God."

ªThe Greek word means either "life" or "soul"; also in Matt. 16:26 and Mark 8:36.

86. THE GLORIOUS TRANSFIGURATION OF JESUS SEEN BY THREE OF HIS DISCIPLES

Probably Mount Hermon

Matt. 17:1-8	Mark 9:2-8	Luke 9:28-36a
1 After six days Jesus took	2 After six days Jesus took	**28 About eight days after Jesus said this, he took**
with him Peter, James and John the brother of James, and led them up a high mountain by themselves.	Peter, James and John with him and led them up a high mountain,	Peter, John and James with him and went up onto a mountain
		to pray. 29 As he was praying, the appearance of his face changed, and
	where they were all alone. There	
2 There he was transfigured before them.	**he was transfigured before them.**	

*Note the different wording in Matt. 16:28.

132

Matt. 17	Mark 9	Luke 9
His face shone like the sun, and his clothes became	3 His clothes became **dazzling white,**	his clothes became
as white as the light.		as bright as a flash of lightning.
	whiter than anyone in the world could bleach them. 4 And there appeared before them Elijah and Moses,	
3 Just then there appeared before them Moses and Elijah, talking with Jesus.	who were talking with Jesus.	30 Two men, Moses and Elijah, 31 appeared in **glorious splendor, talking with Jesus. They spoke about his departure, which he was**

about to bring to fulfillment at Jerusalem. 32 Peter and his companions were very sleepy, but when they became fully awake, they saw his glory

		and the two men standing with him. 33 As the men were leaving **Jesus, Peter said to him, "Master, it is good for us to be here.**
4 Peter said to Jesus, "Lord, it is good for us to be here.	5 Peter said to Jesus, "Rabbi, it is good for us to be here.	
If you wish, I will put up three shelters— one for you, one for Moses and one for Elijah."	**Let us put up three shelters — one for you, one for Moses and one for Elijah." 6 (He did not know what to say, they were so frightened.)**	Let us put up three shelters — one for you, one for Moses and one for Elijah." (He did not know what he was saying.)
5 While he was still speaking, a bright cloud enveloped them,	7 Then a cloud appeared and enveloped them,	34 While he was speaking, a cloud appeared and enveloped them, and they were afraid as they entered the cloud. 35 A voice
and a voice from	and a voice came	

133

Matt. 17	Mark 9	Luke 9
the cloud said, "This is my Son, whom I love;	from the cloud: "This is my be-loved Son.*	came from the cloud, saying, "This is my Son, whom I have cho-sen;
with him I am well pleased. Listen to him!" 6 When the dis-ciples heard this, they fell facedown to the ground, ter-rified. 7 But Jesus came and touched them. "Get up," he said. "Don't be afraid."	Lis-ten to him!"	listen to h i m."
8 When they looked up, they saw no one except Jesus.	8 Suddenly, when they looked a-round, they no longer saw anyone with them except Jesus.	36 When the voice had s p o k e n, they found that Jesus was alone.

87. THE PERPLEXITY OF THE THREE DISCIPLES ABOUT CHRIST'S REFERENCE TO HIS RESURRECTION AND ABOUT THE PROPHECY CONCERNING ELIJAH

On their way down the mountain

Matt. 17:9-13	Mark 9:9-13	Luke 9:36b
9 As they were coming down the mountain, Jesus instructed them, "Don't tell any-	9 As they were coming down the mountain, Jesus gave them orders not to tell any-	

*The NIV reads "my Son, whom I love" — a good translation of the original Greek. The rendering "my beloved Son", which has been used in several English versions, simplifies the reading of the interwoven narrative in this Harmony of the Gospels.

Matt. 17	Mark 9	Luke 9
one what you have seen, until the Son of Man has been raised from the dead."	one what they had seen until the Son of Man had risen from the dead.	
	10 They kept the matter to themselves,	36 b The disciples kept this to themselves,
	discussing what "rising from the dead" meant.	
10 The disciples asked him, "Why then do the teachers of the law say that Elijah must come first?"	11 And they asked him, "Why do the teachers of the law say that Elijah must come first?"	
11 Jesus replied, "To be sure, Elijah comes and will restore all things.	12 Jesus replied, "To be sure, Elijah does come first, and restores all things. Why then is it written that the Son of Man must suffer much and be rejected?	
12 But I tell you, Elijah has already come, and they did not recognize him, but have done to him everything they wished.	13 But I tell you, Elijah has come, and they have done to him everything they wished, just as it is written about him."	
In the same way the Son of Man is going to suffer at their hands." 13 Then the disciples understood that he was talking to them about John the Baptist.		

135

Luke 9

		and they* told no one at that time what they had seen.

88. A DEMONIAC BOY HEALED

The region of Caesarea Philippi

Matt. 17:14-20	Mark 9:14-29	Luke 9:37-43a
		37 The next day, when they came down from the mountain,
14 When they came to the crowd,	14 When they came to the other disciples, they saw a large crowd around them and the teachers of the law arguing with them. 15 As soon as all the people saw Jesus, they were over-whelmed with wonder and ran to greet him.	
		a large crowd met him.
	16 "What are you arguing with them about?" he asked.	
a man	17 A man in the crowd	38 A man in the crowd called out,
approached Jesus and knelt before him. 15 "Lord, have mercy on my	answered, "Teacher, I brought you my son,	"Teacher, I beg you to look at my son, for he is my only child.
son," he said.	who is pos-sessed by a spirit that has robbed	

*The NIV omits the word "they"; it is inserted here to improve the reading of the composite narrative.

Matt. 17	Mark 9	Luke 9
"He is an epileptic and is suffering greatly.	him of speech.	
	18 Whenever it seizes him, it throws him to the ground. He foams at the mouth, gnashes his teeth and becomes rigid.	39 A spirit seizes him and he suddenly screams; it throws him into convulsions so that he foams at the mouth. It scarcely ever leaves him and is destroying him.
He often falls into the fire or into the water. 16 I brought him to your disciples, but they could not heal him."	I asked your disciples to drive out the spirit, but they could not."	40 I begged your disciples to drive it out, but they could not."
17 "O unbelieving and perverse generation," Jesus replied, "how long shall I stay with you? How long shall I put up with you? Bring the boy here to me."	19 "O unbelieving generation," Jesus replied, "how long shall I stay with you? How long shall I put up with you? Bring the boy to me."	41 "O unbelieving and perverse generation," Jesus replied, "how long shall I stay with you and put up with you? Bring your son here."
	20 So they brought him. When the spirit saw Jesus, it immediately threw the boy into a convulsion. He fell to the ground	42 Even while the boy was coming, the demon threw him to the ground in a convulsion.

Matt. 17	Mark 9	Luke 9
	and rolled around, foaming at the mouth. 21 Jesus asked	

the boy's father, "How long has he been like this?"
"From childhood," he answered. 22 "It has often thrown him into fire or water to kill him. But if you can do anything, take pity on us and help us."
23 "'If you can'?" said Jesus. "Everything is possible for him who believes."
24 Immediately the boy's father exclaimed, "I do believe; help me over-

Matt. 17	Mark 9	Luke 9
	come my unbe-lief!"	
18 Jesus rebuked the demon,	25 When Jesus saw that a crowd was running to the scene, he rebuked the evil^a spirit. "You deaf and dumb spirit," he said, "I command you, come out of him and never enter him again." 26 The spirit shrieked, convuls-ed him violently	But Je-sus rebuked the evil^a spirit,
and it came out of the boy, and he was healed from that moment.	and came out.	
		healed the boy
	The boy looked so much like a corpse that many said, "He's dead." 27 But Jesus took him by the hand and lifted him to his feet, and he stood up.	
		and he* gave him back to his father. 43 And they were all amazed at the greatness of God.

*The NIV omits "he". It is inserted here to improve the read-ing of the composite narrative.

138

Matt. 17	Mark 9	
19 Then the disciples came to Jesus in private and asked, "Why couldn't we drive it out?"	28 After Jesus had gone indoors, his disciples asked him privately, "Why couldn't we drive it out?"	
20 He replied, "Because you have so little faith. I	29 He replied,	

tell you the truth, if you have faith as small as a mustard seed, you can say to this mountain, 'Move from here to there' and it will move. Nothing will be impossible for you.b"

"This kind can come out only by prayer.c"

aGreek "unclean".   bSome manuscripts "you. 21 But this kind does not go out except by prayer and fasting".   cSome manuscripts "prayer and fasting".

89. THE QUIET RETURN OF JESUS AND THE TWELVE TO GALILEE, ENDING THE SERIES OF WITHDRAWALS — CHRIST'S REPEATED FORECAST OF HIS DEATH AND RESURRECTION

Matt. 17:22-23	Mark 9:30-32	Luke 9:43b-45
		43b While everyone was marveling at all that Jesus did,
22 When they came together in Galilee,	30 They left that place and passed through Galilee. Jesus did not want anyone to know where they were, 31 because he was teaching his disciples. He said to them,	he said to his disciples,
he said to them, "The Son of Man is	"The Son of Man is	44 "Listen carefully to what I am about to tell you: The Son of Man is

139

Matt. 17	Mark 9	Luke 9
going to be be-trayed into the hands of men. 23 They will kill him, and	**going to be betrayed into the hands of men. They will kill him, and**	going to be betrayed into the hands of men."
on the third day he will be raised to life." And the disciples were filled with grief.	after three days he will rise."	
	32 But they did not understand	45 But they did not understand
	what he meant	**what this meant. It was hidden from them, so that they did not grasp it, and**
	and were afraid to ask him about it.	**they were afraid to ask him about it.**

90. JESUS PAYS THE TEMPLE TAX WITH A SHEKEL FROM A FISH'S MOUTH

Capernaum

Matt. 17:24-27   Mark 9:33a

24 After Jesus and his disciples arrived in Caper-naum, the col-lectors of the	33 They came to Capernaum.	

two-drachma tax came to Peter and asked, "Doesn't your teacher pay the temple tax[a]?"

25 "Yes, he does," he replied.

When Peter came into the house, Jesus was the first to speak. "What do you think, Simon?" he asked. "From whom do the kings of the earth collect duty and taxes — from their own sons or from others?"

26 "From others," Peter answered.

"Then the sons are exempt," Jesus said to him. 27 "But so that we may not offend them, go to the lake and throw out your line. Take the first fish you catch; open its mouth and you will find a four-drachma coin. Take it and give it to them for my tax and yours."

[a]Greek "the two drachmas".

91. JESUS REJECTS THE ADVICE OF HIS UNBELIEVING BROTHERS TO APPEAR WITHOUT DELAY IN JERUSALEM

John 7:1-9

1 After this, Jesus went around in Galilee, purposely staying away from Judea because the Jews there were waiting to take his life. 2 But when the Jewish Feast of Tabernacles was near, 3 Jesus' brothers said to him, "You ought to leave here and go to Judea, so that your disciples may see the miracles you do. 4 No one who wants to become a public figure acts in secret. Since you are doing these things, show yourself to the world." 5 For even his own brothers did not believe in him.

6 Therefore Jesus told them, "The right time for me has not yet come; for you any time is right. 7 The world cannot hate you, but it hates me because I testify that what it does is evil. 8 You go to the Feast. I am not yet[a] going up to this Feast, because for me the right time has not yet come." 9 Having said this, he stayed in Galilee.

[a]Some early manuscripts do not have "yet".

92. A PERTINENT DISCOURSE TO THE DISCIPLES ON THE NECESSITY FOR CHILDLIKENESS, TOLERANCE AND FORGIVENESS

Capernaum

Matt. 18:1-35	Mark 9:33b-50	Luke 9:46-50
1 At that time the disciples came to Jesus and asked, "Who is the greatest in the kingdom of heaven?"		46 An argument started among the disciples as to which of them would be the greatest.
	33b When he was in the house, he asked them, "What were you arguing about on the road?" 34 But they kept quiet because on the way they had argued about who	

141

Matt. 18	Mark 9	Luke 9
	was the greatest. **35 Sitting down,** Jesus	**47 Je-**sus, knowing their thoughts,
	called the Twelve and said, "If anyone wants to be first, he must be the very last, and the servant of all."	
2 He called a little child and had him stand among them. 3 And he said:	**36 He took a little child and had him stand among them. Taking him in his arms, he said to them,**	took a little child and had him stand beside him. **48 Then he said** to them,

"I tell you the truth, unless you change and become like little children, you will never enter the kingdom of heaven. 4 Therefore, whoever humbles himself like this child is

Matt. 18	Mark 9	Luke 9
the greatest in the kingdom of heaven. 5 And whoever welcomes a little child like this in my name welcomes me.	37 "Whoever welcomes one of these little children in my name welcomes **me; and whoever welcomes me does not welcome me but** the one who sent me."	"Whoever welcomes this little child in my name welcomes me; and whoever welcomes me welcomes **the one who sent me. For he who is least among you all — he is the greatest."**
	38 "Teacher," said John, "we saw a man driving out demons in your name and we told him to stop, because he was not one of us."	**49 "Master," said John, "we saw a man driving out demons in your name and we tried to stop him, because he is not one of us."**
	39 "Do not stop him," Jesus said. "No one who does	50 "Do not stop him," Jesus said,

142

Matt. 18	Mark 9	Luke 9
	a miracle in my name can in the next moment say anything bad about me, 40 for whoever is not against us is for us. 41 I tell you the truth, anyone who gives you a cup of water in my name because you belong to Christ will certainly not lose his reward.	"for whoever is not against you is for you."
6 "But if anyone causes one of these little ones who believe in me to sin, it would be better for him to have a large millstone hung around his neck and to be drowned in the depths of the sea. 7 Woe to the world because of the things that cause people to sin! Such things must come, but woe to the man through whom they come!	42 "And if anyone causes one of these little ones who believe in me to sin, it would be better for him to be thrown into the sea with a large millstone tied around his neck.	
8 If your hand or your foot causes you to sin, cut it off and throw it away. It is better for you to enter life maimed or crippled than to have two hands	43 If your hand causes you to sin, cut it off. It is better for you to enter life maimed than with two hands to go into hell, where the fire never goes out.[a] 45 And if your foot causes you to sin,	

Matt. 18 **Mark 8**

Mark 8: cut it off. It is better for you to enter life crippled than to have two feet and be thrown into

Matt. 18: or two feet and be thrown into eternal fire. 9 And if your eye causes you to sin, gouge it out and throw it away. It is better for you to

Mark 8: hell.^b 47 And if your eye causes you to sin, pluck it out. It is better for you to

Matt. 18: enter life with one eye than to have two eyes and be thrown into the fire of hell.

Mark 8: enter the kingdom of God with one eye than to have two eyes and be thrown into hell, 48 where

> "'their worm does not die,
> and the fire is not quenched.'

49 Everyone will be salted with fire.

50 "Salt is good, but if it loses its saltiness, how can you make it salty again? Have salt in yourselves, and be at peace with each other."

Matt. 18: 10 "See that you do not look down on one of these little ones. For I tell you that their angels in heaven always see the face of my Father in heaven.^c

12 "What do you think? If a man owns a hundred sheep, and one of them wanders away, will he not leave the ninety-nine on the hills and go to look for the one that wandered off? 13 And if he finds it, I tell you the truth, he is happier about that one sheep than about the ninety-nine that did not wander off. 14 In the same way your Father in heaven is not willing that any of these little ones should be lost.

15 "If your brother sins against you,^d go and show him his fault, just between the two of you. If he listens to you, you have won your brother over. 16 But if he will not listen, take one or two others along, so that 'every matter may be established by the testimony of two or three witnesses.'^e

Matt. 18

17 If he refuses to listen to them, tell it to the church; and if he refuses to listen even to the church, treat him as you would a pagan or a tax collector.

18 "I tell you the truth, whatever you bind on earth will be bound in heaven, and whatever you loose on earth will be loosed in heaven.

19 "Again, I tell you that if two of you on earth agree about anything you ask for, it will be done for you by my Father in heaven. 20 For where two or three come together in my name, there am I with them."

21 Then Peter came to Jesus and asked, "Lord, how many times shall I forgive my brother when he sins against me? Up to seven times?"

22 Jesus answered, "I tell you, not seven times, but seventy-seven times.[f]

23 "Therefore, the kingdom of heaven is like a king who wanted to settle accounts with his servants. 24 As he began the settlement, a man who owed him ten thousand talents[g] was brought to him. 25 Since he was not able to pay, the master ordered that he and his wife and his children and all that he had be sold to repay the debt.

26 "The servant fell on his knees before him. 'Be patient with me,' he begged, 'and I will pay back everything.' 27 The servant's master took pity on him, canceled the debt and let him go.

28 "But when that servant went out, he found one of his fellow servants who owed him a hundred denarii.[h] He grabbed him and began to choke him. 'Pay back what you owe me!' he demanded.

29 "His fellow servant fell to his knees and begged him, 'Be patient with me, and I will pay you back.'

30 "But he refused. Instead, he went off and had the man thrown into prison until he could pay the debt. 31 When the other servants saw what had happened, they were greatly distressed and went and told their master everything that had happened.

32 "Then the master called the servant in. 'You wicked servant,' he said, 'I canceled all that debt of yours because you begged me to. 33 Shouldn't you have had mercy on your fellow servant just as I had on you?' 34 In anger his master turned him over to the jailers until he should pay back all he owed.

35 "This is how my heavenly Father will treat each of you unless you forgive your brother from your heart."

[a]Some manuscripts "out, 44 where 'their worm does not die, and the fire is not quenched'". [b]Some manuscripts "hell, 46 where 'their worm does not die, and the fire is not quenched'". [c]Some manuscripts "heaven. 11 The Son of Man came to save what was lost." [d]Some manuscripts do not have "against you". [e]Deut. 19:15. [f]Or "seventy times seven". [g]That is, several million dollars. [h]That is, a few dollars.

93. THE MISTAKEN ZEAL OF JAMES AND JOHN ON THE WAY TO THE FESTIVAL OF TABERNACLES AT JERUSALEM

Samaria. Probably September, A.D. 29

Luke 9:51-56	John 7:10
51 As the time approached for him to be taken up to heaven,	10 However,
	after his brothers had left for the Feast,
Je-sus resolutely set out for Jerusalem,	he went
	also, not publicly, but in secret.
52 and he sent messengers on	

ahead. They went into a Samaritan village to get things ready for him, 53 but the people there did not welcome him, because he was heading for Jerusalem. 54 When the disciples James and John saw this, they asked, "Lord, do you want us to call fire down from heaven to destroy them[a]?" 55 But Jesus turned and rebuked them, 56 and[b] they went to another village.

[a]Some manuscripts "them, even as Elijah did". [b]Some manuscripts "them. And he said, 'You do not know what kind of spirit you are of, for the Son of Man did not come to destroy men's lives, but to save them. 56 And".

94. THE REACTION OF JESUS TO THE CASUAL ATTITUDE OF THREE WOULD-BE FOLLOWERS

Samaria or Judea

Matt. 8:19-22	Luke 9:57-62
19 Then	57 As they were walking along the road,
a teacher of the law came to him and said, "Teacher, I will follow you wherever you go."	a man said to him, "I will follow you wherever you go."
20 Jesus replied, "Foxes have holes and birds of the air have nests, but the Son of Man has no place to lay his head."	58 Jesus replied, "Foxes have holes and birds of the air have nests, but the Son of Man has no place to lay his head."

Matt. 8	Luke 9
21 Another man,	59 He said to an- other man,
one of his disciples,	**"Fol-**
said to him, "Lord, first let me go and bury my father."	**low me."** But the man replied, "Lord, first let me go and bury my father."
22 But Jesus told him, "Follow me, and let the	60 Jesus said to him, "Let the
dead bury their own dead."	**dead bury their own dead, but you go and proclaim the kingdom of God."** 61 Still another said, "I will follow you, Lord; but first let me go back and say good-by to my family."

62 Jesus replied, "No one who puts his hand to the plow and looks back
is fit for service in the kingdom of God."

PART VIII

CHRIST'S LATER JUDEAN MINISTRY

OCTOBER TO DECEMBER, A.D. 29

95. JESUS AT THE FESTIVAL OF TABERNACLES — ANIMATED DISCUSSIONS GENERATED BY HIS MESSIANIC ASSERTIONS

The temple, Jerusalem

John 7:11-52

11 Now at the Feast the Jews were watching for him and asking, "Where is that man?"

12 Among the crowds there was widespread whispering about him. Some said, "He is a good man."

Others replied, "No, he deceives the people." 13 But no one would say anything publicly about him for fear of the Jews.

14 Not until halfway through the Feast did Jesus go up to the temple courts and begin to teach. 15 The Jews were amazed and asked, "How did this man get such learning without having studied?"

16 Jesus answered, "My teaching is not my own. It comes from him who sent me. 17 If any one chooses to do God's will, he will find out whether my teaching comes from God or whether I speak on my own. 18 He who speaks on his own does so to gain honor for himself, but he who works for the honor of the one who sent him is a man of truth; there is nothing false about him. 19 Has not Moses given you the law? Yet not one of you keeps the law. Why are you trying to kill me?"

20 "You are demon-possessed," the crowd answered. "Who is trying to kill you?"

21 Jesus said to them, "I did one miracle, and you are all astonished. 22 Yet, because Moses gave you circumcision (though actually it did not come from Moses, but from the patriarchs), you circumcise a child on the Sabbath. 23 Now if a child can be circumcised on the Sabbath so that the law of Moses may not be broken, why are you angry with me for healing the whole man on the Sabbath? 24 Stop judging by mere appearances, and make a right judgment."

25 At that point some of the people of Jerusalem began to ask, "Isn't this the man they are trying to kill? 26 Here he is, speaking publicly, and

they are not say-
ing a word to him.

Have the authorities really concluded that he is the Christ[a]? 27 But we know where this man is from; when the Christ comes, no one will know where he is from."

28 Then Jesus, still teaching in the temple courts, cried out, "Yes, you know me, and you know where I am from. I am not here on my own, but he who sent me is true. You do not know him, 29 but I know him because I am from him and he sent me."

30 At this they tried to seize him, but no one laid a hand on him, because his time had not yet come. 31 Still, many in the crowd put their faith in him. They said, "When the Christ comes, will he do more miraculous signs than this man?"

32 The Pharisees heard the crowd whispering such things about him. Then the chief priests and the Pharisees sent temple guards to arrest him.

33 Jesus said, "I am with you for only a short time, and then I go to the one who sent me. 34 You will look for me, but you will not find me; and where I am, you cannot come."

35 The Jews said to one another, "Where does this man intend to go that we cannot find him? Will he go where our people live scattered among the Greeks, and teach the Greeks? 36 What did he mean when he said, 'You will look for me, but you will not find me,' and 'Where I am, you cannot come'?"

37 On the last and greatest day of the Feast, Jesus stood and said in a loud voice, "If a man is thirsty, let him come to me and drink. 38 Whoever believes in me,[b] as the Scripture has said, streams of living water will flow from within him." 39 By this he meant the Spirit, whom those who believed in him were later to receive. Up to that time the Spirit had not been given, since Jesus had not yet been glorified.

40 On hearing his words, some of the people said, "Surely this man is the Prophet."

41 Others said, "He is the Christ."

Still others asked, "How can the Christ come from Galilee? 42 Does not the Scripture say that the Christ will come from David's family[c] and from Bethlehem, the town where David lived?" 43 Thus the people were divided because of Jesus. 44 Some wanted to seize him, but no one laid a hand on him.

45 Finally the temple guards went back to the chief priests and Pharisees, who asked them, "Why didn't you bring him in?"

46 "No one ever spoke the way this man does," the guards declared.

47 "You mean he has deceived you also?" the Pharisees retorted. 48 "Has any of the rulers or of the Pharisees believed in him? 49 No! But this mob that knows nothing of the law — there is a curse on them."

50 Nicodemus, who had gone to Jesus earlier and who was one of their own number, asked, 51 "Does our law condemn a man without first hearing him to find out what he is doing?"

52 They replied, "Are you from Galilee, too? Look into it, and you will

John 7

| | | |find that a pro-
phet[d] does not
come out of Gal-
ilee." |

[a]Or "Messiah"; also in verses 27, 31, 41 and 42.   [b]Or "If a man is thirsty, let him come to me. And let him drink, who believes in me."
[c]Greek "seed".   [d]Two early manuscripts "the Prophet".

96. CHRIST'S SKILLFUL HANDLING OF SOME HOSTILE RELIGIOUS LEADERS WHO BROUGHT AN ADULTERESS TO HIM FOR JUDGMENT

The temple, Jerusalem

John 7:53-8:11

53 Then each went to his own home.

1 But Jesus went to the Mount of Olives. 2 At dawn he appeared again in the temple courts, where all the people gathered around him, and he sat down to teach them. 3 The teachers of the law and the Pharisees brought in a woman caught in adultery. They made her stand before the group 4 and said to Jesus, "Teacher, this woman was caught in the act of adultery. 5 In the Law Moses commanded us to stone such women. Now what do you say?" 6 They were using this question as a trap, in order to have a basis for accusing him.

But Jesus bent down and started to write on the ground with his finger. 7 When they kept on questioning him, he straightened up and said to them, "If any one of you is without sin, let him be the first to throw a stone at her." 8 Again he stooped down and wrote on the ground.

9 At this, those who heard began to go away one at a time, the older ones first, until only Jesus was left, with the woman still standing there. 10 Jesus straightened up and asked her, "Woman, where are they? Has no one condemned you?"

11 "No one, sir," she said.

"Then neither do I condemn you," Jesus declared. "Go now and leave your life of sin."*

---

*The earliest and most reliable Greek manuscripts do not have John 7:53 - 8:11.

97. HOSTILE RELIGIOUS LEADERS CHALLENGE CHRIST'S DIVINE CLAIMS — INFURIATED BY HIS STRAIGHTFORWARD DECLARATIONS, THEY ATTEMPT TO STONE HIM

The temple, Jerusalem

John 8:12-59

12 When Jesus spoke again to the people, he said, "I am the light of the world. Whoever follows me will never walk in darkness, but will have the light of life."

13 The Pharisees challenged him, "Here you are, appearing as your own witness; your testimony is not valid."

14 Jesus answered, "Even if I testify on my own behalf, my testimony is valid, for I know where I came from and where I am going. But you have no idea where I come from or where I am going. 15 You judge by human standards; I pass judgment on no one. 16 But if I do judge, my decisions are right, because I am not alone. I stand with the Father who sent me. 17 In your own Law it is written that the testimony of two men is valid. 18 I am one who testifies for myself; my other witness is the one who sent me — the Father."

19 Then they asked him, "Where is your father?"

"You do not know me or my Father," Jesus replied. "If you knew me, you would know my Father also." 20 He spoke these words while teaching in the temple area near the place where the offerings were put. Yet no one seized him, because his time had not yet come.

21 Once more Jesus said to them, "I am going away, and you will look for me, and you will die in your sin. Where I go, you cannot come."

22 This made the Jews ask, "Will he kill himself? Is that why he says, 'Where I go, you cannot come'?"

23 But he continued, "You are from below; I am from above. You are of this world; I am not of this world. 24 I told you that you would die in your sins; if you do not believe that I am the one I claim to be,[a] you will indeed die in your sins."

25 "Who are you?" they asked.

"Just what I have been claiming all along," Jesus replied. 26 "I have much to say in judgment of you. But he who sent me is reliable, and what I have heard from him I tell the world."

27 They did not understand that he was telling them about his Father. 28 So Jesus said, "When you have lifted up the Son of Man, then you will know who I am[b] and that I do nothing on my own but speak just what the Father has taught me. 29 The one who sent me is with me; he has not left me alone, for I always do what pleases him." 30 Even as he spoke, many put their faith in him.

31 To the Jews who had believed him, Jesus said, "If you hold to my teaching, you are really my disciples. 32 Then you will know the truth, and the truth will set you free."

John 8

33 They answered
him, "We are Abra-
ham's descendants[c] and have never been slaves of anyone. How can you say
that we shall be set free?"

34 Jesus replied, "I tell you the truth, everyone who sins is a slave to sin.
35 Now a slave has no permanent place in the family, but a son belongs to
it forever. 36 So if the Son sets you free, you will be free indeed. 37 I know
you are Abraham's descendants. Yet you are ready to kill me, because you
have no room for my word. 38 I am telling you what I have seen in the
Father's presence, and you do what you have heard from your father.[dn]

39 "Abraham is our father," they answered.

"If you were Abraham's children," said Jesus, "then you would[e] do the
things Abraham did. 40 As it is, you are determined to kill me, a man who
has told you the truth that I heard from God. Abraham did not do such
things. 41 You are doing the things your own father does."

"We are not illegitimate children," they protested. "The only Father we
have is God himself."

42 Jesus said to them, "If God were your Father, you would love me, for
I came from God and now am here. I have not come on my own; but he
sent me. 43 Why is my language not clear to you? Because you are unable
to hear what I say. 44 You belong to your father, the devil, and you want
to carry out your father's desire. He was a murderer from the beginning,
not holding to the truth, for there is no truth in him. When he lies, he
speaks his native language, for he is a liar and the father of lies. 45 Yet
because I tell the truth, you do not believe me! 46 Can any of you prove
me guilty of sin? If I am telling the truth, why don't you believe me?
47 He who belongs to God hears what God says. The reason you do not
hear is that you do not belong to God."

48 The Jews answered him, "Aren't we right in saying that you are a
Samaritan and demon-possessed?"

49 "I am not possessed by a demon," said Jesus, "but I honor my Father
and you dishonor me. 50 I am not seeking glory for myself; but there is
one who seeks it, and he is the judge. 51 I tell you the truth, if a man
keeps my word, he will never see death."

52 At this the Jews exclaimed, "Now we know that you are demon-
possessed! Abraham died and so did the prophets, yet you say that if a
man keeps your word, he will never taste death. 53 Are you greater than
our father Abraham? He died, and so did the prophets. Who do you think
you are?"

54 Jesus replied, "If I glorify myself, my glory means nothing. My Father,
whom you claim as your God, is the one who glorifies me. 55 Though you
do not know him, I know him. If I said I did not, I would be a liar like you,
but I do know him and keep his word. 56 Your father Abraham rejoiced at
the thought of seeing my day; he saw it and was glad."

57 "You are not yet fifty years old," the Jews said to him, "and you have
seen Abraham!"

58 "I tell you the truth," Jesus answered, "before Abraham was born,

John 8

I am!" 59 At this,
they picked up
stones to stone him, but Jesus hid himself, slipping away from the temple
grounds.

ªOr "I am he".   bOr "know that I am he".   cGreek "seed"; also in
verse 37.   dOr "presence. Therefore do what you have heard from the
Father".   eSome manuscripts "'If you are Abraham's children,' said
Jesus, 'then,"

98. A MAN BORN BLIND, HEALED ON THE SABBATH, CONFOUNDS AND ANGERS THE PHARISEES — USING THE ALLEGORY OF A GOOD SHEPHERD, JESUS TRIES TO EXPLAIN HIS REDEMPTIVE MINISTRY

Jerusalem

John 9:1-10:21

1 As he went
along, he saw a
man blind from
birth. 2 His disciples asked him, "Rabbi, who sinned, this man or his parents, that he was born blind?"

3 "Neither this man nor his parents sinned," said Jesus, "but this happened
so that the work of God might be displayed in his life. 4 As long as it is
day, we must do the work of him who sent me. Night is coming, when no
one can work. 5 While I am in the world, I am the light of the world."

6 Having said this, he spit on the ground, made some mud with the saliva,
and put it on the man's eyes. 7 "Go," he told him, "wash in the pool of
Siloam" (this word means Sent). So the man went and washed, and came
home seeing.

8 His neighbors and those who had formerly seen him begging asked,
"Isn't this the same man who used to sit and beg?" 9 Some claimed that he
was.

Others said, "No, he only looks like him."

But he himself insisted, "I am the man."

10 "How then were your eyes opened?" they demanded.

11 He replied, "The man they call Jesus made some mud and put it on my
eyes. He told me to go to Siloam and wash. So I went and washed, and
then I could see."

12 "Where is this man?" they asked him.

"I don't know," he said.

13 They brought to the Pharisees the man who had been blind. 14 Now
the day on which Jesus had made the mud and opened the man's eyes was
a Sabbath. 15 Therefore the Pharisees also asked him how he had received
his sight. "He put mud on my eyes," the man replied, "and I washed, and

now I see."
16 Some of the Pharisees said, "This man is not from God, for he does not keep the Sabbath."

But others asked, "How can a sinner do such miraculous signs?" So they were divided.

17 Finally they turned again to the blind man, "What have you to say about him? It was your eyes he opened."

The man replied, "He is a prophet."

18 The Jews still did not believe that he had been blind and had received his sight until they sent for the man's parents. 19 "Is this your son?" they asked. "Is this the one you say was born blind? How is it that now he can see?"

20 "We know he is our son," the parents answered, "and we know he was born blind. 21 But how he can see now, or who opened his eyes, we don't know. Ask him. He is of age; he will speak for himself." 22 His parents said this because they were afraid of the Jews, for already the Jews had decided that anyone who acknowledged that Jesus was the Christ[a] would be put out of the synagogue. 23 That was why his parents said, "He is of age; ask him."

24 A second time they summoned the man who had been blind. "Give glory to God,[b]" they said. "We know this man is a sinner."

25 He replied, "Whether he is a sinner or not, I don't know. One thing I do know. I was blind but now I see!"

26 Then they asked him, "What did he do to you? How did he open your eyes?"

27 He answered, "I have told you already and you did not listen. Why do you want to hear it again? Do you want to become his disciples, too?"

28 Then they hurled insults at him and said, "You are this fellow's disciple! We are disciples of Moses! 29 We know that God spoke to Moses, but as for this fellow, we don't even know where he comes from."

30 The man answered, "Now that is remarkable! You don't know where he comes from, yet he opened my eyes. 31 We know that God does not listen to sinners. He listens to the godly man who does his will. 32 Nobody has ever heard of opening the eyes of a man born blind. 33 If this man were not from God, he could do nothing."

34 To this they replied, "You were steeped in sin at birth; how dare you lecture us!" And they threw him out.

35 Jesus heard that they had thrown him out, and when he found him, he said, "Do you believe in the Son of Man?"

36 "Who is he, sir?" the man asked. "Tell me so that I may believe in him."

37 Jesus said, "You have now seen him; in fact, he is the one speaking with you."

38 Then the man said, "Lord, I believe," and he worshiped him.

39 Jesus said, "For judgment I have come into this world, so that the blind will see and those who see will become blind."

John 9–10

40 Some Phari-
sees who were with
him heard him say this and asked, "What? Are we blind too?"

41 Jesus said, "If you were blind, you would not be guilty of sin; but now that you claim you can see, your guilt remains.

1 "I tell you the truth, the man who does not enter the sheep pen by the gate, but climbs in by some other way, is a thief and a robber. 2 The man who enters by the gate is the shepherd of his sheep. 3 The watchman opens the gate for him, and the sheep listen to his voice. He calls his own sheep by name and leads them out. 4 When he has brought out all his own, he goes on ahead of them, and his sheep follow him because they know his voice. 5 But they will never follow a stranger; in fact, they will run away from him because they do not recognize a stranger's voice." 6 Jesus used this figure of speech, but they did not understand what he was telling them.

7 Therefore Jesus said again, "I tell you the truth, I am the gate for the sheep. 8 All who ever came before me were thieves and robbers, but the sheep did not listen to them. 9 I am the gate; whoever enters through me will be saved.^{c} He will come in and go out, and find pasture. 10 The thief comes only to steal and kill and destroy; I have come that they may have life, and have it to the full.

11 "I am the good shepherd. The good shepherd lays down his life for the sheep. 12 The hired hand is not the shepherd who owns the sheep. So when he sees the wolf coming, he abandons the sheep and runs away. Then the wolf attacks the flock and scatters it. 13 The man runs away because he is a hired hand and cares nothing for the sheep.

14 "I am the good shepherd; I know my sheep and my sheep know me — 15 just as the Father knows me and I know the Father — and I lay down my life for the sheep. 16 I have other sheep that are not of this sheep pen. I must bring them also. They too will listen to my voice, and there shall be one flock and one shepherd. 17 The reason my Father loves me is that I lay down my life — only to take it up again. 18 No one takes it from me, but I lay it down of my own accord. I have authority to lay it down and authority to take it up again. This command I received from my Father."

19 At these words the Jews were again divided. 20 Many of them said, "He is demon-possessed and raving mad. Why listen to him?"

21 But others said, "These are not the sayings of a man possessed by a demon. Can a demon open the eyes of the blind?"

^{a}Or "Messiah". ^{b}A solemn charge to tell the truth (see Joshua 7:19).
^{c}Or "kept safe".

99. SEVENTY-TWO PREACHERS INSTRUCTED AND SENT OUT IN PAIRS — THE EXULTATION OF JESUS ON THEIR RETURN

Probably in Judea*

Luke 10:1-24

1 After this the Lord appointed seventy-two[a] others

and sent them two by two ahead of him to every town and place where he was about to go. 2 He told them, "The harvest is plentiful, but the workers are few. Ask the Lord of the harvest, therefore, to send out workers into his harvest field. 3 Go! I am sending you out like lambs among wolves. 4 Do not take a purse or bag or sandals; and do not greet anyone on the road.

5 "When you enter a house, first say, 'Peace to this house.' 6 If a man of peace is there, your peace will rest on him; if not, it will return to you. 7 Stay in that house, eating and drinking whatever they give you, for the worker deserves his wages. Do not move around from house to house.

8 "When you enter a town and are welcomed, eat what is set before you. 9 Heal the sick who are there and tell them, 'The kingdom of God is near you.' 10 But when you enter a town and are not welcomed, go into its streets and say, 11 'Even the dust of your town that sticks to our feet we wipe off against you. Yet be sure of this: The kingdom of God is near.' 12 I tell you, it will be more bearable on that day for Sodom than for that town.

13 "Woe to you, Korazin! Woe to you, Bethsaida! For if the miracles that were performed in you had been performed in Tyre and Sidon, they would have repented long ago, sitting in sackcloth and ashes. 14 But it will be more bearable for Tyre and Sidon at the judgment than for you. 15 And you, Capernaum, will you be lifted up to the skies? No, you will go down to the depths.[b]

16 "He who listens to you listens to me; he who rejects you rejects me; but he who rejects me rejects him who sent me."

17 The seventy-two returned with joy and said, "Lord, even the demons submit to us in your name."

18 He replied, "I saw Satan fall like lightning from heaven. 19 I have given you authority to trample on snakes and scorpions and to overcome all the power of the enemy; nothing will harm you. 20 However, do not rejoice that the spirits submit to you, but rejoice that your names are written in heaven."

---

*New Testament scholars hold different opinions about the time and place of events recorded in a large part of Luke's Gospel. Strong arguments support the probability that the events described in Luke 10:1-13:21 occurred in Judea during the three months' interval between Christ's appearances in Jerusalem at the Festival of Tabernacles and the Festival of Dedication.

Luke 10

| 21 At that time |
| Jesus, full of joy |

through the Holy Spirit, said, "I praise you, Father, Lord of heaven and earth, because you have hidden these things from the wise and learned, and revealed them to little children. Yes, Father, for this was your good pleasure.

22 "All things have been committed to me by my Father. No one knows who the Son is except the Father, and no one knows who the Father is except the Son and those to whom the Son chooses to reveal him."

23 Then he turned to his disciples and said privately, "Blessed are the eyes that see what you see. 24 For I tell you that many prophets and kings wanted to see what you see but did not see it, and to hear what you hear but did not hear it."

aSome manuscripts "seventy"; also in verse 17.   bGreek "Hades".

100. JESUS ANSWERS A TEST QUESTION POSED BY AN EXPERT IN THE LAW — THE PARABLE OF A GOOD SAMARITAN

Luke 10:25-37

| 25 On one occa- |
| sion an expert in |
| the law stood up |

to test Jesus. "Teacher," he asked, "what must I do to inherit eternal life?"

26 "What is written in the Law?" he replied. "How do you read it?"

27 He answered: " 'Love the Lord your God with all your heart and with all your soul and with all your strength and with all your mind'; and, 'Love your neighbor as yourself.' "

28 "You have answered correctly," Jesus replied. "Do this and you will live."

29 But he wanted to justify himself, so he asked Jesus, "And who is my neighbor?"

30 In reply Jesus said: "A man was going down from Jerusalem to Jericho, when he fell into the hands of robbers. They stripped him of his clothes, beat him and went away, leaving him half dead. 31 A priest happened to be going down the same road, and when he saw the man, he passed by on the other side. 32 So too, a Levite, when he came to the place and saw him, passed by on the other side. 33 But a Samaritan, as he traveled, came where the man was; and when he saw him, he took pity on him. 34 He went to him and bandaged his wounds, pouring on oil and wine. Then he put the man on his own donkey, took him to an inn and took care of him. 35 The next day he took out two silver coinsᵃ and gave them to the innkeeper. 'Look after him,' he said, 'and when I return, I will reimburse you for any extra expense you may have.'

Luke 10

| 36 "Which of these
| three do you think |

was a neighbor to the man who fell into the hands of robbers?"
37 The expert in the law replied, "The one who had mercy on him."
Jesus told him, "Go and do likewise."

ªGreek "two denarii".

101. JESUS AT THE HOME OF MARTHA AND MARY

Bethany, near Jerusalem

Luke 10:38-42

| 38 As Jesus and |
| his disciples were |
| on their way, he |

came to a village where a woman named Martha opened her home to him.
39 She had a sister called Mary, who sat at the Lord's feet listening to
what he said. 40 But Martha was distracted by all the preparations that
had to be made. She came to him and asked, "Lord, don't you care that my
sister has left me to do the work by myself? Tell her to help me!"
41 "Martha, Martha," the Lord answered, "you are worried and upset
about many things, 42 but only one thing is needed.ª Mary has chosen
what is better, and it will not be taken away from her."

ªSome manuscripts "but few things are needed — or only one".

102. A DISCOURSE TO THE DISCIPLES ON PRAYER — THE PARABLE OF A PERSISTENT FRIEND

Luke 11:1-13

| 1 One day Jesus |
| was praying in a |
| certain place. |

When he finished, one of his disciples said to him, "Lord, teach us to pray,
just as John taught his disciples."
2 He said to them, "When you pray, say:
   " 'Father,ª
   hallowed be your name,
   your kingdom come.ᵇ
  3 Give us each day our daily bread.
  4 Forgive us our sins,
      for we also forgive everyone who sins against us.ᶜ
  And lead us not into temptation.ᵈ' "

158

Luke 11

| 5 Then he said
| to them, "Suppose

one of you has a friend, and he goes to him at midnight and says, 'Friend, lend me three loaves of bread, 6 because a friend of mine on a journey has come to me, and I have nothing to set before him.'

7 "Then the one inside answers, 'Don't bother me. The door is already locked, and my children are with me in bed. I can't get up and give you anything.' 8 I tell you, though he will not get up and give him the bread because he is his friend, yet because of the man's persistence he will get up and give him as much as he needs.

9 "So I say to you: Ask and it will be given to you; seek and you will find; knock and the door will be opened to you. 10 For everyone who asks receives; he who seeks finds; and to him who knocks, the door will be opened.

11 "Which of you fathers, if your son asks for[e] a fish, will give him a snake instead? 12 Or if he asks for an egg, will give him a scorpion? 13 If you then, though you are evil, know how to give good gifts to your children, how much more will your Father in heaven give the Holy Spirit to those who ask him!"

[a]Some manuscripts "Our Father in heaven". [b]Some manuscripts "come. May your will be done on earth as it is in heaven". [c]Greek "everyone who is indebted to us". [d]Some manuscripts "temptation but deliver us from evil". [e]Some manuscripts "for bread, will give him a stone; or if he asks for".

103. THE HEALING OF A DUMB DEMONIAC PRECIPITATES ANOTHER CLASH WITH THE PHARISEES

Luke 11:14-36

| 14 Jesus was driv-
| ing out a demon
| that was mute.

When the demon left, the man who had been dumb spoke, and the crowd was amazed. 15 But some of them said, "By Beelzebub,[a] the prince of demons, he is driving out demons." 16 Others tested him by asking for a sign from heaven.

17 Jesus knew their thoughts and said to them: "Any kingdom divided against itself will be ruined, and a house divided against itself will fall. 18 If Satan is divided against himself, how can his kingdom stand? I say this because you claim that I drive out demons by Beelzebub. 19 Now if I drive out demons by Beelzebub, by whom do your followers drive them out? So then, they will be your judges. 20 But if I drive out demons by the finger of God, then the kingdom of God has come to you.

21 "When a strong man, fully armed, guards his own house, his possessions are safe. 22 But when someone stronger attacks and overpowers him, he takes away the armor in which the man trusted and divides up the spoils.

159

Luke 11

| 23 "He who is|
| not with me is|

against me, and he who does not gather with me, scatters.

24 "When an evil[b] spirit comes out of a man, it goes through arid places seeking rest and does not find it. Then it says, 'I will return to the house I left.' 25 When it arrives, it finds the house swept clean and put in order. 26 Then it goes and takes seven other spirits more wicked than itself, and they go in and live there. And the final condition of that man is worse than the first."

27 As Jesus was saying these things, a woman in the crowd called out, "Blessed is the mother who gave you birth and nursed you."

28 He replied, "Blessed rather are those who hear the word of God and obey it."

29 As the crowds increased, Jesus said, "This is a wicked generation. It asks for a miraculous sign, but none will be given it except the sign of Jonah. 30 For as Jonah was a sign to the Ninevites, so also will the Son of Man be to this generation. 31 The Queen of the South will rise at the judgment with the men of this generation and condemn them, for she came from the ends of the earth to listen to Solomon's wisdom, and now one[c] greater than Solomon is here. 32 The men of Nineveh will stand up at the judgment with this generation and condemn it, for they repented at the preaching of Jonah, and now one greater than Jonah is here.

33 "No one lights a lamp and puts it in a place where it will be hidden, or under a bowl. Instead he puts it on its stand, so that those who come in may see the light. 34 Your eye is the lamp of your body. When your eyes are good, your whole body also is full of light. But when they are bad, your body also is full of darkness. 35 See to it, then, that the light within you is not darkness. 36 Therefore, if your whole body is full of light, and no part of it dark, it will be completely lighted, as when the light of a lamp shines on you."

[a]Greek "Beezeboul" or "Beelzeboul"; also in verses 18 and 19.   [b]Greek "unclean".   [c]Or "something"; also in verse 32.

104. BY DINING CEREMONIALLY UNBATHED IN A PHARISEE'S HOUSE, JESUS AROUSES CRITICAL SURPRISE — HE RESPONDS WITH A DENUNCIATION OF RELIGIOUS HYPOCRISY

Luke 11:37–12:12

| 37 When Jesus|
| had finished|
| speaking, a Phar-|

isee invited him to eat with him; so he went in and reclined at the table. 38 But the Pharisee, noticing that Jesus did not first wash before the meal, was surprised.

Luke 11-12

| 39 Then the Lord
said to him, "Now

then, you Pharisees clean the outside of the cup and dish, but inside you are full of greed and wickedness. 40 You foolish people! Did not the one who made the outside make the inside also? 41 But give what is inside the dish[a] to the poor, and everything will be clean for you.

42 "Woe to you Pharisees, because you give God a tenth of your mint, rue and all other kinds of garden herbs, but you neglect justice and the love of God. You should have practiced the latter without leaving the former undone.

43 "Woe to you Pharisees, because you love the most important seats in the synagogues and greetings in the marketplaces.

44 "Woe to you, because you are like unmarked graves, which men walk over without knowing it."

45 One of the experts in the law answered him, "Teacher, when you say these things, you insult us also."

46 Jesus replied, "And you experts in the law, woe to you, because you load people down with burdens they can hardly carry, and you yourselves will not lift one finger to help them.

47 "Woe to you, because you build tombs for the prophets, and it was your forefathers who killed them. 48 So you testify that you approve of what your forefathers did; they killed the prophets, and you build their tombs. 49 Because of this, God in his wisdom said, 'I will send them prophets and apostles, some of whom they will kill and others they will persecute.' 50 Therefore this generation will be held responsible for the blood of all the prophets that has been shed since the beginning of the world, 51 from the blood of Abel to the blood of Zechariah, who was killed between the altar and the sanctuary. Yes, I tell you, this generation will be held responsible for it all.

52 "Woe to you experts in the law, because you have taken away the key to knowledge. You yourselves have not entered, and you have hindered those who were entering."

53 When Jesus left there, the Pharisees and the teachers of the law began to oppose him fiercely and to besiege him with questions, 54 waiting to catch him in something he might say.

1 Meanwhile, when a crowd of many thousands had gathered, so that they were trampling on one another, Jesus began to speak first to his disciples, saying: "Be on your guard against the yeast of the Pharisees, which is hypocrisy. 2 There is nothing concealed that will not be disclosed, or hidden that will not be made known. 3 What you have said in the dark will be heard in the daylight, and what you have whispered in the ear in the inner rooms will be proclaimed from the housetops.

4 "I tell you, my friends, do not be afraid of those who kill the body and after that can do no more. 5 But I will show you whom you should fear: Fear him who, after the killing of the body, has power to throw you into hell. Yes, I tell you, fear him. 6 Are not five sparrows sold for two pennies[b]? Yet not one of them is forgotten by God. 7 Indeed, the very hairs of

Luke 12

|
| your head are all |
| numbered. Don't |

be afraid; you are worth more than many sparrows.

8 "I tell you, whoever acknowledges me before men, the Son of Man will also acknowledge him before the angels of God. 9 But he who disowns me before men will be disowned before the angels of God. 10 And everyone who speaks a word against the Son of Man will be forgiven, but anyone who blasphemes against the Holy Spirit will not be forgiven.

11 "When you are brought before synagogues, rulers and authorities, do not worry about how you will defend yourselves or what you will say, 12 for the Holy Spirit will teach you at that time what you should say."

ᵃOr "what you have".   ᵇGreek "two assaria".

105. PARABLES ON THE FOLLY OF WORLDLINESS AND THE NEED FOR SPIRITUAL ALERTNESS

Luke 12:13-59

|
| 13 Someone in |
| the crowd said to |
| h i m, "Teacher, |

tell my brother to divide the inheritance with me."

14 Jesus replied, "Man, who appointed me a judge or an arbiter between you?" 15 Then he said to them, "Watch out! Be on your guard against all kinds of greed; a man's life does not consist in the abundance of his possessions."

16 And he told them this parable: "The ground of a certain rich man produced a good crop. 17 He thought to himself, 'What shall I do? I have no place to store my crops.'

18 "Then he said, 'This is what I'll do. I will tear down my barns and build bigger ones, and there I will store all my grain and my goods. 19 And I'll say to myself, "You have plenty of good things laid up for many years. Take life easy; eat, drink and be merry." '

20 "But God said to him, 'You fool! This very night your life will be demanded from you. Then who will get what you have prepared for yourself?'

21 "This is how it will be with anyone who stores up things for himself but is not rich toward God."

22 Then Jesus said to his disciples: "Therefore I tell you, do not worry about your life, what you will eat; or about your body, what you will wear. 23 Life is more than food, and the body more than clothes. 24 Consider the ravens: They do not sow or reap, they have no storeroom or barn; yet God feeds them. And how much more valuable you are than birds! 25 Who of you by worrying can add a single hour to his lifeᵃ? 26 Since you cannot do this very little thing, why do you worry about the rest?

162

Luke 12

| 27 "Consider how |
| the lilies grow. |

They do not labor or spin. Yet I tell you, not even Solomon in all his splendor was dressed like one of these. 28 If that is how God clothes the grass of the field, which is here today, and tomorrow is thrown into the fire, how much more will he clothe you, O you of little faith! 29 And do not set your heart on what you will eat or drink; do not worry about it. 30 For the pagan world runs after all such things, and your Father knows that you need them. 31 But seek his kingdom, and these things will be given to you as well.

32 "Do not be afraid, little flock, for your Father has been pleased to give you the kingdom. 33 Sell your possessions and give to the poor. Provide purses for yourselves that will not wear out, a treasure in heaven that will not be exhausted, where no thief comes near and no moth destroys. 34 For where your treasure is, there your heart will be also.

35 "Be dressed ready for service and keep your lamps burning, 36 like men waiting for their master to return from a wedding banquet, so that when he comes and knocks they can immediately open the door for him. 37 It will be good for those servants whose master finds them watching when he comes. I tell you the truth, he will dress himself to serve, will have them recline at the table and will come and wait on them. 38 It will be good for those servants whose master finds them ready, even if he comes in the second or third watch of the night. 39 But understand this: If the owner of the house had known at what hour the thief was coming, he would not have let his house be broken into. 40 You also must be ready, because the Son of Man will come at an hour when you do not expect him."

41 Peter asked, "Lord, are you telling this parable to us, or to everyone?"

42 The Lord answered, "Who then is the faithful and wise manager, whom the master puts in charge of his servants to give them their food allowance at the proper time? 43 It will be good for that servant whom the master finds doing so when he returns. 44 I tell you the truth, he will put him in charge of all his possessions. 45 But suppose the servant says to himself, 'My master is taking a long time in coming,' and he then begins to beat the menservants and womenservants and to eat and drink and get drunk. 46 The master of that servant will come on a day when he does not expect him and at an hour he is not aware of. He will cut him to pieces and assign him a place with the unbelievers.

47 "That servant who knows his master's will and does not get ready or does not do what his master wants will be beaten with many blows. 48 But the one who does not know and does things deserving punishment will be beaten with few blows. From everyone who has been given much, much will be demanded; and from the one who has been entrusted with much, much more will be asked.

49 "I have come to bring fire on the earth, and how I wish it were already kindled! 50 But I have a baptism to undergo, and how distressed I am until it is completed! 51 Do you think I came to bring peace on earth? No, I tell you, but division. 52 From now on there will be five in one family divided

Luke 12

|against each other, |
|three against two |

and two against three. 53 They will be divided, father against son and son against father, mother against daughter and daughter against mother, mother-in-law against daughter-in-law and daughter-in-law against mother-in-law."

54 He said to the crowd: "When you see a cloud rising in the west, immediately you say, 'It's going to rain,' and it does. 55 And when the south wind blows, you say, 'It's going to be hot,' and it is. 56 Hypocrites! You know how to interpret the appearance of the earth and the sky. How is it that you don't know how to interpret this present time?

57 "Why don't you judge for yourselves what is right? 58 As you are going with your adversary to the magistrate, try hard to be reconciled to him on the way, or he may drag you off to the judge, and the judge turn you over to the officer, and the officer throw you into prison. 59 I tell you, you will not get out until you have paid the last penny.[b]"

[a]Or "single cubit to his height".   [b]Greek "lepton".

106. JESUS USES TWO CURRENT CALAMITIES TO ILLUSTRATE THE IMPERATIVENESS OF REPENTANCE — THE PARABLE OF A FRUITLESS FIG TREE

Luke 13:1-9

|1 Now there were |
|some present at|
|that time who told|

Jesus about the Galileans whose blood Pilate had mixed with their sacrifices. 2 Jesus answered, "Do you think that these Galileans were worse sinners than all the other Galileans because they suffered this way? 3 I tell you, no! But unless you repent, you too will all perish. 4 Or those eighteen who died when the tower in Siloam fell on them — do you think they were more guilty than all the others living in Jerusalem? 5 I tell you, no! But unless you repent, you too will all perish."

6 Then he told this parable: "A man had a fig tree, planted in his vineyard, and he went to look for fruit on it, but did not find any. 7 So he said to the man who took care of the vineyard, 'For three years now I've been coming to look for fruit on this fig tree and haven't found any. Cut it down! Why should it use up the soil?'

8 "'Sir,' the man replied, 'leave it alone for one more year, and I'll dig around it and fertilize it. 9 If it bears fruit next year, fine! If not, then cut it down.'"

107. CRITICISED FOR HEALING A CRIPPLED WOMAN IN A SYNAGOGUE ON A SABBATH DAY, JESUS DEFENDS HIMSELF

Luke 13:10-21

10 On a Sabbath Jesus was teaching in one of the synagogues, 11 and a woman was there who had been crippled by a spirit for eighteen years. She was bent over and could not straighten up at all. 12 When Jesus saw her, he called her forward and said to her, "Woman, you are set free from your infirmity." 13 Then he put his hands on her, and immediately she straightened up and praised God.

14 Indignant because Jesus had healed on the Sabbath, the synagogue ruler said to the people, "There are six days for work. So come and be healed on those days, not on the Sabbath."

15 The Lord answered him, "You hypocrites! Doesn't each of you on the Sabbath untie his ox or donkey from the stall and lead it out to give it water? 16 Then should not this woman, a daughter of Abraham, whom Satan has kept bound for eighteen long years, be set free on the Sabbath day from what bound her?"

17 When he said this, all his opponents were humiliated, but the people were delighted with all the wonderful things he was doing.

18 Then Jesus asked, "What is the kingdom of God like? What shall I compare it to? 19 It is like a mustard seed, which a man took and planted in his garden. It grew, became a tree, and the birds of the air perched in its branches."

20 Again he asked, "What shall I compare the kingdom of God to? 21 It is like yeast that a woman took and mixed into a large amount[a] of flour until it worked all through the dough."

[a]Greek "three satas" (probably about ½ bushel or 22 liters).

108. JESUS AT THE FESTIVAL OF DEDICATION — ANOTHER CONFRONTATION WITH HOSTILE JEWISH LEADERS, ON THE QUESTION OF HIS MESSIAHSHIP

The temple, Jerusalem

John 10:22-39

22 Then came the Feast of Dedication[a] at Jerusalem. It was winter, 23 and Jesus was in the temple area walking in Solomon's Colonnade. 24 The Jews gathered around him, saying, "How long will you keep us in suspense? If you are the Christ,[b] tell us plainly."

John 10

25 Jesus answered, "I did tell you, but you do not believe. The miracles I do in my Father's name speak for me, 26 but you do not believe because you are not my sheep. 27 My sheep listen to my voice; I know them, and they follow me. 28 I give them eternal life, and they shall never perish; no one can snatch them out of my hand. 29 My Father, who has given them to me, is greater than all[c]; no one can snatch them out of my Father's hand. 30 I and the Father are one."

31 Again the Jews picked up stones to stone him, 32 but Jesus said to them, "I have shown you many great miracles from the Father. For which of these do you stone me?"

33 "We are not stoning you for any of these," replied the Jews, "but for blasphemy, because you, a mere man, claim to be God."

34 Jesus answered them, "Is it not written in your Law, 'I have said you are gods'? 35 If he called them 'gods,' to whom the word of God came — and the Scripture cannot be broken — 36 what about the one whom the Father set apart as his very own and sent into the world? Why then do you accuse me of blasphemy because I said, 'I am God's Son'? 37 Do not believe me unless I do what my Father does. 38 But if I do it, even though you do not believe me, believe the miracles, that you may learn and understand that the Father is in me, and I in the Father." 39 Again they tried to seize him, but he escaped their grasp.

[a]That is, Hanukkah.   [b]Or "Messiah".   [c]Many early manuscripts "What my Father has given me is greater than all".

PART IX

CHRIST'S PEREAN MINISTRY

JANUARY TO MARCH, A.D. 30

A. THE FIRST PEREAN TOUR

109. LEAVING JUDEA, JESUS MOVES EASTWARD INTO PEREA, ACROSS THE JORDAN RIVER

John 10:40-42

40 Then Jesus went back across the Jordan to the place where John had been baptizing in the early days. Here he stayed 41 and many people came to him. They said, "Though John never performed a miraculous sign, all that John said about this man was true." 42 And in that place many believed in Jesus.

110. AN OUTLINE OF THE FIRST PEREAN TOUR

Luke 13:22

22 Then Jesus went through the towns and vil-lages, teaching as he made his way to Jerusalem.*

---

*This tour through Perea seems to have been a circular one. After preaching in many towns and villages as He journeyed northward, Jesus apparently turned southward. From then on, his listeners probably included people traveling toward Jerusalem by the Perean route; it was the route commonly used by Jews from northern regions, who preferred not to pass through Samaria.

111. THE PARABOLIC ANSWER OF JESUS TO A QUESTION WHETHER FEW WILL BE SAVED

Probably in Perea*

Luke 13:23-30

> 23 Someone asked him, "Lord, are only a few people going to be saved?"

He said to them, 24 "Make every effort to enter through the narrow door, because many, I tell you, will try to enter and will not be able to. 25 Once the owner of the house gets up and closes the door, you will stand outside knocking and pleading, 'Sir, open the door for us.'

"But he will answer, 'I don't know you or where you come from.'

26 "Then you will say, 'We ate and drank with you, and you taught in our streets.'

27 "But he will reply, 'I don't know you or where you come from. Away from me, all you evildoers!'

28 "There will be weeping there, and gnashing of teeth, when you see Abraham, Isaac and Jacob and all the prophets in the kingdom of God, but you yourselves thrown out. 29 People will come from east and west and north and south, and will take their places at the feast in the kingdom of God. 30 Indeed there are those who are last who will be first, and first who will be last."

112. CHRIST'S REACTION WHEN SOME PHARISEES WARNED HIM AGAINST HEROD ANTIPAS

Luke 13:31-35

> 31 At that time some Pharisees came to Jesus and

said to him, "Leave this place and go somewhere else. Herod wants to kill you."

32 He replied, "Go tell that fox, 'I will drive out demons and heal people today and tomorrow, and on the third day I will reach my goal.' 33 In any

---

*In relation to Christ's later Judean ministry it was noted that New Testament scholars are divided in their opinions about the time and location of events recorded in a large section of Luke's Gospel (see the footnote on page 156). Strong arguments support the probability that the events described in Luke 13:22-17:10 occurred in Perea during the early part of A.D. 30.

Luke 13

| case, I must keep |
| going today and |

tomorrow and the next day — for surely no prophet can die outside Jerusalem!

34 "O Jerusalem, Jerusalem, you who kill the prophets and stone those sent to you, how often I have longed to gather your children together, as a hen gathers her chicks under her wings, but you were not willing! 35 Look, your house is left to you desolate. I tell you, you will not see me again until you say, 'Blessed is he who comes in the name of the Lord.'"

113. INVITED TO DINE AT THE HOME OF A PROMINENT PHARISEE ON A SABBATH DAY, JESUS HEALS A MAN SUFFERING FROM DROPSY — HE SILENCES HIS ADVERSARIES AND ADMONISHES THEM WITH PERTINENT ADVICE AND PARABOLIC TEACHING

Luke 14:1-24

| 1 One Sabbath, |
| when Jesus went |
| to eat in the house |

of a prominent Pharisee, he was being carefully watched. 2 There in front of him was a man suffering from dropsy. 3 Jesus asked the Pharisees and experts in the law, "Is it lawful to heal on the Sabbath or not?" 4 But they remained silent. So taking hold of the man, he healed him and sent him away.

5 Then he asked them, "If one of you has a son[a] or an ox that falls into a well on the Sabbath day, will you not immediately pull him out?" 6 And they had nothing to say.

7 When he noticed how the guests picked the places of honor at the table, he told them this parable: 8 "When someone invites you to a wedding feast, do not take the place of honor, for a person more distinguished than you may have been invited. 9 If so, the host who invited both of you will come and say to you, 'Give this man your seat.' Then, humiliated, you will have to take the least important place. 10 But when you are invited, take the lowest place, so that when your host comes, he will say to you, 'Friend, move up to a better place.' Then you will be honored in the presence of all your fellow guests. 11 For everyone who exalts himself will be humbled, and he who humbles himself will be exalted."

12 Then Jesus said to his host, "When you give a luncheon or dinner, do not invite your friends, your brothers or relatives, or your rich neighbors; if you do, they may invite you back and so you will be repaid. 13 But when you give a banquet, invite the poor, the crippled, the lame, the blind, 14 and you will be blessed. Although they cannot repay you, you will be repaid at the resurrection of the righteous."

15 When one of those at the table with him heard this, he said to Jesus, "Blessed is the man who will eat at the feast in the kingdom of God."

Luke 14

| 16 Jesus replied:
| "A certain man

was preparing a great banquet and invited many guests. 17 At the time of the banquet he sent his servant to tell those who had been invited, 'Come, for everything is now ready.'

18 "But they all alike began to make excuses. The first said, 'I have just bought a field, and I must go and see it. Please excuse me.'

19 "Another said, 'I have just bought five yoke of oxen, and I'm on my way to try them out. Please excuse me.'

20 "Still another said, 'I just got married, so I can't come.'

21 "The servant came back and reported this to his master. Then the owner of the house became angry and ordered his servant, 'Go out quickly into the streets and alleys of the town and bring in the poor, the crippled, the blind and the lame.'

22 "'Sir,' the servant said, 'what you ordered has been done, but there is still room.'

23 "Then the master told his servant, 'Go out to the roads and country lanes and make them come in, so that my house will be full. 24 I tell you, not one of those men who were invited will get a taste of my banquet.'"

aSome manuscripts "donkey".

114. THREE PARABLES, ADDRESSED TO A CROWD OF FOLLOWERS, ON THE DEMANDS OF TRUE DISCIPLESHIP

Luke 14:25-35

| 25 Large crowds
| were traveling with
| Jesus, and turning

to them he said: 26 "If anyone comes to me and does not hate his father and mother, his wife and children, his brothers and sisters — yes, even his own life — he cannot be my disciple. 27 And anyone who does not carry his cross and follow me cannot be my disciple.

28 "Suppose one of you wants to build a tower. Will he not first sit down and estimate the cost to see if he has enough money to complete it? 29 For if he lays the foundation and is not able to finish it, everyone who sees it will ridicule him, 30 saying, 'This fellow began to build and was not able to finish.'

31 "Or suppose a king is about to go to war against another king. Will he not first sit down and consider whether he is able with ten thousand men to oppose the one coming against him with twenty thousand? 32 If he is not able, he will send a delegation while the other is still a long way off and will ask for terms of peace. 33 In the same way, any of you who does not give up everything he has cannot be my disciple.

34 "Salt is good, but if it loses its saltiness, how can it be made salty again? 35 It is fit neither for the soil nor for the manure pile; it is thrown out.

"He who has ears to hear, let him hear."

115. CHRIST'S DEFENCE OF HIS COMPASSIONATE ATTITUDE TOWARD RELIGIOUS OUTCASTS — PARABLES ABOUT A LOST SHEEP, A LOST COIN AND A WAYWARD SON

Luke 15:1-32

1 Now the tax collectors and "sinners" were all gathering around to hear him. 2 But the Pharisees and the teachers of the law muttered, "This man welcomes sinners and eats with them."

3 Then Jesus told them this parable: 4 "Suppose one of you has a hundred sheep and loses one of them. Does he not leave the ninety-nine in the open country and go after the lost sheep until he finds it? 5 And when he finds it, he joyfully puts it on his shoulders 6 and goes home. Then he calls his friends and neighbors together and says, 'Rejoice with me; I have found my lost sheep.' 7 I tell you that in the same way there is more rejoicing in heaven over one sinner who repents than over ninety-nine righteous persons who do not need to repent.

8 "Or suppose a woman has ten silver coins[a] and loses one. Does she not light a lamp, sweep the house and search carefully until she finds it? 9 And when she finds it, she calls her friends and neighbors together and says, 'Rejoice with me; I have found my lost coin.' 10 In the same way, I tell you, there is rejoicing in the presence of the angels of God over one sinner who repents."

11 Jesus continued: "There was a man who had two sons. 12 The younger one said to his father, 'Father, give me my share of the estate.' So he divided his property between them.

13 "Not long after that, the younger son got together all he had, set off for a distant country and there squandered his wealth in wild living. 14 After he had spent everything, there was a severe famine in that whole country, and he began to be in need. 15 So he went and hired himself out to a citizen of that country, who sent him to his fields to feed pigs. 16 He longed to fill his stomach with the pods that the pigs were eating, but no one gave him anything.

17 "When he came to his senses, he said, 'How many of my father's hired men have food to spare, and here I am starving to death! 18 I will set out and go back to my father and say to him: Father, I have sinned against heaven and against you. 19 I am no longer worthy to be called your son; make me like one of your hired men.' 20 So he got up and went to his father.

"But while he was still a long way off, his father saw him and was filled with compassion for him; he ran to his son, threw his arms around him and kissed him.

21 "The son said to him, 'Father, I have sinned against heaven and against you. I am no longer worthy to be called your son.[b]'

22 "But the father said to his servants, 'Quick! Bring the best robe and put it on him. Put a ring on his finger and sandals on his feet. 23 Bring the

Luke 15

| fattened calf and |
| kill it. Let's have |

a feast and celebrate. 24 For this son of mine was dead and is alive again; he was lost and is found.' So they began to celebrate.

25 "Meanwhile, the older son was in the field. When he came near the house, he heard music and dancing. 26 So he called one of the servants and asked him what was going on. 27 'Your brother has come,' he replied, 'and your father has killed the fattened calf because he has him back safe and sound.'

28 "The older brother became angry and refused to go in. So his father went out and pleaded with him. 29 But he answered his father, 'Look! All these years I've been slaving for you and never disobeyed your orders. Yet you never gave me even a young goat so I could celebrate with my friends. 30 But when this son of yours who has squandered your property with prostitutes comes home, you kill the fattened calf for him!'

31 " 'My son,' the father said, 'you are always with me, and everything I have is yours. 32 But we had to celebrate and be glad, because this brother of yours was dead and is alive again; he was lost and is found.' "

[a]Greek "ten drachmas", each worth about a day's wages.   [b]Some early manuscripts "son. Make me like one of your hired men".

116. TWO PARABLES ON THE ADVANTAGEOUS USE OF MONEY — STORIES ABOUT A SHREWD PROPERTY MANAGER, AND A RICH MAN AND A BEGGAR

Luke 16:1-31

| 1 Jesus told his |
| disciples: "There |
| was a rich man |

whose manager was accused of wasting his possessions. 2 So he called him in and asked him, 'What is this I hear about you? Give an account of your management, because you cannot be manager any longer.'

3 "The manager said to himself, 'What shall I do now? My master is taking away my job. I'm not strong enough to dig, and I'm ashamed to beg — 4 I know what I'll do so that, when I lose my job here, people will welcome me into their houses.'

5 "So he called in each one of his master's debtors. He asked the first, 'How much do you owe my master?'

6 " 'Eight hundred gallons[a] of olive oil,' he replied.

"The manager told him, 'Take your bill, sit down quickly, and make it four hundred.'

7 "Then he asked the second, 'And how much do you owe?'

" 'A thousand bushels[b] of wheat,' he replied.

"He told him, 'Take your bill and make it eight hundred.'

Luke 16

| 8 "The master
| commended the|

dishonest manager because he had acted shrewdly. For the people of this world are more shrewd in dealing with their own kind than are the people of the light. 9 I tell you, use worldly wealth to gain friends for yourselves, so that when it is gone, you will be welcomed into eternal dwellings.

10 "Whoever can be trusted with very little can also be trusted with much, and whoever is dishonest with very little will also be dishonest with much. 11 So if you have not been trustworthy in handling worldly wealth, who will trust you with true riches? 12 And if you have not been trustworthy with someone else's property, who will give you property of your own?

13 "No servant can serve two masters. Either he will hate the one and love the other, or he will be devoted to the one and despise the other. You cannot serve both God and Money."

14 The Pharisees, who loved money, heard all this and were sneering at Jesus. 15 He said to them, "You are the ones who justify yourselves in the eyes of men, but God knows your hearts. What is highly valued among men is detestable in God's sight.

16 "The Law and the Prophets were proclaimed until John. Since that time, the good news of the kingdom of God is being preached, and everyone is forcing his way into it. 17 It is easier for heaven and earth to disappear than for the least stroke of a pen to drop out of the Law.

18 "Anyone who divorces his wife and marries another woman commits adultery, and the man who marries a divorced woman commits adultery.

19 "There was a rich man who was dressed in purple and fine linen and lived in luxury every day. 20 At his gate was laid a beggar named Lazarus, covered with sores 21 and longing to eat what fell from the rich man's table. Even the dogs came and licked his sores.

22 "The time came when the beggar died and the angels carried him to Abraham's side. The rich man also died and was buried. 23 In hell,[c] where he was in torment, he looked up and saw Abraham far away, with Lazarus by his side. 24 So he called to him, 'Father Abraham, have pity on me and send Lazarus to dip the tip of his finger in water and cool my tongue, because I am in agony in this fire.'

25 "But Abraham replied, 'Son, remember that in your lifetime you received your good things, while Lazarus received bad things, but now he is comforted here and you are in agony. 26 And besides all this, between us and you a great chasm has been fixed, so that those who want to go from here to you cannot, nor can anyone cross over from there to us.'

27 "He answered, 'Then I beg you, father, send Lazarus to my father's house, 28 for I have five brothers. Let him warn them, so that they will not also come to this place of torment.'

29 "Abraham replied, 'They have Moses and the Prophets; let them listen to them.'

30 " 'No, father Abraham,' he said, 'but if someone from the dead goes to them, they will repent.'

31 "He said to him, 'If they do not listen to Moses and the Prophets, they

Luke 16

| will not be con- |
| vinced even if |

someone rises from the dead.'"

[a]Greek "one hundred batous" (probably about 3 kiloliters).   [b]Greek "one hundred korous" (probably about 35 kiloliters).   [c]Greek "Hades".

117. STRAIGHTFORWARD TEACHING TO THE DISCIPLES ABOUT FORGIVENESS, FAITH AND SERVICE

Luke 17:1-10

| 1 Jesus said to |
| his disciples: |
| "Things that cause |

people to sin are bound to come, but woe to that person through whom they come. 2 It would be better for him to be thrown into the sea with a millstone tied around his neck than for him to cause one of these little ones to sin. 3 So watch yourselves.

"If your brother sins, rebuke him, and if he repents, forgive him. 4 If he sins against you seven times in a day, and seven times comes back to you and says, 'I repent,' forgive him."

5 The apostles said to the Lord, "Increase our faith!"

6 He replied, "If you have faith as small as a mustard seed, you can say to this mulberry tree, 'Be uprooted and planted in the sea,' and it will obey you.

7 "Suppose one of you had a servant plowing or looking after the sheep. Would he say to the servant when he comes in from the field, 'Come along now and sit down to eat'? 8 Would he not rather say, 'Prepare my supper, get yourself ready and wait on me while I eat and drink; after that you may eat and drink'? 9 Would he thank the servant because he did what he was told to do? 10 So you also, when you have done everything you were told to do, should say, 'We are unworthy servants; we have only done our duty.'"

B. AN INTERLUDE IN JUDEA, SAMARIA AND GALILEE

118. LAZARUS MIRACULOUSLY RAISED FROM THE DEAD

Bethany, near Jerusalem

John 11:1-44

| 1 Now a man |
| named Lazarus |
| was sick. He was |

from Bethany, the village of Mary and her sister Martha. 2 This Mary,

| | |whose brother
| | |Lazarus now lay

sick, was the same one who poured perfume on the Lord and wiped his feet with her hair. 3 So the sisters sent word to Jesus, "Lord, the one you love is sick."

4 When he heard this, Jesus said, "This sickness will not end in death. No, it is for God's glory so that God's Son may be glorified through it." 5 Jesus loved Martha and her sister and Lazarus. 6 Yet when he heard that Lazarus was sick, he stayed where he was two more days.

7 Then he said to his disciples, "Let us go back to Judea."

8 "But Rabbi," they said, "a short while ago the Jews tried to stone you, and yet you are going back there?"

9 Jesus answered, "Are there not twelve hours of daylight? A man who walks by day will not stumble, for he sees by this world's light. 10 It is when he walks by night that he stumbles, for he has no light."

11 After he had said this, he went on to tell them, "Our friend Lazarus has fallen asleep; but I am going there to wake him up."

12 His disciples replied, "Lord, if he sleeps, he will get better." 13 Jesus had been speaking of his death, but his disciples thought he meant natural sleep.

14 So then he told them plainly, "Lazarus is dead, 15 and for your sake I am glad I was not there, so that you may believe. But let us go to him."

16 Then Thomas (called Didymus) said to the rest of the disciples, "Let us also go, that we may die with him."

17 On his arrival, Jesus found that Lazarus had already been in the tomb for four days. 18 Bethany was less than two miles[a] from Jerusalem, 19 and many Jews had come to Martha and Mary to comfort them in the loss of their brother. 20 When Martha heard that Jesus was coming, she went out to meet him, but Mary stayed at home.

21 "Lord," Martha said to Jesus, "if you had been here, my brother would not have died. 22 But I know that even now God will give you whatever you ask."

23 Jesus said to her, "Your brother will rise again."

24 Martha answered, "I know he will rise again in the resurrection at the last day."

25 Jesus said to her, "I am the resurrection and the life. He who believes in me will live, even though he dies; 26 and whoever lives and believes in me will never die. Do you believe this?"

27 "Yes, Lord," she told him, "I believe that you are the Christ,[a] the Son of God, who was to come into the world."

28 And after she had said this, she went back and called her sister Mary aside. "The Teacher is here," she said, "and is asking for you." 29 When Mary heard this, she got up quickly and went to him. 30 Now Jesus had not yet entered the village, but was still at the place where Martha had met him. 31 When the Jews who had been with Mary in the house, comforting her, noticed how quickly she got up and went out, they followed her, supposing she was going to the tomb to mourn there.

John 11

| | | 32 When Mary
reached the place
where Jesus was and saw him, she fell at his feet and said, "Lord, if you had been here, my brother would not have died."

33 When Jesus saw her weeping, and the Jews who had come along with her also weeping, he was deeply moved in spirit and troubled. 34 "Where have you laid him?" he asked.

"Come and see, Lord," they replied.

35 Jesus wept.

36 Then the Jews said, "See how he loved him!"

37 But some of them said, "Could not he who opened the eyes of the blind man have kept this man from dying?"

38 Jesus, once more deeply moved, came to the tomb. It was a cave with a stone laid across the entrance. 39 "Take away the stone," he said.

"But, Lord," said Martha, the sister of the dead man, "by this time there is a bad odor, for he has been there four days."

40 Then Jesus said, "Did I not tell you that if you believed, you would see the glory of God?"

41 So they took away the stone. Then Jesus looked up and said, "Father, I thank you that you have heard me. 42 I knew that you always hear me, but I said this for the benefit of the people standing here, that they may believe that you sent me."

43 When he had said this, Jesus called in a loud voice, "Lazarus, come out!" 44 The dead man came out, his hands and feet wrapped with strips of linen, and a cloth around his face.

Jesus said to them, "Take off the grave clothes and let him go."

aGreek "fifteen stadia" (about 3 kilometers).   bOr "Messiah".

119. CONSEQUENCES OF THE RAISING OF LAZARUS — POPULAR BELIEF, PHARISAIC PLOTS, AND THE DEPARTURE OF JESUS TO EPHRAIM IN NORTHERN JUDEA

John 11:45-54

| | | 45 Therefore
many of the Jews
who had come to
visit Mary, and had seen what Jesus did, put their faith in him. 46 But some of them went to the Pharisees and told them what Jesus had done. 47 Then the chief priests and the Pharisees called a meeting of the Sanhedrin.

"What are we accomplishing?" they asked. "Here is this man performing many miraculous signs. 48 If we let him go on like this, everyone will believe in him, and then the Romans will come and take away both our place^a and our nation."

49 Then one of them, named Caiaphas, who was high priest that year, spoke up, "You know nothing at all! 50 You do not realize that it is better

John 11

| | | for you that one |
| | | man die for the |

people than that the whole nation perish."

51 He did not say this on his own, but as high priest that year he prophesied that Jesus would die for the Jewish nation, 52 and not only for that nation but also for the scattered children of God, to bring them together and make them one. 53 So from that day on they plotted to take his life.

54 Therefore Jesus no longer moved about publicly among the Jews. Instead he withdrew to a region near the desert, to a village called Ephraim, where he stayed with his disciples.

aOr "temple".

120. TEN LEPERS HEALED — GRATITUDE EXPRESSED BY ONLY ONE OF THEM

Probably in Galilee, near the northeastern border of Samaria

Luke 17:11-19

	11 Now on his way
	to Jerusalem, Je-
	sus traveled along

the border between Samaria and Galilee.* 12 As he was going into a village, ten men who had leprosy^a met him. They stood at a distance 13 and called out in a loud voice, "Jesus, Master, have pity on us!"

14 When he saw them, he said, "Go, show yourselves to the priests." And as they went, they were cleansed.

15 One of them, when he saw he was healed, came back, praising God in a loud voice. 16 He threw himself at Jesus' feet and thanked him — and he was a Samaritan.

17 Jesus asked, "Were not all ten cleansed? Where are the other nine? 18 Was no one found to return and give praise to God except this foreigner?" 19 Then he said to him, "Rise and go; your faith has made you well."

aThe Greek word was used for various diseases affecting the skin — not necessarily leprosy.

---

*On his departure from Ephraim (sec. 119), Jesus apparently continued northward through Samaria and Galilee, probably with the intention of meeting the Passover crowds in northern Perea. He could teach them as they journeyed slowly southward through Perea on their way to Jerusalem.

121. CHRIST'S SOLEMN REPLY TO A QUESTION ABOUT THE COMING OF GOD'S KINGDOM

Probably in south-eastern Galilee

Luke 17:20-37

> 20 Once, having been asked by the Pharisees when

the kingdom of God would come, Jesus replied, "The kingdom of God does not come visibly, 21 nor will people say, 'Here it is,' or 'There it is,' because the kingdom of God is within[a] you."

22 Then he said to his disciples, "The time is coming when you will long to see one of the days of the Son of Man, but you will not see it. 23 Men will tell you, 'There he is!' or 'Here he is!' Do not go running off after them. 24 For the Son of Man in his day[b] will be like the lightning, which flashes and lights up the sky from one end to the other. 25 But first he must suffer many things and be rejected by this generation.

26 "Just as it was in the days of Noah, so also will it be in the days of the Son of Man. 27 People were eating, drinking, marrying and being given in marriage up to the day Noah entered the ark. Then the flood came and destroyed them all.

28 "It was the same in the days of Lot. People were eating and drinking, buying and selling, planting and building. 29 But the day Lot left Sodom, fire and sulfur rained down from heaven and destroyed them all.

30 "It will be just like this on the day the Son of Man is revealed. 31 On that day no one who is on the roof of his house, with his goods inside, should go down to get them. Likewise, no one in the field should go back for anything. 32 Remember Lot's wife! 33 Whoever tries to keep his life will lose it, and whoever loses his life will preserve it. 34 I tell you, on that night two people will be in one bed; one will be taken and the other left. 35 Two women will be grinding grain together; one will be taken and the other left.[c]"

37 "Where, Lord?" they asked.

He replied, "Where there is a dead body, there the vultures will gather."

[a]Or "among".   [b]Some manuscripts do not have "in his day".   [c]Some manuscripts "left. 36 Two men will be in the field; one will be taken and the other left."

122. PARABOLIC TEACHING ON PRAYER — STORIES ABOUT A PERSISTENT WIDOW, AND A PHARISEE AND A TAX COLLECTOR

Probably in south-eastern Galilee

Luke 18:1-14

> 1 Then Jesus told his disciples a parable to show

them that they should always pray and not give up. 2 He said: "In a certain

Luke 18

| town there was a |
| judge who neither |

feared God nor cared about men. 3 And there was a widow in that town who kept coming to him with the plea, 'Grant me justice against my adversary.'

4 "For some time he refused. But finally he said to himself, 'Even though I don't fear God or care about men, 5 yet because this widow keeps bothering me, I will see that she gets justice, so that she won't eventually wear me out with her coming!'"

6 And the Lord said, "Listen to what the unjust judge says. 7 And will not God bring about justice for his chosen ones, who cry out to him day and night? Will he keep putting them off? 8 I tell you, he will see that they get justice, and quickly. However, when the Son of Man comes, will he find faith on the earth?"

9 To some who were confident of their own righteousness and looked down on everybody else, Jesus told this parable: 10 "Two men went up to the temple to pray, one a Pharisee and the other a tax collector. 11 The Pharisee stood up and prayed about[a] himself; 'God, I thank you that I am not like all other men — robbers, evildoers, adulterers — or even like this tax collector. 12 I fast twice a week and give a tenth of all I get.'

13 "But the tax collector stood at a distance. He would not even look up to heaven, but beat his breast and said, 'God, have mercy on me, a sinner.'

14 "I tell you that this man, rather than the other, went home justified before God. For everyone who exalts himself will be humbled, and he who humbles himself will be exalted."

[a]Or "to".

C. THE SECOND PEREAN TOUR

123. CHRIST'S ARRIVAL IN PEREA AGAIN, FROM GALILEE — HIS HEALING AND TEACHING MINISTRY

Matt. 19:1-2	Mark 10:1	
1 When Jesus had finished saying these things, he left Galilee and went into the region of Judea to the other side of the Jordan.* 2 Large crowds fol-	1 Jesus then left that place and went into the region of Judea and across the Jordan. Again crowds of people	

*The Perean route was commonly used by Jews traveling from Galilee to Judea (see the footnote on page 167).

179

Matt. 19	Mark 10
lowed him, and he healed them there.	came to him, and as was his custom, he taught them.

124. IN REPLY TO A QUESTION OF SOME PHARISEES, JESUS TEACHES CONCERNING DIVORCE

Perea

Matt. 19:3-12   Mark 10:2-12

Matt. 19:3-12	Mark 10:2-12
3 Some Pharisees came to him to test him. They asked, "Is it lawful for a man to divorce his wife for any and every reason?" 4 "Haven't you read," he replied, "that at the beginning the Creator 'made them male and female,' 5 and said, 'For this reason a man will leave his father and mother and be united to his wife, and the two will become one flesh'? 6 So they are no longer two, but one. Therefore what God has joined together, let man not separate." 7 "Why then," they asked, "did Moses command that a man give his wife a certificate of	2 Some Pharisees came and tested him by asking, "Is it lawful for a man to divorce his wife?" 3 "What did Moses command you?" he replied. 4 They said, "Moses permitted a man to write a certificate of divorce and send her away." 5 "It was because your hearts were hard that Moses wrote you this law," Jesus replied. 6 "But at the beginning of creation God 'made them male and female.' 7 'For this reason a man will leave his father and mother and be united to his wife,[a] 8 and the two will become one flesh.' So they are no longer two, but one.

180

Matt. 19	Mark 10

divorce and send
her away?"

8 Jesus replied,
"Moses permitted
you to divorce
your wives because
your hearts were
hard. But it was
not this way from
the beginning.

9 Therefore
what God has
joined together,
let man not sep-
arate."

10 When they
were in the house
again, the disci-
ples asked Jesus
about this. 11 He
answered,

9 I
tell you that any-
one who divorces
his wife, except
for marital un-
faithfulness, and
marries another
woman commits

"Anyone
who divorces his
wife and marries
another woman
commits

adultery."

adultery
against her. 12
And if she divor-
ces her husband
and marries an-
other man, she
commits adultery."

10 The disciples
said to him, "If
this is the situation between a husband and wife, it is better not to marry."

11 Jesus replied, "Not everyone can accept this teaching, but only those
to whom it has been given. 12 For some are eunuchs because they were born
that way; others were made that way by men; and others have renounced
marriage[b] because of the kingdom of heaven. The one who can accept this
should accept it."

[a]Some early manuscripts do not have "and be united to his wife."
[b]Or "have made themselves eunuchs".

125. JESUS BLESSES LITTLE CHILDREN

Matt. 19:13-15   Mark 10:13-16   Luke 18:15-17

13 Then little children were brought to Jesus for him to place his hands on them and pray for them.

13 People were bringing little children to Jesus

15 People were also bringing babies to Jesus to have him touch them. When the disciples saw this, they rebuked them.

But the disciples rebuked those who brought them.

to have him touch them, but the disciples rebuked them.

14 When Jesus saw this, he was indignant. He

16 But Jesus

called the children to him and said, "Let the little children come to me, and do not hinder them, for the kingdom of God belongs to such as these. 17 I tell you the truth, anyone who will not receive the kingdom of God like a little child will never enter it."

14 Jesus said, "Let the little children come to me, and do not hinder them, for the kingdom of heaven belongs to such as these."

said to them, "Let the little children come to me, and do not hinder them, for the kingdom of God belongs to such as these. 15 I tell you the truth, anyone who will not receive the kingdom of God like a little child will never enter it."

16 And he took the children in his arms, put his hands on them and blessed them.

15 When he had placed his hands on them, he went on from there.

126. A RICH YOUNG RULER'S FALTERING FAITH — JESUS WARNS HIS DISCIPLES ABOUT THE PERILS OF WEALTH, AND GIVES THEM PARABOLIC TEACHING ABOUT THE REWARDS OF CHRISTIAN SERVICE

Matt. 19:16-20:16   Mark 10:17-31   Luke 18:18-30

Matt. 19:16-20:16	Mark 10:17-31	Luke 18:18-30
	17 As Jesus started on his way, a	18 A
16 Now a man	man	certain ruler
came up to Jesus	ran up to him and fell on	
and asked,	his knees before	
"Teacher, what	him. "Good teach-	asked him,
	er," he asked,	"Good teacher,
good thing must I	"what	what must I do
do to get eternal	must I do	to inherit eter-
life?"	to inherit eter-	nal life?"
17 "Why do you	nal life?"	
ask me about what		
is good?" Jesus		
replied.		
	18 "Why do you	19 "Why do you
	call me good?"	call me good?"
"There is		Jesus answered.
only One who is	Jesus answered.	"No one is good
good.		— except God
	"No one is good —	alone.
	except God alone.	
If you want		
to enter life, obey		
the command-		
ments."		
18 "Which ones?"		
the man inquired.		
Jesus replied,		
	19 You know the	20 You
	commandments:	know the com-
"'Do not murder,	'Do not murder,	mandments: 'Do
do not commit	do not commit	not commit adul-
adultery, do not	adultery, do not	tery, do not
steal, do not	steal, do not give	murder, do not
give false tes-	false testimony,	steal, do not
timony, 19 honor	do not defraud,	give false tes-
your father	honor your fa-	timony, honor

183

Matt. 19	Mark 10	Luke 18
and mother,' and 'love your neighbor as yourself.'"	ther ␣ ␣ **a n d moth-er.'"**	your father and mother.'"
20 "All these I have kept," the young man said.	**20 "Teacher," he declared, "all these I have kept since I was a boy."**	21 "All these I have kept since I was a boy," he said.
"What do I still lack?"		
21 Jesus an-swered,	**21 Jesus looked at him and loved him. "One thing you lack," he said.**	22 When Jesus heard this, he said to him, "You still lack one thing. Sell
"If you want to be perfect, go, sell your pos-sessions	**"Go, sell everything you have**	everything you have and give to the poor, and you will have
and give to the poor, and you will have treasure in heav-en. Then come, follow me."	and give to the poor, and you will have treasure in heaven. Then come, follow me."	treasure in heaven. Then come, f o l l o w me."
22 When the young man heard this,	22 At this	23 When he heard
he w e n t away sad, because he h a d great wealth.	**his face fell.* He went away** sad, because he had great wealth.	this, he became **very sad, because he was a man of great wealth. 24**
23 Then Jesus said to his dis-ciples, "I tell you the truth, it is hard for a rich man to en-	23 Jesus looked around and **said to his disciples, "How hard it is for the rich to enter**	**Jesus looked at him and** said, "How hard it is for the rich to en-

*The NIV correctly reads "the man's face fell." The pronoun has been substituted to make the composite narrative run smoothly.

184

Matt. 19	Mark 10	Luke 18
ter the kingdom of heaven.	the kingdom of God!"	ter the kingdom of God!
24 Again I tell you,	**24 The disciples were amazed at his words. But Jesus said again, "Children, how hard it is**[a] **to enter the kingdom of God!** 25 It is	
it is easier for a camel to go through the eye of a needle than for a rich man	**easier for a camel to go through the eye of a needle than for a rich man**	25 Indeed, it is easier for a camel to go through the eye of a needle than for
to enter the kingdom of God."	to enter the kingdom of God."	a rich man to enter the kingdom of God."
25 **When the disciples heard this, they were greatly astonished and**	26 The disciples were even more amazed, and	
asked, "Who then can be saved?"	**said to each other, "Who then can be saved?"**	26 Those who heard this asked, "Who then can be saved?"
26 Jesus looked at them and said, "With man this is impossible, but with God all things are possible."	**27 Jesus looked at them and said, "With man this is impossible, but not with God; all things are possible with God."**	27 Jesus replied, "What is impossible with men is possible with God."
27 **Peter answered him, "We have left everything to follow you! What then will there be for us?"**	28 Peter said to him, "We have left everything to follow you!"	28 Peter said to him, "We have left all we had to follow you!"
28 **Jesus said to them, "I tell you the truth, at the renewal of all things, when the Son of Man sits on his glorious throne, you who have followed me will also**	29 "I tell you the truth," Jesus replied,	29 "I tell you the truth," Jesus said to them,

185

Matt. 19-20	Mark 10	Luke 18
sit on twelve thrones, judging the twelve tribes of Israel. 29 And everyone who has left houses or brothers or sisters or father or mother or children or fields for my sake will receive a hundred times as much and will inherit eternal life. 30 But many who are first will be last, and many who are last will be first. 1 "For the kingdom of heaven is	"No one who has left home or broth- ers or sisters or mother or father or children or fields for me and the gospel 30 will fail to re- ceive a hundred times as much in this present age (homes, brothers, sisters, mothers, children and fields — and with them, persecutions) and in the age to come, eternal life. 31 But many who are first will be last, and the last first."	"no one who has left home or wife or brothers or parents or children for the sake of the king- dom of God 30 will fail to receive many times as much in this age and, in the age to come, eternal life."

like a landowner who went out early in the morning to hire men to work in his vineyard. 2 He agreed to pay them a denarius for the day and sent them into his vineyard.

3 "About the third hour he went out and saw others standing in the marketplace doing nothing. 4 He told them, 'You also go and work in my vineyard, and I will pay you whatever is right.' 5 So they went.

"He went out again about the sixth hour and the ninth hour and did the same thing. 6 About the eleventh hour he went out and found still others standing around. He asked them, 'Why have you been standing here all day long doing nothing?'

7 " 'Because no one has hired us,' they answered.

"He said to them, 'You also go and work in my vineyard.'

Matt. 20

8 "When evening
came, the owner
of the vineyard said to his foreman, 'Call the workers and pay them their
wages, beginning with the last ones hired and going on to the first.'

9 "The workers who were hired about the eleventh hour came and each
received a denarius. 10 So when those came who were hired first, they
expected to receive more. But each one of them also received a denarius.
11 When they received it, they began to grumble against the landowner.
12 'These men who were hired last worked only one hour,' they said, 'and
you have made them equal to us who have borne the burden of the work
and the heat of the day.'

13 "But he answered one of them, 'Friend, I am not being unfair to you.
Didn't you agree to work for a denarius? 14 Take your pay and go. I want
to give the man who was hired last the same as I gave you. 15 Don't I have
the right to do what I want with my own money? Or are you envious because I am generous?'

16 "So the last will be first, and the first will be last."

aSome manuscripts "is for those who trust in riches".

127. JESUS AGAIN TELLS HIS TWELVE DISCIPLES PRIVATELY ABOUT HIS APPROACHING DEATH AND RESURRECTION

Matt. 20:17-19	Mark 10:32-34	Luke 18:31-34
17 Now as Jesus was going up to Jerusalem,	32 They were on their way up to Jerusalem, with Jesus leading the way, and the disciples were astonished, while those who followed were afraid. Again he	
he took the twelve disciples aside and said to them, 18 "We are going up to Jerusalem,	took the Twelve aside and told them what was going to happen to him. 33 "We are going up to Jerusalem," he said, "and	31 Jesus took the Twelve aside and told them, "We are going up to Jerusalem, and everything that is written by the prophets about the
and the Son of Man will	the Son of Man will	Son of Man will be fulfilled. 32 He will

187

Matt. 20	Mark 10	Luke 18
be betrayed to the chief	be betrayed to the chief	
priests		
and the teachers of the law. They will condemn him to death 19 and will turn him over to the Gentiles to be mocked	priests and teachers of the law. They will condemn him to death and will hand him over to the Gentiles, 34 who will mock him	be handed over to the Gentiles.
	and spit on	They will mock him, insult him, spit on
and flogged and crucified. On the third day he will be raised to life!"*	him, flog him and kill him. Three days later he will rise."	him, flog him and kill him. 33 On the third day he will rise again."
		34 The disciples did not understand

any of this. Its meaning was hidden from them, and they did not know what he was talking about.

128. SELFISH AMBITION EXPRESSED BY JAMES AND JOHN AND THEIR MOTHER PRECIPITATES DISCORD AMONG THE DISCIPLES — JESUS TALKS TO THEM PLAINLY ABOUT HUMBLE UNSELFISH SERVICE

Matt. 20:20-28	Mark 10:35-45	
20 Then the mother of Zebedee's sons came to Jesus with her sons	35 Then	
	James and John, the sons of Zebedee, came to	
and, kneeling down, asked a favor of		
him.	him. **"Teacher,"** they said, "we want you to do for	

---

*Twice previously (sec. 85 and 89) Jesus had foretold his death and resurrection, but this was the first time that he disclosed precise details. With reference to the resurrection, on all three occasions Mark says "after three days", while Matthew and Luke say "the third day". As Matthew elsewhere (27:63) also uses the expression "after three days", it seems obvious that these words are not to be interpreted in a strictly literal sense.

Matt. 20   Mark 10

us whatever we ask."

21 "What is it you want?" he asked.

36 "What do you want me to do for you?" he asked.

She said, "Grant that one of these two sons of mine may sit at your right and the other at your left in your kingdom."

37 They replied, "Let one of us sit at your right and the other at your left in your glory."

22 "You don't know what you are asking," Jesus said to them. "Can you drink the cup I am going to

drink?"

38 "You don't know what you are asking," Jesus said. "Can you drink the cup I

drink or be baptized with the baptism I am baptized with?"

"We can," they answered.

39 "We can," they answered. Jesus said to them, "You will drink the cup I drink

23 Jesus said to them, "You will indeed drink from my cup,

and be baptized with the baptism I am baptized with,

but to sit at my right or left is not for me to grant. These places belong to those for whom they have been

40 but to sit at my right or left is not for me to grant. These places belong to those for whom they have been

pre-pared by my Father."

prepared."

24 When the ten heard about this, they were indignant with the two brothers. 25 Jesus called

41 When the ten heard about this, they became indignant with James and John. 42 Jesus called them to—

Matt. 20	Mark 10
t h e m together and said, "You know that the rulers of the Gentiles lord it over them, and their high officials exercise authority over them.	gether and said, "You know that those who are regarded as rulers of the Gentiles lord it over them, and their high officials exercise authority over
26 Not so with you. Instead, w h o ever wants to become great among you must be your servant, 27 and whoever w a n t s t o b e first must be your slave —	them. 43 Not so with you. Instead, whoever wants to b e c o m e great among you must be your servant, 44 and whoever wants to be first must be slave of
28 just as the Son of M a n d i d not come to be served, but to serve, and to give his life as a ransom for many."	all. 45 For even the Son of Man did not come to be served, but to serve, and to give his life as a ransom for many."

D. A POSTLUDE: EXCITING EVENTS AS JESUS RE-ENTERS JUDEA, TERMINATING HIS MINISTRY IN PEREA

129. THE HEALING OF BLIND BARTIMAEUS

Probably on the way out of Old Jericho

Matt. 20:29-34	Mark 10:46-52	Luke 18:35-43
29 As Jesus and his disciples w e r e leaving Jericho, a large crowd followed h i m.	46 Then they came to Jericho. As Jesus and his disciples, together with a large crowd, were leaving the city,	35 As J e s u s approached Jericho,*

*Luke's statement seems to contradict the other two Gospel accounts. Matthew and Mark say that Jesus was leaving Jericho, but Luke says that Jesus was approaching Jericho. Apparently He was leaving Old Jericho and was on his way to the new city built by Herod the Great.

Matt. 20	Mark 10	Luke 18
30 Two blind men were sitting by the roadside,	a blind man,* Bartimaeus (that is, the Son of Timaeus), was sitting by the roadside begging.	a blind man was sitting by the roadside begging. 36 When he heard the crowd going by, he asked what was happening. 37 They told him, "Jesus of Nazareth is passing by."
and when they heard that Jesus was going by, they shouted,	47 When he heard that it was Jesus of Nazareth, he began to shout,	38 He called out, "Jesus, Son of David, have mercy on me!"
"Lord, Son of David, have mercy on us!"	"Jesus, Son of David, have mercy on me!"	
31 The crowd rebuked them and told them to be quiet, but they shouted all the louder, "Lord, Son of David, have mercy on us!"	48 Many rebuked him and told him to be quiet, but he shouted all the more, "Son of David, have mercy on me!"	39 Those who led the way rebuked him and told him to be quiet, but he shouted all the more, "Son of David, have mercy on me!"
32 Jesus stopped and called them.	49 Jesus stopped and said, "Call him." So they called to the blind man, "Cheer up! On your feet! He's calling you." 50 Throwing his cloak aside, he jumped to his feet and came to Jesus.	40 Jesus stopped and ordered the man to be brought to him.

*Matthew mentions two blind men. Probably the one described by Mark and Luke was the more prominent one (cf. sec. 64).

Matt. 20	Mark 10	Luke 18
"What do you want me to do for you?" he asked. 33 "Lord," they answered, "we want our sight." 34 Jesus had compassion on them and touched their eyes.* Immediately they received their sight and followed him.	51 "What do you want me to do for you?" Jesus asked him. The blind man said. "Rabbi, I want to see." 52 "Go," said Jesus, "your faith has healed you." Immediately he received his sight and followed Jesus along the road.	**When he came near, Jesus asked him, 41 "What do you want me to do for you?"** **"Lord, I want to see," he replied.** **42 Jesus said to him, "Receive your sight; your faith has healed you."** **43 Immediately he received his sight and followed Jesus, praising God. When all the people saw it, they also praised God.**

130. JESUS AND ZACCHAEUS

Probably New Jericho

Luke 19:1-10

1 Jesus entered Jericho and was passing through.

2 A man was there by the name of Zacchaeus; he was a chief tax collector and was wealthy. 3 He wanted to see who Jesus was, but being a short man he could not, because of the crowd. 4 So he ran ahead and climbed a sycamore-fig tree to see him, since Jesus was coming that way.

5 When Jesus reached the spot, he looked up and said to him, "Zacchaeus, come down immediately. I must stay at your house today." 6 So he came down at once and welcomed him gladly.

7 All the people saw this and began to mutter, "He has gone to be the guest of a 'sinner.'"

8 But Zacchaeus stood up and said to the Lord, "Look, Lord! Here and now I give half of my possessions to the poor, and if I have cheated anybody out of anything, I will pay back four times the amount."

9 Jesus said to him, "Today salvation has come to this house, because this man, too, is a son of Abraham. 10 For the Son of Man came to seek and to save what was lost."

---

*Unfortunately, because of the plural pronouns this sentence in Matthew's account could not be included in the boldfaced composite narrative.

131. AS HE APPROACHES JERUSALEM, JESUS ENDEAVORS TO CORRECT POPULAR MISUNDERSTANDING ABOUT THE COMING OF THE KINGDOM — THE PARABLE OF THE TEN MINAS

Luke 19:11-28

11 While they were listening to this, he went on to tell them a parable, because he was near Jerusalem and the people thought that the kingdom of God was going to appear at once. 12 He said: "A man of noble birth went to a distant country to have himself appointed king and then to return. 13 So he called ten of his servants and gave them ten minas.[a] 'Put this money to work,' he said, 'until I come back.'

14 "But his subjects hated him and sent a delegation after him to say, 'We don't want this man to be our king.'

15 "He was made king, however, and returned home. Then he sent for the servants to whom he had given the money, in order to find out what they had gained with it.

16 "The first one came and said, 'Sir, your mina has earned ten more.'

17 " 'Well done, my good servant!' his master replied. 'Because you have been trustworthy in a very small matter, take charge of ten cities.'

18 "The second came and said, 'Sir, your mina has earned five more.'

19 "His master answered, 'You take charge of five cities.'

20 "Then another servant came and said, 'Sir, here is your mina; I have kept it laid away in a piece of cloth. 21 I was afraid of you, because you are a hard man. You take out what you did not put in and reap what you did not sow.'

22 "His master replied, 'I will judge you by your own words, you wicked servant! You knew, did you, that I am a hard man, taking out what I did not put in, and reaping what I did not sow? 23 Why then didn't you put my money on deposit, so that when I came back, I could have collected it with interest?'

24 "Then he said to those standing by, 'Take his mina away from him and give it to the one who has ten minas.'

25 " 'Sir,' they said, 'he already has ten!'

26 "He replied, 'I tell you that to everyone who has, more will be given, but as for the one who has nothing, even what he has will be taken away. 27 But those enemies of mine who did not want me to be king over them — bring them here and kill them in front of me.'"

28 After Jesus had said this, he went on ahead, going up to Jerusalem.

[a]A mina was about three months' wages.

132. A HOSTILE PROCLAMATION OF THE SANHEDRIN CREATES SUSPENSE IN JERUSALEM ABOUT THE COMING OF JESUS TO THE PASSOVER

John 11:55-57

55 When it was almost time for the Jewish Passover, many went up from the country to Jerusalem for their ceremonial cleansing before the Passover. 56 They kept looking for Jesus, and as they stood in the temple area they asked one another, "What do you think? Isn't he coming to the Feast at all?" 57 But the chief priests and Pharisees had given orders that if anyone found out where Jesus was, he should report it so that they might arrest him.

133. THE ARRIVAL OF JESUS AT BETHANY GIVES RISE TO POPULAR INTEREST AND PRIESTLY PLOTS

John 12:1,9-11

1 Six days before the Passover, Jesus arrived at Bethany, where Lazarus lived, whom Jesus had raised from the dead.

9 Meanwhile a large crowd of Jews found out that Jesus was there and came, not only because of him but also to see Lazarus, whom he had raised from the dead. 10 So the chief priests made plans to kill Lazarus as well, 11 for on account of him many of the Jews were going over to Jesus and putting their faith in him.

PART X

CHRIST'S FINAL MINISTRY IN JERUSALEM
A CULMINATING CLASH WITH THE JEWISH LEADERS

SUNDAY TO WEDNESDAY MORNING, APRIL 2-5, A.D. 30

134. RIDING INTO JERUSALEM, JESUS DRAMATIZES HIS MESSIAHSHIP AND WINS POPULAR SUPPORT

Sunday, April 2

Matt. 21:1-11	Mark 11:1-11	Luke 19:29-44	John 12:12-19
			12 The next day
1 As they approached Jerusalem and came to Bethphage on the Mount of Olives, Jesus sent two disciples, 2 saying to them, "Go to the village ahead of you, and at once **you will find a donkey tied there, with her colt** by her. **Untie them and bring them to me. 3 If anyone says anything to you, tell him that the**	1 As they approached **Jerusalem and came to Bethphage and Bethany at the Mount of Olives, Jesus sent two of his disciples, 2 saying to them, "Go to the village ahead of you, and just as you enter it,** you will find a colt tied there, **which no one has ever ridden.** Untie it and bring it here. 3 If anyone asks you, 'Why are you doing this?' tell him, 'The Lord	29 As he approached Bethphage and Bethany at the hill called the Mount of Olives, he sent two of his disciples, saying to them, 30 "Go to the village ahead of you, and as you enter it, you will find a colt tied there, which no one has ever ridden. Untie it and bring it here. 31 If anyone asks you, 'Why are you untying it?' tell him,	

195

Matt. 21	Mark 11	Luke 19	John 12
Lord needs them, and he will send them right away." 6 The disciples went and did as Jesus had instructed them.	needs it and will send it back here shortly.'"	'The Lord needs it.'"	
	4 They went and found a colt outside in the street, tied at a doorway.	32 Those who were sent ahead went and found it	
	As they untied it, 5 some people	just as he had told them. 33 As they were untying the colt, its owners	
	standing there asked, "What are you doing, untying that colt?" 6 They answered as Jesus had told them to,	asked them, "Why are you untying the colt?" 34 They replied,	
		"The Lord needs it."	
	and the people let them go.		
7 They brought the donkey and the	7 When they brought the colt to Jesus and	35 They brought it to Jesus,	
colt, placed their cloaks on them, and Jesus sat on them. 8 A very large crowd spread their cloaks on the road, while others cut branches from the trees and spread them on the road.	threw their cloaks over it, he sat on it. 8 Many people spread their cloaks on the road, while others spread branches they had cut in the fields.	threw their cloaks on the colt and put Jesus on it. 36 As he went along, people spread their cloaks on the road.	
		37 When he came near the place where the road goes down the Mount of Olives,	
			the great crowd that had come for

Matt. 21	Mark 11	Luke 19	. John 12

the Feast heard that Jesus was on his way to Jerusalem. 13 They took palm branches and went out to meet him, shouting,

"Hosanna![a]"

"Blessed is he who comes in the name of the Lord!"

"Blessed is the King of Israel!"

Matt. 21	Mark 11	Luke 19
9 The crowds that went ahead of him and those that followed shouted,	9 Those who went ahead and those who followed shouted,	the whole crowd of disciples began joyfully to praise God in loud voices for all the miracles they had seen:
	"Hosanna![a]"	
"Hosanna[a] to the Son of David!"		
"Blessed is he who comes in the name of the Lord!"	"Blessed is he who comes in the name of the Lord!" 10 "Blessed is the coming kingdom of our father David!"	38 "Blessed is the king who comes in the name of the Lord!"
"Hosanna[a] in the highest!"	"Hosanna[a] in the highest!"	"Peace in heaven and glory in the highest!"

17 Now the crowd that was with him had continued to spread the word that he had called Lazarus from the tomb, raising him from the dead.[b] 18 Many people, because they had heard that he had given this miraculous sign, went out to meet him. 19 So the Pharisees said to one another, "See, this is getting us nowhere. Look how the whole world has gone after him!"

39 Some of the Pharisees in the crowd said to Jesus, "Teacher, rebuke your disciples!"

40 "I tell you," he replied, "if they keep quiet, the stones will cry out."

Matt. 21	Mark 11	Luke 19	John 12
4 This took place to fulfill what was spoken through the prophet: 5 "Say to the Daughter of Zion,			14 Jesus found a young donkey and sat upon it, as it is written,
'See, your king			15 "Do not be afraid, O Daughter of Zion; see, your king
comes to you, gentle and riding on a donkey, on a colt, the foal of a donkey.'"			is coming, seated on a donkey's colt."
			16 At first his disciples did not

understand all this. Only after Jesus was glorified did they realize that these things had been written about him and that they had done these things to him.

| | | 41 As he ap-proached Jerusa- | |

lem and saw the city, he wept over it 42 and said, "If you, even you, had only known on this day what would bring you peace — but now it is hidden from your eyes. 43 The days will come upon you when your enemies will build an embankment against you and encircle you and hem you in on every side. 44 They will dash you to the ground, you and the children within your walls. They will not leave one stone on another, because you

	11 Jesus en-tered Jerusalem	did not recognize the time of God's coming to you."	
10 When Jesus entered Jerusalem,			
	and went to the temple.		
the whole city was stirred and asked, "Who is this?" 11 The crowds answered, "This is Jesus, the prophet			

Matt. 21   Mark 11

from Nazareth in
Galilee."

                                    He looked
                    around at every-
thing, but since it was already late, he went out to Bethany with the
Twelve.

aA Hebrew expression meaning "Save!" which became an exclamation of
praise.   bOr "Now the crowd that had been with him when he called
Lazarus from the tomb and raised him from the dead were telling everyone".

135. JESUS CONDEMNS A FRUITLESS FIG TREE

Monday, April 3

Matt. 21:18-19   Mark 11:12-14

18 Early in the morning, as he was	12 The next day as they were leaving Bethany,
on his way back to the city, he was hungry. 19 Seeing	Jesus was hungry. 13 Seeing
a fig tree	in the distance a fig tree
by the road,	
he went	in leaf, he went to find out if it had any
up to it but found nothing on it except leaves. Then he said to it, "M a y y o u never bear fruit again!"	fruit. When he reached it, he found nothing but leaves, because it was not the season for figs. 14 Then he said to the tree, "May no one ever eat fruit from you again." And his disciples heard him say it.
Imme- diately the tree withered.	

136. THE SECOND* CLEANSING OF THE TEMPLE

Monday, April 3

Matt. 21:12-16	Mark 11:15-18	Luke 19:45-48
12 Jesus entered the temple area and drove out	15 On reaching Jerusalem, Jesus entered the temple area and began driving out	45 Then he entered the temple area and began driving out
all who were buying and selling there. He overturned the tables of the money changers	those who were buying and selling there. He overturned the tables of the money changers	those who were selling.
and the benches of those selling doves.	and the benches of those selling doves, 16 and would not allow anyone to carry merchandise through the temple courts. 17	
13 "It is written," he said to them,	And as he taught them, he said, "Is it not written:	46 "It is written," he said to them,
"'My house will be called a house of prayer,'	"'My house will be called a house of prayer for all nations'?	"'My house will be a house of prayer';
but you are making it a 'den of robbers.'"	But you have made it 'a den of robbers.'"	but you have made it 'a den of robbers.'"
14 The blind and the lame came to		

him at the temple, and he healed them. 15 But when the chief priests and the teachers of the law saw the wonderful things he did and the children shouting in the temple area, "Hosanna to the Son of David," they were indignant.

16 "Do you hear what these children are saying?" they asked him.

"Yes," replied Jesus, "have you never read,

"'From the lips of children and infants
you have ordained praise'?"

---

*See sec. 31 (on page 28), especially the footnote.

Mark 11	Luke 19
18 The chief priests and the teachers of the law	47 Every day he was teaching at the temple. But the chief priests, the teachers of the law and the leaders among the people
heard this and began looking for a way to kill him, for they feared him, because the whole crowd was amazed at his teaching.	were try-ing to kill him.
	48 Yet they could not find any way to do it, because all the people hung on his words.

137. THE DESIRE OF SOME GREEKS TO SEE JESUS OCCASIONS A GREAT DISCOURSE ON THE SIGNIFICANCE OF HIS APPROACHING DEATH

Monday, April 3

Matt. 21:17   Mark 11:19   John 12:20-50

20 Now there were some Greeks among those who went up to worship at the Feast. 21 They came to Philip, who was from Bethsaida in Galilee, with a request. "Sir," they said, "we would like to see Jesus." 22 Philip went to tell Andrew; Andrew and Philip in turn told Jesus.

23 Jesus replied, "The hour has come for the Son of Man to be glorified. 24 I tell you the truth, unless a kernel of wheat falls to the ground and dies, it remains only a single seed. But if it dies, it produces many seeds. 25 The man who loves his life will lose it, while the man who hates his life in this world will keep it for eternal life. 26 Whoever serves me must follow me; and where I am, my servant also will be. My Father will honor the one who serves me.

27 "Now my heart is troubled, and what shall I say? 'Father, save me from this hour'? No, it was for this very reason I came to this hour. 28 Father, glorify your name!"

Then a voice came from heaven, "I have glorified it, and will glorify it again." 29 The crowd that was there and heard it said it had thundered; others said an angel had spoken to him.

30 Jesus said, "This voice was for your benefit, not mine. 31 Now is the time for judgment on this world; now the prince of this world will be driven out. 32 But I, when I am lifted up from the earth, will draw all men to myself." 33 He said this to show the kind of death he was going to die.

34 The crowd spoke up, "We have heard from the Law that the Christ[a] will remain forever, so how can you say, 'The Son of Man must be lifted up'? Who is this 'Son of Man'?"

35 Then Jesus told them, "You are going to have the light just a little while longer. Walk while you have the light, before darkness overtakes you. The man who walks in the dark does not know where he is going. 36 Put your trust in the light while you have it, so that you may become sons of light." When he had finished speaking, Jesus left and hid himself from them.

37 Even after Jesus had done all these miraculous signs in their presence, they still would not believe in him. 38 This was to fulfill the word of Isaiah the prophet:

"Lord, who has believed our message
and to whom has the arm of the Lord been revealed?"

39 For this reason they could not believe, because, as Isaiah says elsewhere:

40 "He has blinded their eyes
and deadened their hearts,
so they can neither see with their eyes,
nor understand with their hearts,
nor turn — and I would heal them."

41 Isaiah said this because he saw Jesus' glory and spoke about him.

42 Yet at the same time many even among the leaders believed in him. But because of the Pharisees they would not confess their faith for fear they would be put out of the synagogue; 43 for they loved praise from men more than praise from God.

44 Then Jesus cried out, "When a man believes in me, he does not believe in me only, but in the one who sent me. 45 When he looks at me, he sees the one who sent me. 46 I have come into the world as a light, so that no one who believes in me should stay in darkness.

47 "As for the person who hears my words but does not keep them, I do not judge him. For I did not come to judge the world, but to save it. 48 There is a judge for the one who rejects me and does not accept my words; that very word which I spoke will condemn him at the last day. 49 For I did not speak of my own accord, but the Father who sent me commanded me what to say and how to say it. 50 I know that his command leads to eternal life. So whatever I say is just what

Matt. 21	Mark 11	John 12
		the Father has told me to say."
17 And	19 When evening came,	
he left them and went out of the city to Bethany, where he spent the night.	they[b] went out of the city.	

^aOr "Messiah".   ^bSome early manuscripts "he".

138. THE WITHERED FIG TREE — A LESSON ON FAITH

Tuesday, April 4

Matt. 21:20-22	Mark 11:20-25	
	20 In the morning, as they went along, they saw the fig tree withered from the roots.	
20 When the disciples saw this, they were amazed. "How did the fig tree wither so quickly?" they asked.		
	21 Peter remembered and said to Jesus, "Rabbi, look! The fig tree you cursed has withered!"	
21 Jesus replied,	22 "Have[a] faith in God," Jesus answered.	
"I tell you the truth, if you have faith and do not doubt, not only can you do what was done to the fig tree, but also you can say to	23 "I tell you the truth, if anyone says to this	

Matt. 21	Mark 11	
this mountain, 'Go, throw your- self into the sea,' and it will be done. 22 If you believe, you will receive whatever you ask for in prayer."	mountain, 'Go, throw yourself into the sea,' and does not doubt in his heart but be- lieves that what he says will happen, it will be done for him. 24 Therefore I tell you, what- ever you ask for in prayer, believe that you have re- ceived it, and it will be yours. 25 And when you	

stand praying, if you hold anything against anyone, forgive him, so that your Father in heaven may forgive you your sins.[b]"

[a]Some early manuscripts "If you have".   [b]Some manuscripts "sins. 26 But if you do not forgive, neither will your Father who is in heaven for- give your sins."

139. CHALLENGED BY THE SANHEDRIN AS TO HIS AUTHORITY, JESUS REPLIES WITH A SHREWD QUESTION AND PERTINENT PARABLES

Tuesday, April 4

Matt. 21:23—22:14   Mark 11:27—12:12   Luke 20:1-19

Matt. 21:23—22:14	Mark 11:27—12:12	Luke 20:1-19
23 Jesus en- tered the temple courts, and, while he was teaching, the chief priests and the elders of the people came to him. "By what authority are you doing these things?"	27 They arrived again in Jerusalem, and while Jesus was walking in the temple courts, the chief priests, the teachers of the law and the elders came to him. 28 "By what authority are you doing these things?" they	1 One day as he was teaching the people in the temple courts and preaching the gospel, the chief priests and the teachers of the law, together with the elders, came up to him. 2 "Tell us by what authority you are doing these things," they

Matt. 21	Mark 11-12	Luke 20
they asked. "And who gave you this authority?"	asked. **"And who gave you authority to do this?"**	said. "Who gave you this authority?"
24 Jesus replied, "I will also ask you one question. If you answer me, I will tell you by what authority I am doing these things. 25 John's baptism— where did it come from? Was it from heaven, or from men?"	29 Jesus replied, "I will ask you one question. Answer me, and I will tell you by what authority I am doing these things. 30 John's baptism — was it **from heaven, or from men? Tell me!"**	3 He replied, "I will also ask you a question. Tell me, 4 John's baptism — was it from heaven, or from men?"
They discussed it among themselves and said, "If we say, 'From heaven,' he will ask, 'Then why didn't you believe him?' 26 But if we say, 'From men'— we are afraid of the people, for they all hold that John was a prophet."	**31 They discussed it among themselves and said, "If we say, 'From heaven,' he will ask, 'Then why didn't you believe him?' 32 But if we say,** 'From men'...." (They feared the people, for everyone held that John really was a prophet.)	5 They discussed it among themselves and said, "If we say, 'From heaven', he will ask, 'Why didn't you believe him?' 6 But if we say, 'From men,' all the people will stone us, because they are persuaded that John was a prophet."
27 So they answered Jesus, "We don't know." Then he said, "Neither will I tell you by what authority I am doing these things.	33 So they answered Jesus, "We don't know." Jesus said, "Neither will I tell you by what authority I am doing these things."	7 So they answered, "We don't know where it was from." 8 Jesus said, "Neither will I tell you by what authority I am doing these things."
	1 He then began to speak to them in parables:	9 He went on to tell the people this parable:
28 "What do you think? There was		

a man who had two sons. He went to the first and said, 'Son, go and work today in the vineyard.'

Matt. 21	Mark 12	Luke 20

29 "'I will not,' he answered, but later he changed his mind and went.

30 "Then the father went to the other son and said the same thing. He answered, 'I will, sir,' but he did not go.

31 "Which of the two did what his father wanted?"

"The first," they answered.

Jesus said to them, "I tell you the truth, the tax collectors and the prostitutes are entering the kingdom of God ahead of you. 32 For John came to you to show you the way of righteousness, and you did not believe him, but the tax collectors and the prostitutes did. And even after you saw this, you did not repent and believe him.

---

33 "Listen to another parable: There was a land-owner who planted

"A man planted

"A man planted a vineyard,

a vineyard. He put a wall a-round it, dug a winepress in it and built a watchtower. Then he rented the vineyard to some farmers and went away on a journey.

a vineyard. He put a wall around it, dug a pit for the winepress and built a watchtower. Then he rented the vineyard to some farmers and went away on a journey.

rented it to

some farmers and went away for a long time. 10 At harvest time he sent a servant to the

34 When the harvest time approached, he sent his ser-vants to the tenants to col-lect his fruit.

2 At harvest time he sent a servant to the **tenants to collect from them some of the fruit of the vineyard.**

tenants so they would give him some of the fruit of the vineyard. But the tenants beat him and sent him away empty-handed.

35 "The tenants seized his ser-vants; they beat one,

3 But they seized him, beat him and sent him away empty-handed. 4 Then he sent another servant to them; **they struck this man on the head and treated him**

11 He sent another servant, but that one also they beat and treated

killed another,

shamefully.

shame-**fully and sent away empty-handed. 12 He sent still a**

Matt. 21	Mark 12	Luke 20
and stoned a third. 36 Then he sent other servants to them, more than the first time, and the tenants treated them the same way.	5 He sent still another, and that one they killed. He sent many others; some of them they beat, others they killed.	third, and they wounded him and threw him out.
37 Last of all, he sent his son to them. 'They will respect my son,' he said. 38 "But when the tenants saw the son, they said to each other, 'This is the heir. Come, let's kill him and take his inheritance.'	6 "He had one left to send, a son, whom he loved. He sent him last of all, saying, 'They will respect my son.' 7 "But the tenants said to one another, 'This is the heir. Come, let's kill him, and the inheritance will be ours.'	13 "Then the owner of the vineyard said, 'What shall I do? I will send my son, whom I love; perhaps they will respect him.' 14 "But when the tenants saw him, they talked the matter over. 'This is the heir,' they said. 'Let's kill him, and the inheritance will be ours.' 15 So
39 So they took him and threw him out of the vineyard and killed him. 40 "Therefore, when the owner of the vineyard comes, what will he do to those tenants?" 41 "He will bring those wretches to a wretched end," they replied, "and he will rent the vineyard to other tenants, who will give him his share of the crop at	8 So they took him and killed him, and threw him out of the vineyard. 9 "What then will the owner of the vineyard do? He will come and kill those tenants and give the vineyard to others.	they threw him out of the vineyard and killed him. "What then will the owner of the vineyard do to them? 16 He will come and kill those tenants and give the vineyard to others."

Matt. 21–22	Mark 12	Luke 20
harvest time."		
		When the people heard this, they said, "May this never be!"
42 Jesus said to them, "Have you never read in the Scriptures:	10 Haven't you read this scripture:	17 Jesus looked directly at them and asked, "Then what is the meaning of that which is written:
" 'The stone the builders rejected has become the capstone[a]; the Lord has done this, and it is marvelous in our eyes'?	" 'The stone the builders rejected has become the capstone[a]; 11 the Lord has done this, and it is marvelous in our eyes'?"	" 'The stone the builders rejected has become the capstone[a]'?
43 "Therefore I tell you that the kingdom of God will be taken away from you and given to a people who will produce its fruit. 44 He who falls on this stone will be broken to pieces, but he on whom it falls will be crushed."[b]		18 Everyone who falls on that stone will be broken to pieces, but he on whom it falls will be crushed."
45 When the chief priests and the		

Pharisees heard Jesus' parables, they knew he was talking about them. 46 They looked for a way to arrest him, but they were afraid of the crowd because the people held that he was a prophet.

1 Jesus spoke to them again in parables, saying: 2 "The kingdom of heaven is like a king who prepared a wedding banquet for his son. 3 He sent his servants to those who had been invited to the banquet to tell them to come, but they refused to come.

4 "Then he sent some more servants and said, 'Tell those who have been invited that I have prepared my dinner: My oxen and fattened cattle have been butchered, and everything is ready. Come to the wedding banquet.'

Matt. 22	Mark 12	Luke 20

5 "But they paid no attention and went off — one to his field, another to his business. 6 The rest seized his servants, mistreated them and killed them. 7 The king was enraged. He sent his army and destroyed those murderers and burned their city.

8 "Then he said to his servants, 'The wedding banquet is ready, but those I invited did not deserve to come. 9 Go to the street corners and invite to the banquet anyone you find.' 10 So the servants went out into the streets and gathered all the people they could find, both good and bad, and the wedding hall was filled with guests.

11 "But when the king came in to see the guests, he noticed a man there who was not wearing wedding clothes. 12 'Friend,' he asked, 'how did you get in here without wedding clothes?' The man was speechless.

13 "Then the king told the attendants, 'Tie him hand and foot, and throw him outside, into the darkness, where there will be weeping and gnashing of teeth.'

14 "For many are invited, but few are chosen."

	Mark	Luke
		19 The teachers of the law and the chief priests looked for a way to arrest him immediately,
	12 Then they looked for a way to arrest him	
	because they knew he had spoken the parable against them. But they were afraid of the crowd; so they left him and went away.	because they knew he had spoken this parable against them. But they were afraid of the people.

aOr "cornerstone".   bSome manuscripts do not have Matt. 21:44.

140. SOME PHARISEES AND HERODIANS TRY IN VAIN TO ENSNARE JESUS WITH A QUESTION ABOUT PAYING TAXES TO CAESAR

Tuesday, April 4

Matt. 22:15-22	Mark 12:13-17	Luke 20:20-26

15 Then the Pharisees went out and laid plans to trap him in his words.

Matt. 22	Mark 12	Luke 20
16 They sent	13 Later they sent some of	20 Keeping a close watch on him, they
their disciples to him along with the	the Pharisees and Herodians	sent spies,
Herodians.	to Jesus to catch him in his words.	who pretended to be honest. They hoped to catch Jesus in something he said so that they might hand him over to the power and authority of the governor. 21 So the spies
	14 They came to him and said,	questioned
"Teacher," they said, "we know you are a man of integrity and that you teach the way of God in accordance with the truth.	"Teacher, we know you are a man of integrity. You aren't swayed by men, because you pay no attention to who they are; but	him: "Teacher, we know that
You aren't swayed by men, because you pay no attention to who they are.	you teach the way of God in accordance with the truth.	you speak and teach what is right, and that you do not show partiality but teach the way of God in accordance with the truth. 22 Is
17 Tell us then, what is your opinion? Is it right to pay taxes to Caesar	Is it right to pay taxes to Caesar or not? 15 Should we pay or shouldn't we?"	it right for us to pay taxes to Caesar or not?"
or not?"		
18 But Jesus, knowing their evil intent, said, "You hypocrites, why are you trying to trap me? 19 Show	But Jesus knew their hypocrisy. "Why are you trying to trap me?" he asked.	23 He saw through their duplicity and said to them,

210

Matt. 22	Mark 12	Luke 20
me the coin used for paying the tax." They brought him a denarius, 20 and he asked them, "Whose portrait is this? And whose inscription?"	"Bring me a denarius and let me look at it." 16 They brought the coin, and he asked them, "Whose portrait is this? And whose inscription?"	24 "Show me a denarius. Whose portrait and inscription are on it?"
21 "Caesar's," they replied. Then he said to them, "Give to Caesar what is Caesar's, and to God what is God's."	"Caesar's," they replied. 17 Then Jesus said to them, "Give to Caesar what is Caesar's and to God what is God's."	25 "Caesar's," they replied. He said to them, "Then give to Caesar what is Caesar's, and to God what is God's."
22 When they heard this, they were amazed.	And they were amazed at him.	26 They were unable to trap him in what he had said there in public. And astonished by his answer, they became silent.
So they left him and went away.		

141. JESUS REPLIES TO A SKEPTICAL QUESTION FROM SOME SADDUCEES ABOUT THE RESURRECTION

Tuesday, April 4

Matt. 22:23-33	Mark 12:18-27	Luke 20:27-40
23 That same day the Sadducees, who say there is no resurrection, came to him with a question. 24 "Teacher," they said, "Moses told us that if	18 Then the Sadducees, who say there is no resurrection, came to him with a question. 19 "Teacher," they said, "Moses wrote for us	27 Some of the Sadducees, who say there is no resurrection, came to Jesus with a question. 28 "Teacher," they said, "Moses wrote for us that

Matt. 22	Mark 12	Luke 20
a man dies without having children, his brother must marry the widow and have children for him. 25 Now there were seven **brothers among us. The first one married and died, and since he had no children, he left his wife to his brother.**	that if a man's brother dies and leaves a wife but no children, the man must marry the widow and have children for his brother. **20 Now there were seven** brothers. The first one married and died without leaving any children.	**if a man's brother dies and leaves a wife but no child-ren, the man must marry the widow and have children for his brother.** 29 Now there were seven brothers. The first one mar-ried a woman and died childless.
26 The same thing hap-pened to the second and **third brother, right on down to the sev-enth.**	**21 The second one married the widow, but he also died, leaving no child. It was the same with the** third.	30 The second 31 and then the third married her, and in the same way the seven died,
27 Finally, the woman died.	**22 In fact, none of the seven left any children. Last of all, the woman died too.**	leaving no child ren. 32 Finally, the woman died too.
28 Now then, at the resurrection, whose wife will she be of the seven, since all of them were married to her?" 29 Jesus re-plied, "You are in error because you do not know the Scriptures or the power of God.	23 At the resurrec-tion[a] whose wife will she be, since the seven were married to her?" **24 Jesus replied,** **"Are you not in error because you do not know the Scriptures or the power of God?**	33 Now then, at the resurrec-tion whose wife will she be, since the seven were married to her?" 34 Jesus re-plied, **"The peo-ple of this age**

212

Matt. 22	Mark 12	Luke 20
		marry and are given in marriage. 35 But those who are considered worthy of taking part in that age and in the resur-
30 At the resurrection people will neither marry nor be given in marriage; they will be like the angels in heaven.	25 When the dead rise, they will neither marry nor be given in marriage; they will be like the angels in heaven.	rection from the dead will neither marry nor be giv- en in marriage, 36 and they can no longer die; for they are like the angels. They are God's children, since they are children of the resurrection.
31 But about the resurrection of the dead — have you not read what God said to you, 32 'I am the God of Abra- ham, the God of Isaac, and the God of Jacob'? He is not the God of the dead but of the liv- ing."	26 Now about the dead rising— have you not read in the book of Moses, in the account of the bush, how God said to him, 'I am the God of Abra- ham, the God of Isaac, and the God of Jacob'? 27 He is not the God of the dead, but of the living. You are badly mistaken!"	37 But in the ac- count of the bush, even Moses showed that the dead rise, for he calls the Lord 'the God of Abraham, and the God of Isaac, and the God of Jacob.' 38 He is not the God of the dead, but of the living, for to him all are alive."
33 When the crowds heard this, they were as- tonished at his teaching.		39 Some of the

213

Luke 20

| teachers of the law |
| responded, "Well|
said, teacher!" 40 And no one dared to ask him any more questions.

ªSome manuscripts "resurrection, when men rise from the dead".

142. JESUS ANSWERS A PHARISAIC TEACHER'S QUESTION ABOUT THE GREATEST COMMANDMENT

Tuesday afternoon, April 4

Matt. 22:34-40   Mark 12:28-34   Luke 21:37

Matt. 22:34-40	Mark 12:28-34	Luke 21:37
34 Hearing that Jesus had silenced the Sadducees, the Pharisees got together. 35 One of them, an expert in the law,	28 One of the teachers of the law came and heard them debating. Noticing that Jesus had given them a good answer, he	
tested him with this question: 36 "Teacher, which is the greatest commandment in the Law?"	asked him, "Of all the commandments, which is the most important?"	
37 Jesus replied: " 'Love the Lord your God with all your heart and with all your soul and with all your mind.'	29 "The most important one," answered Jesus, "is this: 'Hear, O Israel, the Lord our God, the Lord is one.ª 30 Love the Lord your God with all your heart and with all your soul and with all your mind and with all your strength.'	
38 This is the first and greatest commandment. 39 And the second is like it: 'Love your	31 The second is this: 'Love your	

214

Matt. 22	Mark 12	Luke 21

neighbor as your- | n e i g h b o r as
self.' 40 All the | yourself.'
Law and the Proph-
ets hang on these
two command-
ments."

There
is no command-
ment greater than these."

32 "Well said, teacher," the man replied. "You are right in saying that God is one and there is no other but him. 33 To love him with all your heart, with all your understanding and with all your strength, and to love your neighbor as yourself is more important than all burnt offerings and sacrifices."

34 When Jesus saw that he had answered wisely, he said to him, "You are not far from the kingdom of God." And from then on no one dared ask him any more questions.

37 Each day Jesus was teaching at the temple, and each evening he went out to spend the night on the hill called the Mount of Olives.

aOr "the Lord our God is one Lord".

143. JESUS FINALLY SILENCES THE PHARISEES WITH A QUESTION ABOUT THE MESSIAH

Wednesday,* April 5

Matt. 22:41-46	Mark 12:35-37a	Luke 21:38; 20:41-44

**38 And all the people came early

---

*According to some Harmonies of the Gospels, all the events recorded in sec. 138-149 of this Harmony took place on Tuesday, with nothing said about Wednesday; presumably Jesus rested in Bethany on that day.

Instead of thus overcrowding Tuesday, it seems better to adopt the alternative advanced by Moffatt and some other New Testament scholars. In Moffatt's view the language of Matt. 22:41 and Mark 12:35 suggests the occurrence of an interval after Tuesday's incident described in sec. 142 of this Harmony. If so, Jesus probably concluded His final ministry in Jerusalem on Wednesday morning with the events recorded in sec. 143-145

**The NIV begins Luke 21:38 with "and" (a small "a"), after a comma at the end of vs. 37.

Matt. 22	Mark 12	Luke 21-20
		in the morning to hear him at the temple.
41 While the Pharisees were gathered together,		
	35 While Jesus was teaching in the temple courts, he	
Jesus		
asked them, 42 "What do you think about the Christ[a]? Whose son is he?" **"The son of David," they replied.**	asked, "How is it that the teachers of the law say that the Christ[a] is the son of David?	20:41 Then Jesus said to them, "How is it that they say the Christ[a] is the Son of David?
43 He said to them, "How is it then that David, speaking by the Spirit, calls him 'Lord'? For	**36** David himself, speaking by the Holy Spirit, declared:	**42**
		David himself declares in the Book of Psalms:
he says, 44 "'The Lord said to my Lord: "Sit at my right hand until I put your enemies under your feet."'	"'The Lord said to my Lord: "Sit at my right hand until I put your enemies under your feet."'	"'The Lord said to my Lord: "Sit at my right hand 43 until I make your enemies a footstool for your feet."'
45 If then David calls him 'Lord,' how can he be his son?" **46 No** one could say a	**37 David himself calls him 'Lord.' How then can he be his son?"**	44 David calls him 'Lord.' How then can he be his son?"

word in reply, and from that day on no one dared to ask him any more questions.

[a]Or "Messiah".

144. JESUS PUBLICLY DENOUNCES THE TEACHERS OF THE LAW AND THE PHARISEES

Wednesday, April 5

Matt. 23:1-39	Mark 12:37b-40	Luke 20:45-47
	37b The large crowd listened to him with delight.	45 While all the people were listening, Jesus said to his disciples, 46
1 Then Jesus said to the crowds and to his disciples:	38 As he taught, Jesus said,	
2 "The teachers of the law	**"Watch out for the teachers of the law. They**	"Beware of the teachers of the law.
and the Pharisees sit		

in Moses' seat. 3 So you must obey them and do everything they tell you. But do not do what they do, for they do not practice what they preach. 4 They tie up heavy loads and put them on men's shoulders, but they themselves are not willing to lift a finger to move them.

5 "Everything they do is done for men to see: They make their phylacteries[a] wide and the tassels of their prayer shawls long; 6 they

	like to walk around in flowing robes and	They like to walk around in flowing robes and love to be
love the place of honor at banquets and the most important seats in the synagogues; 7 they love to be greeted in the marketplaces and to have men call them 'Rabbi.'	be greeted in the marketplaces, 39 and have the most important seats in the synagogues and the places of honor at banquets.	greeted in the marketplaces and have the most important seats in the synagogues and the places of honor at banquets. 47 They
	40 They devour widows' houses and for a show make lengthy prayers. Such men will be punished most severely."	devour widows' houses and for a show make lengthy prayers. Such men will be punished most severely."

217

Matt. 23

8 "But you are
not to be called
'Rabbi,' for you have only one Master and you are all brothers. 9 And do not call anyone on earth 'father,' for you have one Father, and he is in heaven. 10 Nor are you to be called 'teacher,' for you have one Teacher, the Christ.[b] 11 The greatest among you will be your servant. 12 For whoever exalts himself will be humbled, and whoever humbles himself will be exalted.

13 "Woe to you, teachers of the law and Pharisees, you hypocrites! You shut the kingdom of heaven in men's faces. You yourselves do not enter, nor will you let those enter who are trying to.[c]

15 "Woe to you, teachers of the law and Pharisees, you hypocrites! You travel over land and sea to win a single convert, and when he becomes one, you make him twice as much a son of hell as you are.

16 "Woe to you, blind guides! You say, 'If anyone swears by the temple, it means nothing; but if anyone swears by the gold of the temple, he is bound by his oath.' 17 You blind fools! Which is greater: the gold, or the temple that makes the gold sacred? 18 You also say, 'If anyone swears by the altar, it means nothing; but if anyone swears by the gift on it, he is bound by his oath.' 19 You blind men! Which is greater: the gift, or the altar that makes the gift sacred? 20 Therefore, he who swears by the altar swears by it and by everything on it. 21 And he who swears by the temple swears by it and by the one who dwells in it. 22 And he who swears by heaven swears by God's throne and by the one who sits on it.

23 "Woe to you, teachers of the law and Pharisees, you hypocrites! You give a tenth of your spices — mint, dill and cummin. But you have neglected the more important matters of the law — justice, mercy and faithfulness. You should have practiced the latter, without neglecting the former. 24 You blind guides! You strain out a gnat but swallow a camel.

25 "Woe to you, teachers of the law and Pharisees, you hypocrites! You clean the outside of the cup and dish, but inside they are full of greed and self-indulgence. 26 Blind Pharisee! First clean the inside of the cup and dish, and then the outside also will be clean.

27 "Woe to you, teachers of the law and Pharisees, you hypocrites! You are like whitewashed tombs, which look beautiful on the outside but on the inside are full of dead men's bones and everything unclean. 28 In the same way, on the outside you appear to people as righteous but on the inside you are full of hypocrisy and wickedness.

29 "Woe to you, teachers of the law and Pharisees, you hypocrites! You build tombs for the prophets and decorate the graves of the righteous. 30 And you say, 'If we had lived in the days of our forefathers, we would not have taken part with them in shedding the blood of the prophets.' 31 So you testify against yourselves that you are the descendants of those who murdered the prophets. 32 Fill up, then, the measure of the sin of your forefathers!

33 "You snakes! You brood of vipers! How will you escape being condemned to hell? 34 Therefore I am sending you prophets and wise men

Matt. 23

and teachers.
Some of them you
will kill and crucify; others you will flog in your synagogues and pursue
from town to town. 35 And so upon you will come all the righteous blood
that has been shed on earth, from the blood of righteous Abel to the blood
of Zechariah son of Berakiah, whom you murdered between the temple and
the altar. 36 I tell you the truth, all this will come upon this generation.

37 "O Jerusalem, Jerusalem, you who kill the prophets and stone those
sent to you, how often I have longed to gather your children together, as
a hen gathers her chicks under her wings, but you were not willing. 38 Look,
your house is left to you desolate. 39 For I tell you, you will not see me
again until you say, 'Blessed is he who comes in the name of the Lord.'"

aThat is, boxes containing Scripture verses, which were worn on the
forehead and arms.   bOr "Messiah".   cSome manuscripts "to. 14 Woe to
you, teachers of the law and Pharisees, you hypocrites! You devour widows'
houses and for a show make lengthy prayers. Therefore you will be punished
more severely."

145. A WIDOW'S TWO SMALL COINS

Wednesday, April 5

Mark 12:41-44   Luke 21:1-4

41 Jesus sat down opposite the place where the offerings were put and watched the crowd putting their money into the temple treasury. Many rich people threw in large amounts. 42 But a poor widow came and put in two very small copper coins,a worth only a fraction of a penny.b

43 Calling his disciples to him, Jesus said, "I tell you the truth, this poor widow has put more into

1 As he looked up, Jesus saw the rich putting their gifts into the temple treasury. 2 He also saw a poor widow put in two very small copper coins.a

3 "I tell you the truth," he said, "this poor widow has put

Mark 12	Luke 21
the treasury than all the others.	in more than all the others. 4
44 They all gave out of their wealth;	All these people gave their gifts out of their wealth;
but she, out of her poverty, put in every-thing — all she had to live on."	but she out of her pov-erty put in all she had to live on."

aGreek "two lepta".   bGreek "kodrantes".

PART XI

JESUS WITH THE TWELVE IN THE SHADOW OF THE CROSS

WEDNESDAY AFTERNOON TO THURSDAY NIGHT, APRIL 5-6, A.D. 30

146. A GREAT DISCOURSE TO THE DISCIPLES ABOUT THE DESTRUCTION OF JERUSALEM AND THE END OF THE WORLD

Wednesday afternoon,* April 5, on the Mount of Olives

Matt. 24-25	Mark 13:1-37	Luke 21:5-36
1 Jesus left the temple and was walking away when his disciples came up to him to call his attention to its buildings. 2 "Do you see all these things?" he asked. "I tell you the truth, not one stone here will be left on another; every one will be thrown down."	1 As he was leaving the temple, one of his disciples said to him, "Look, Teacher! What massive stones! What magnificent buildings!" 2 "Do you see all these great buildings?" replied Jesus. "Not one stone here will be left on another; every one will be thrown down."	5 Some of his disciples were remarking about **how the temple was adorned with beautiful stones and with gifts dedicated to God.** But Jesus said, 6 "As for what you see here, the time will come when not one stone will be left on another; every one of them will be thrown down."
3 As Jesus was sitting on the Mount of Olives,	**3 As Jesus was sitting on the Mount of Olives**	

*According to some Harmonies of the Gospels, the events recorded in sec. 146-149 of this Harmony occurred on Tuesday. See the first footnote at the bottom of page 215.

221

Matt. 24	Mark 13	Luke 21
the disciples came to him privately. "Tell us," they said, "when will this happen,	opposite the temple, Peter, James, John and Andrew asked him privately, 4 "Tell us, when will these things happen? And what will be the sign that they are all about to be fulfilled?"	7 "Teacher," they asked, "when will these things happen? And what will be the sign that they are about to take place?"
and what will be the sign of your coming and of the end of the age?"		
4 Jesus answered: "Watch out that no one deceives you. 5 For many will come in my name, claiming, 'I am the Christ,ᵃ'	5 Jesus said to them: "Watch out that no one deceives you. 6 Many will come in my name, claiming, 'I am he,'	8 He replied: "Watch out that you are not deceived. For many will come in my name, claiming, 'I am he,'
		and, 'The time is near.'
and will deceive many.	and will deceive many.	Do not follow them.
6 You will hear of wars and rumors of wars, but see to it that you are not alarmed. Such things must happen, but the end is still to come.	7 When you hear of wars and rumors of wars, do not be alarmed. Such things must happen, but the end is still to come.	9 When you hear of wars and revolutions, do not be frightened. These things must happen first, but the end will not come right away."
7 Nation will rise against nation, and kingdom against kingdom. There will be famines and earthquakes	8 Nation will rise against nation, and kingdom against kingdom. There will be earthquakes in vari-	10 Then he said to them: "Nation will rise against nation, and kingdom against kingdom. 11 There will be great earthquakes, famines

Matt. 24	Mark 13	Luke 21
in various places.	ous places, and famines.	and pestilences in various places, and fearful events and great signs from heaven. 12 "But before all this, they will lay hands on you and persecute you.
8 All these are the beginning of birth pains.	These are the beginning of birth pains. 9 "You must be on your guard. You will be handed over to the local councils and flogged in the	
9 "Then you will be handed over	synagogues. On account of me you will stand before	They will deliver you to synagogues and prisons, and you will be brought before
	governors and kings	kings and governors, and
to be persecuted and put to death,		
	as witnesses to them.	all on account of my name. 13 This will result in your being witnesses to them.
	11 Whenever you are arrested and brought to trial,	14 But
	do not worry beforehand about what to say.	make up your mind not to worry beforehand how you will defend yourselves.
	Just say whatever is given you at the time, for it is not you speaking, but the Holy Spirit.	
		15 For I will give

223

Matt. 24	Mark 13	Luke 21
		you words and wis-dom that none of your adversaries will be able to resist or contra-dict.
and you will be hated by all nations be-cause of me. 10 At that time many will turn away from the faith and will betray and hate each other, 11 and many false prophets will ap-pear and deceive many people.	13 All men will hate you because of me,	17 All men will hate you because of me.
	12 "Brother will betray brother to death, and a fa-ther his child.	
		16 You will be betrayed by par-ents, brothers,
	Children will rebel against their parents and have them put to death.	relatives and friends, and they will put some of you to death. 18 But not a hair of your head will perish.
12 Because of the increase of wicked-ness, the love of most will grow cold, 13 but he who stands firm to the end will be saved. 14 And this gospel of the kingdom	13b but he who stands firm to the end will be saved. 10 And the gospel	19 By standing firm you will save yourselves.
will	must	
be	first	
preached in the	be preached	

Matt. 24	Mark 13	Luke 21
whole world as a testimony to all nations, and then the end will come.	to all nations.	
		20 "When you see Jerusalem surrounded by armies, you will know that its desolation is near.
15 "So when you see standing in the holy place 'the abomination that causes desolation,' spoken of through the prophet Daniel — let the reader	14 "When you see 'the abomination that causes desolation' standing where it[b] does not belong — let the reader	
understand — 16 then let those who are in Judea flee to the mountains.	understand — then let those who are in Judea flee to the mountains.	21 Then let those who are in Judea flee to the mountains, let those in the city get out, and let those in the country not enter the city.
17 Let no one on the roof of his house go down to take anything out of the house. 18 Let no one in the field go back to get his cloak.	15 Let no one on the roof of his house go down or enter the house to take anything out. 16 Let no one in the field go back to get his cloak.	
19 How dreadful it will be in those days for pregnant women and nursing mothers!	17 How dreadful it will be in those days for pregnant women and nursing mothers!	22 For this is the time of punishment in fulfillment of all that has been written. 23 How dreadful it will be in those days for pregnant women and nursing mothers! There will be great

225

Matt. 24	Mark 13	Luke 21

| | | distress in the land and wrath |

against this people. 24 They will fall by the sword and will be taken as prisoners to all the nations. Jerusalem will be trampled on by the Gentiles until the times of the Gentiles are fulfilled.

20 Pray that your flight will not take place in winter or on the Sabbath. 21 For then there	18 Pray that this will not take place in winter, 19 because those	

| will be great distress, un-equaled from the beginning of the world until now — and never to be equaled again. | **will be days of distress unequaled from the beginning, when God created the world, until now — and never to be equaled again. 20 If the Lord had not cut short those days, no one would survive. But for the sake of the elect, whom he has chosen, he has shortened them.** | |

| 22 If those days had not been cut short, no one would survive, but for the sake of the elect those days will be shortened. | | |

| 23 At that time if anyone says to you, 'Look, here is the Christ[a]!' or, 'There he is!' do not believe it. | **21 At that time if anyone says to you, 'Look, here is the Christ[a]!' or, 'Look, there he is!' do not believe it. 22 For false Christs and false prophets will appear and perform** | |

| 24 For false Christs and false prophets will appear and perform | | |

| **great signs and miracles to deceive even the elect —** **if that were** | signs and miracles to deceive the elect — if that were | |

| possible. 25 See, | **possible. 23 So be on your guard;** | |

226

Matt. 24	Mark 13	Luke 21
I have told you ahead of time.	I have told you everything ahead of time.	

26 "So if any-one tells you, 'There he is, out in the desert,' do not go out; or, 'Here he is, in the inner rooms,' do not believe it. **27** For as the lightning comes from the east and flashes to the west, so will be the coming of the Son of Man. **28** Wherever there is a carcass, there the vultures will gather.

29 "Immediately after the distress of those days	**24** "But in those days, following that distress,	
		25 "There will be signs in the sun, moon and stars.
" 'the sun will be darkened, and the moon will not give its light; the stars will fall from the sky,	" 'the sun will be darkened, and the moon will not give its light; **25** the stars will fall from the sky,	
		On the earth, nations will

be in anguish and perplexity at the roaring and tossing of the sea. **26** Men will faint from terror, apprehensive of what is coming on the world,

and the heavenly bodies will be shaken.' **30** "At that time	and the heavenly bodies will be shaken.' **26** "At that time	for the heavenly bodies will be shaken.
the sign of the Son of Man will appear in the sky, and all the nations of the earth will mourn. They will see the Son of Man coming on the clouds of the sky, with power and great glory. **31** And he will send	men will see the Son of Man coming in clouds with great power and glory. **27** And he will	**27** At that time they will see the Son of Man coming in a cloud with power and great glory.

Matt. 24	Mark 13	Luke 21
his angels with a loud trumpet call, and they will gather his elect from the four winds,	send his angels and gather his elect from the four winds,	
from one end of the heavens to the other.	from the ends of the earth to the ends of the heavens.	
		28 When these things begin to take place, stand up and lift up your heads, because your redemption is drawing near." 29 He told them this parable:
32 "Now learn this lesson from the fig tree: As soon as its twigs get tender and its leaves come out,	28 "Now learn this lesson from the fig tree: As soon as its twigs get tender and its leaves come out,	"Look at the fig tree and all the trees. 30 When they sprout leaves,
you know that summer is near.	you know that summer is near.	you can see for yourselves and know that summer is near.
33 Even so, when you see all these things, you know that it[b] is near, right at the door. 34 I tell you the truth, this generation[c] will certainly not pass away until all these things have happened. 35 Heaven and earth will pass away, but my words will never pass away.	29 Even so, when you see these things happening, you know that it[b] is near, right at the door. 30 I tell you the truth, this generation[c] will certainly not pass away until all these things have happened. 31 Heaven and earth will pass away, but my words will	31 Even so, when you see these things happening, you know that the kingdom of God is near. 32 "I tell you the truth, this generation[c] will certainly not pass away until all these things have happened. 33 Heaven and earth will pass away, but my words will never pass away.

Matt. 24   Mark 13   Luke 21

never pass away.

36 "No one knows about that day or hour, not even the angels in heaven, nor the Son,ᵈ but only the Father. 37 As it was in the days of Noah,

32 "No one knows about that day or hour, not even the angels in heaven, nor the Son, but only the Father.

so it will be at the coming of the Son of Man. 38 For in the days before the flood, people were eating and drinking, marrying and giving in marriage, up to the day Noah entered the ark; 39 and they knew nothing about what would happen until the flood came and took them all away. That is how it will be at the coming of the Son of Man. 40 Two men will be in the field; one will be taken and the other left. 41 Two women will be grinding with **a hand mill; one will be taken and the other left.**

33 Be on guard! Be alertᵉ!

34 "Be careful, or your hearts will

be weighed down with dissipation, drunkenness and the anxieties of life, and that day will close on you unexpectedly like a trap. 35 For it will come upon all those who live on the face of the whole earth. 36 Be always on the watch, and pray that you may be able to escape all that is about to

happen, and that you may be able to stand before the Son of Man."

42 "Therefore keep watch, because you do not know on what day your Lord will

You do not know when that time will come. 34 It's like a man going away: He leaves his house

come.

in charge of his servants, each with his assigned task, and tells the one at the door to keep watch.

35 "Therefore keep watch because you do not know when the owner of the house will come back — whether in the evening, or at midnight, or when the rooster crows, or at dawn. 36 If he comes suddenly, do not let him find you sleeping.

43 But understand this:

Matt. 24-25   Mark 13

If the owner of the
house had known
at what time of night the thief was coming, he would have kept watch and
would not have let his house be broken into. 44 So you also must be ready,
because the Son
of Man will come
at an hour when
you do not expect
him.

                  37 What
I say to you, I
say to everyone:
'Watch!' "

45 "Who then is
the faithful and
wise servant, whom the master has put in charge of the servants in his
household to give them their food at the proper time? 46 It will be good
for that servant whose master finds him doing so when he returns. 47 I
tell you the truth, he will put him in charge of all his possessions. 48 But
suppose that servant is wicked and says to himself, 'My master is staying
away a long time,' 49 and he then begins to beat his fellow servants and
to eat and drink with drunkards. 50 The master of that servant will come
on a day when he does not expect him and at an hour he is not aware of.
51 He will cut him to pieces and assign him a place with the hypocrites,
where there will be weeping and gnashing of teeth.

1 "At that time the kingdom of heaven will be like ten virgins who took
their lamps and went out to meet the bridegroom. 2 Five of them were
foolish and five were wise. 3 The foolish ones took their lamps but did not
take any oil with them. 4 The wise, however, took oil in jars along with
their lamps. 5 The bridegroom was a long time in coming, and they all
became drowsy and fell asleep.

6 "At midnight the cry rang out: 'Here's the bridegroom! Come out to
meet him!'

7 "Then all the virgins woke up and trimmed their lamps. 8 The foolish
ones said to the wise, 'Give us some of your oil; our lamps are going out.'

9 " 'No,' they replied, 'there may not be enough for both us and you.
Instead, go to those who sell oil and buy some for yourselves.'

10 "But while they were on their way to buy the oil, the bridegroom
arrived. The virgins who were ready went in with him to the wedding
banquet. And the door was shut.

11 "Later the others also came. 'Sir! Sir!' they said. 'Open the door for
us!'

12 "But he replied, 'I tell you the truth, I don't know you.'

13 "Therefore keep watch, because you do not know the day or the hour.

14 "Again, it will be like a man going on a journey, who called his servants and entrusted his property to them. 15 To one he gave five talents[f]
of money, to another two talents, and to another one talent, each accord-

ing to his ability.
Then he went on
his journey. 16 The man who had received the five talents went at once
and put his money to work and gained five more. 17 So also, the one with
the two talents gained two more. 18 But the man who had received the one
talent went off, dug a hole in the ground and hid his master's money.

19 "After a long time the master of those servants returned and settled
accounts with them. 20 The man who had received the five talents brought
the other five. 'Master,' he said, 'you entrusted me with five talents. See,
I have gained five more.'

21 "His master replied, 'Well done, good and faithful servant! You have
been faithful with a few things; I will put you in charge of many things.
Come and share your master's happiness!'

22 "The man with the two talents also came. 'Master,' he said, 'you entrusted me with two talents; see, I have gained two more.'

23 "His master replied, 'Well done, good and faithful servant! You have
been faithful with a few things; I will put you in charge of many things.
Come and share your master's happiness!'

24 "Then the man who had received the one talent came. 'Master,' he
said, 'I knew that you are a hard man, harvesting where you have not sown
and gathering where you have not scattered seed. 25 So I was afraid and
went out and hid your talent in the ground. See, here is what belongs to
you.'

26 "His master replied, 'You wicked, lazy servant! So you knew that I
harvest where I have not sown and gather where I have not scattered seed?
27 Well then, you should have put my money on deposit with the bankers,
so that when I returned I would have received it back with interest.

28 " 'Take the talent from him and give it to the one who has the ten talents.
29 For everyone who has will be given more, and he will have an abundance.
Whoever does not have, even what he has will be taken from him. 30 And
throw that worthless servant outside, into the darkness, where there will
be weeping and gnashing of teeth.'

31 "When the Son of Man comes in his glory, and all the angels with him,
he will sit on his throne in heavenly glory. 32 All the nations will be
gathered before him, and he will separate the people one from another as
a shepherd separates the sheep from the goats. 33 He will put the sheep
on his right and the goats on his left.

34 "Then the King will say to those on his right, 'Come, you who are blessed by my Father; take your inheritance, the kingdom prepared for you
since the creation of the world. 35 For I was hungry and you gave me
something to eat, I was thirsty and you gave me something to drink, I was
a stranger and you invited me in, 36 I needed clothes and you clothed me,
I was sick and you looked after me, I was in prison and you came to visit
me.'

37 "Then the righteous will answer him, 'Lord, when did we see you
hungry and feed you, or thirsty and give you something to drink? 38 When
did we see you a stranger and invite you in, or needing clothes and clothe

Matt. 25

you? 39 When did
we see you sick
or in prison and go to visit you?'

40 "The King will reply, 'I tell you the truth, whatever you did for one of the least of these brothers of mine, you did for me.'

41 "Then he will say to those on his left, 'Depart from me, you who are cursed, into the eternal fire prepared for the devil and his angels. 42 For I was hungry and you gave me nothing to eat, I was thirsty and you gave me nothing to drink, 43 I was a stranger and you did not invite me in, I needed clothes and you did not clothe me, I was sick and in prison and you did not look after me.'

44 "They also will answer, 'Lord, when did we see you hungry or thirsty or a stranger or needing clothes or sick or in prison, and did not help you?'

45 "He will reply, 'I tell you the truth, whatever you did not do for one of the least of these, you did not do for me.'

46 "Then they will go away to eternal punishment, but the righteous to eternal life."

aOr "Messiah".   bOr "he".   cOr "race".   dSome manuscripts do not have "nor the Son".   eSome manuscripts "alert and pray".   fA talent was worth more than a thousand dollars.

147. WHILE JESUS ON THE MOUNT OF OLIVES IS AGAIN WARNING HIS DISCIPLES ABOUT HIS IMPENDING CRUCIFIXION, THE RELIGIOUS LEADERS IN JERUSALEM PLOT HIS DEATH

Wednesday afternoon, April 5

Matt. 26:1-5	Mark 14:1-2	Luke 22:1-2
1 When Jesus had finished saying all these things, he said to his disciples, 2 "As you know, the Passover is two days away — and the Son of Man will be handed over to be crucified."	1 Now the Passover and the Feast of Unleavened Bread were only two days away,	1 Now the Feast of Unleavened Bread, called the Passover, was approaching, 2

Matt. 26	Mark 14	Luke 22
3 Then the chief priests	and the chief priests	and the chief priests
	and the teachers of the law	and the teachers of the law
and the elders of the people assembled in the palace of the high priest, whose name was Caiaphas, 4 and they plotted to arrest Jesus in some sly way and kill him. 5 "But not during the Feast," they said, "or there may be a riot among the people."	were looking for some sly way to arrest Jesus and kill him. 2 "But not during the **Feast," they said, "or the people may riot."**	were looking for some way to get rid of Jesus, **for they were afraid of the people.**

148. JESUS HONORED AT BETHANY — MARY'S LAVISH EXPRESSION OF DEVOTION

Wednesday evening, April 5

Matt. 26:6-13	Mark 14:3-9	John 12:2-8
6 While Jesus was in Bethany in the home of a man known as Simon the Leper,	3 While he was in Bethany,	2 Here
	re-clining at the table in the home of a man known as Simon the Leper, a wo-man came with	**a dinner was given in Je-sus' honor. Martha served, while Laz-arus was among those reclining at the table with him. 3 Then Mary took**
7 a woman came to him with an alabaster jar	**an alabaster jar**	

233

Matt. 26	Mark 14		John 12
	containing*		**about a pint**[a] **of**
of very expen-sive p e r fume,	**very expensive perfume, made of pure nard. She broke the jar** which she poured **and poured the perfume on**		pure nard, an expensive per-fume; she poured it on
on his head as he was reclining at the table.	h i s head.		**Jesus' feet**** and wiped his feet with her hair. And the house was filled with the fragrance of the perfume.**
8 When the dis-ciples saw this, they were	4 Some of those p r e s e n t were		
indig-nant. "Why this w a s t e ?" they asked.	**saying indignant-ly to one another, "Why this waste of perfume?**		4 B u t one of his disciples,
	5b And they		**Judas Iscariot, who was later to be-tray him,**
	rebuked her harshly.		objected,
9 "This perfume c o u l d have been sold at a high price a n d the money g i v e n to the poor."	5a It could have been sold for more than a year's wages[b] and the money given to the poor."		**5 "Why wasn't this perfume sold and the money given to the poor? It was worth a year's wages.**[b]**" 6 He did not say this be-cause he cared about the poor but because he was a thief; as keeper of the money bag,**

*The NIV reads "of". By substituting the word "containing", which conveys the same meaning, the composite narrative is improved.

**Matthew and Mark state that Mary poured the perfume on Jesus' head also.

Matt. 26	Mark 14	John 12
		he used to help himself to what was put into it.
10 Aware of this, Jesus said to them,	6 "Leave her alone," said Jesus. "Why are you bothering her?	7 "Leave her alone," Jesus replied. "It was meant that she should save this perfume for the day of my burial.
"Why are you bothering this woman?		
She has done a beautiful thing to me. 11 The poor you will always have with you, but you will not always have me.	She has done a beautiful thing to me. 7 The poor you will always have with you, and you can help them any time you want. But you will not always have me. 8 She did what she could.	8 You will always have the poor among you, but you will not always have me."
12 When she poured this perfume on my body, she did it	She poured perfume on my body	
to prepare me for burial. 13 I tell you the truth, wherever this gospel is preached throughout the world, what she has done will also be told, in memory of her."	beforehand to prepare for my burial. 9 I tell you the truth, wherever the gospel is preached throughout the world, what she has done will also be told, in memory of her."	

aGreek "a litra" (probably about 0.5 liter). bGreek "three hundred denarii".

149. JUDAS BARGAINS WITH THE JEWISH LEADERS TO BETRAY JESUS

Jerusalem. Wednesday night, April 5

Matt. 26:14-16	Mark 14:10-11	Luke 22:3-6
		3 Then Satan entered Judas, called

Matt. 26	Mark 14	Luke 22
		Iscariot, one of the Twelve. 4 And
14 Then one of the Twelve — the one called Judas Iscariot — went to the chief priests 15 and	10 Then Judas Iscariot, one of the Twelve, went to the chief priests to	Judas went to the chief priests and the officers of the temple guard and discussed with them how he might
	betray Jesus to them. 11 They were delighted to hear this and promised to give him money. So he	betray Jesus. 5 They were delighted and agreed to give him money.
asked, "What are you willing to give me if I hand him over to you?" So they counted out for him thirty silver coins.		
16 From then on Judas watched for an opportunity to hand him over.	watched for an opportunity to hand him over.	6 He consented, and watched for an opportunity to hand Jesus over to them when no crowd was present.

150. PREPARING FOR THE PASSOVER MEAL IN AN UPPER ROOM

Jerusalem. Thursday, April 6

Matt. 26:17-19	Mark 14:12-16	Luke 22:7-13
17 On the first day of the Feast of Unleavened Bread,	12 On the first day of the Feast of Unleavened Bread, when it was customary to sacrifice the Passover lamb,	7 Then came the day of Unleavened Bread on which the Passover lamb had to be sacrificed.
		8 Jesus sent Peter and John, saying, "Go and make

Matt. 26	Mark 14	Luke 22
the disciples came to Jesus and asked, "Where do you want us to make preparations for you to eat the Passover?"	Jesus' disciples asked him, "Where do you want us to go and make preparations for you to eat the Passover?" 13 So he sent two of his disciples, telling them, "Go into the city, and a man carrying a jar of water will meet you. Follow him.	preparations for us to eat the Passover." 9 "Where do you want us to prepare for it?" they asked.
18 He replied, "Go into the city to a certain man and tell him, 'The Teacher says: My appointed time is near.	14 Say to the owner of the house he enters, 'The Teacher asks:	10 He replied, "As you enter the city, a man carrying a jar of water will meet you. Follow him to the house that he enters, 11 and say to the owner of the house, 'The Teacher asks:
I am going to celebrate the Passover with my disciples at your house.'"	Where is my guest room, where I may eat the Passover with my disciples?' 15 He will show you a large upper room, furnished and ready. Make preparations for us there."	Where is the guest room, where I may eat the Passover with my disciples?' 12 He will show you a large upper room, all furnished. Make preparations there."
19 So the disciples did as Jesus had directed them and prepared the Passover.	16 The disciples left, went into the city and found things just as Jesus had told them. So they prepared the Passover.	13 They left and found things just as Jesus had told them. So they prepared the Passover.

151. AT THE BEGINNING OF THE PASSOVER JESUS WASHES THE FEET OF HIS UNWILLING DISCIPLES, AND GENTLY REBUKES THEM FOR THEIR SELFISH PRIDE

Jerusalem. Thursday evening,* April 6

Matt. 26:20	Mark 14:17	Luke 22:14-16,24-30	John 13:1-20
20 When evening came,	17 **When evening came, Jesus arrived with the Twelve.**	14 When the hour came,	

1 It was just before the Passover Feast. Jesus knew that the time had come for him to leave this world and go to the Father. Having loved his own who were in the world, he now showed them the full extent of his love.

Jesus was reclining at the table with the Twelve.

Jesus and his apostles reclined at the table.

3 Jesus knew that the Father had put all things under his power, and that he had come from God and was returning to God;

15 And he said to them, "I have eagerly desired to eat this Passover with you before I suffer. 16 For I tell you, I will not eat it again until it finds fulfillment in the kingdom of God."

2 The evening meal was being served, and the devil had already prompted Judas Iscariot, son of Simon, to betray Jesus.

*After 6 p.m. it was Friday by Jewish time, the 14th day of the month Nissan.

Luke 22   John 13

24 Also a dispute arose among them as to which of them was considered to be greatest.

4 so he got up from the meal, took off his outer clothing, and wrapped a towel around his waist. 5 After that, he poured water into a basin and began to wash his disciples' feet, drying them with the towel that was wrapped around him.

6 He came to Simon Peter, who said to him, "Lord, are you going to wash my feet?"

7 Jesus replied, "You do not realize now what I am doing, but later you will understand."

8 "No," said Peter, "you shall never wash my feet."

Jesus answered, "Unless I wash you, you have no part with me."

9 "Then, Lord," Simon Peter replied, "not just my feet but my hands and my head as well!"

10 Jesus answered, "A person who has had a bath needs only to wash his feet; his whole body is clean. And you are clean, though not every one of you." 11 For he knew who was going to betray him, and that was why he said not every one was clean.

12 When he had finished washing their feet, he put on his clothes and returned to his place. "Do you understand what I have done for you?" he asked them. 13 "You call me 'Teacher' and 'Lord,' and rightly so, for that is what I am. 14 Now that I, your Lord and Teacher, have washed your feet, you also should wash one another's feet. 15 I have set you an example that you should do as I have done for you. 16 I tell you the truth, no servant is greater than his master, nor is a messenger greater than the one who sent him.

25 Jesus said to them,

"The kings of the Gentiles lord it over them; and those who exercise authority over them call themselves Benefactors. 26 But you are not to be like that. Instead, the greatest among you should be like the youngest, and the one who rules like the one who serves.

17 Now that you know these things, you will be blessed if you do them.

27 For who is greater,

239

Luke 22   John 13

| | the one who is at |
| | the table or the |

one who serves? Is it not the one who is at the table? But I am among you as one who serves. 28 You are those who have stood by me in my trials. 29 And I confer on you a kingdom, just as my Father conferred one on me, 30 so that you may eat and drink at my table in my kingdom and sit on thrones,

| | judging the twelve |
| | tribes of Israel. |

18 "I am not referring to all of you; I know those I have chosen. But this is to fulfill the scripture: 'He who shares my bread has lifted up his heel against me.'

19 "I am telling you now before it happens, so that when it does happen you will believe that I am He. 20 I tell you the truth, whoever accepts anyone I send accepts me; and whoever accepts me accepts the one who sent me."

152. DURING THE PASSOVER MEAL, JESUS MAKES A FINAL UNSUCCESSFUL APPEAL TO JUDAS, BY INTIMATING THAT HE IS AWARE OF HIS INTENTIONS

Jerusalem. Thursday evening, April 6

Matt. 26:21-25   Mark 14:18-21   Luke 22:21-23   John 13:21-30

			21 After he had said this,
21 And while they were eating,	18 While they were reclining at the table eating,		
he said, "I tell you the truth, one of you will betray me."	he said, "I tell you the truth, one of you will betray		Jesus was troubled in spirit and testified, "I tell you the truth, one of you is going to betray
	me — one who is eating with me."		me."
24 The Son of Man will go just as it is written about him. But woe to that man	21 The Son of Man will go just as it is written about him. But woe to that man	22 The Son of Man will go as it has been decreed, but woe to that man	

240

Matt. 26	Mark 14	Luke 22	John 13
who betrays the Son of Man! It would be better for him if he had not been born."	**who betrays the Son of Man! It would be better for him if he had not been born."**	who betrays him."	
		21 But the hand of him who is going to betray me is with mine on the table.	
			22 His disciples stared at one another, at a loss to know which of them he meant.
22 They		23 They	
were very sad and			
	19 They were saddened,	began to question among themselves which of them it might be who would do this.	
began to say to him one after the other,	and one by one they said to him,		
"Surely not I, Lord?"	"Surely not I?"		
23 Jesus replied, "The one who has dipped his hand into the	20 "It is one of the Twelve," he replied, "one who dips bread into the		
bowl with me will betray me.	bowl with me.		
			23 One of them, the disciple whom

Jesus loved, was reclining next to him. 24 Simon Peter motioned to this disciple and said, "Ask him which one he means."

25 Leaning back against Jesus, he asked him, "Lord, who is it?"

26 Jesus answered, "It is the one to whom I will give this piece of bread when I have dipped it in the dish." Then, dipping the piece of bread, he

			gave it to Judas Iscariot, son of Simon.
25 Then Judas, the one who would			

Matt. 26   John 13

betray him, said,
"Surely not I,
Rabbi?"
  Jesus answered,
"Yes, it is you."[a]

27 As soon
as Judas took the

bread, Satan entered into him.
  "What you are about to do, do quickly," Jesus told him, 28 but no one at
the meal understood why Jesus said this to him. 29 Since Judas had charge
of the money, some thought Jesus was telling him to buy what was needed
for the Feast, or to give something to the poor. 30 As soon as Judas had
taken the bread, he went out. And it was night.

[a]Or "You yourself have said it".

153. AFTER THE DEPARTURE OF JUDAS, JESUS INSTITUTES THE ORDINANCE OF THE LORD'S SUPPER

Jerusalem. Thursday night, April 6

Matt. 26:26-29	Mark 14:22-25	Luke 22:17-20	John 13:31-32
			31 When he was gone, Jesus said, "Now is the Son of Man glorified and God is glorified in him. 32 If God is glorified in him,[a] God will glorify the Son in himself, and will glorify him at once.
26 While they were eating, Jesus took bread, gave thanks and broke it, and gave it to his disciples, saying, "Take and eat; this is my body."	22 While they were eating, Jesus took bread, gave thanks and broke it, and gave it to his disciples, saying, "Take it; this is my body."	19 And he took bread, gave thanks and broke it, and gave it to them, saying, "This is my body given for you; do this in remembrance of me."	

Matt. 26	Mark 14	Luke 22
		20 In the same way, after the supper he took the cup,
27 Then he took the cup, gave thanks and offered it to	23 Then he took the cup, **gave thanks and offered it to**	
		17 After taking the cup, he gave thanks and said, "Take this and divide it among you.
them, saying, "Drink from it, all of you.	them,	
	and they all drank from it.	20b saying,
28 This is my blood of the[b] covenant, which is poured out	24 **"This is my blood of the[b] covenant,** which **is poured out**	"This cup is the **new covenant** in my blood, which is poured out for you.
for **many for the forgiveness of sins.**	**for** many," **he said to them.**	
29 I tell you,	25 **"I tell you the truth,**	
I will not drink of this fruit of the vine from now on until that day when I drink it anew with you in my Father's kingdom."	I will not drink again of the fruit of the vine until that day when I drink it anew in the kingdom of God."	18 For I tell you I will not drink again of the fruit of the vine until the kingdom of God comes."

[a]Many early manuscripts do not have "If God is glorified in him".
[b]Some manuscripts "the new".

154. JESUS BEGINS HIS FAREWELL DISCOURSE TO THE DISCIPLES IN THE UPPER ROOM

Jerusalem. Thursday night, April 6

Matt. 26:31-35	Mark 14:27-31	Luke 22:31-38	John 13:33—14:31
31 Then Jesus told them,			
			33 "My children, I will be with you

Matt. 26	Mark 14	Luke 22	John 13

only a little long- er. You will look for me, and just as I told the Jews, so I tell you now: Where I am going, you cannot come.

34 "A new command I give you: Love one another. As I have loved you, so you must love one another. 35 All men will know that you are my dis- ciples if you love one another."

36 Simon Peter asked him, "Lord, where are you going?"

Jesus replied, "Where I am going, you cannot follow now, but you will follow later."

37 Peter asked, "Lord, why can't I follow you now? I will lay down my life for you."

38 Then Jesus answered, "Will you really lay down your life for me?

"This very night you will all fall away on account of me, for it is written:

"'I will strike the shepherd, and the sheep of the flock will be scattered.'

32 But after I have risen, I will go ahead of you into Galilee."

27 "You will all fall away," Je- sus told them, "for it is writ- ten:

"'I will strike the shep- herd, and the sheep will be scattered.'

28 But after I have risen, I will go ahead of you into Galilee."

33 Peter re- plied,

29 Peter de- clared,

"Even if all fall away on account of you, I never will."

"Even if all fall away, I will not."

30 "I tell you the truth," Jesus answered,

31 "Simon, Simon, Satan has asked to sift you[a] as wheat. 32 But I have prayed for you, Simon, that your faith may not fail. And when you have turned back, strengthen your brothers."

33 But he replied, "Lord, I am ready to go with you to pris- on and to death."

34 "I tell you the truth," Je- sus answered,

34 Jesus answer- ed, "I tell you, Peter,

I tell you the truth,

"today— yes, to-

Matt. 26	Mark 14	Luke 22	John 13-14
"this very night, before the roòst-er crows, you will disown me three times."	**night — before the rooster crows twice**[b] **you your-self will** disown me three times."	before the rooster crows today, you will **deny three times**	before the roost-er crows, you will disown me three times!
	31 But Peter	**that you know me."**	
35 But Peter declared, "Even if I have to die with you, I will never disown you."	**insisted emphati-cally, "Even if I have to die with you, I will never disown you."**		
And all the other disciples said the same.	And all the others said the same.		
		35 Then Jesus asked them, "When	

I sent you without purse, bag or sandals, did you lack anything?"
"Nothing," they answered.

36 He said to them, "But now if you have a purse, take it, and also a bag; and if you don't have a sword, sell your cloak and buy one. 37 It is written: 'And he was numbered with the transgressors'; and I tell you that this must be fulfilled in me. Yes, what is written about me is reaching its fulfill-ment."

38 The disciples said, "See, Lord, here are two swords."

"That is enough," he replied.

1 "Do not let your hearts be troubled. Trust in God[c]; trust also in me. 2 In my Father's house are many rooms; if it were not so, I would have told you. I am going there to pre-pare a place for you. 3 And if I go and prepare a place for you, I will come back and take you to be with me that you also may be where I am. 4 You know the way to the place where I am going."

5 Thomas said to him, "Lord, we don't know where you are going, so how can we know the way?"

6 Jesus answered, "I am the way and the truth and the life. No one comes to the Father except through me. 7 If you really knew me, you would know[d] my Father as well. From now on, you do know him and have seen him."

8 Philip said, "Lord, show us the Father and that will be enough for us."

9 Jesus answered: "Don't you know me, Philip, even after I have been among you such a long time? Anyone who has seen me has seen the Father. How can you say, 'Show us the Father'? 10 Don't you believe that I am in the Father, and that the Father is in me? The words I say to you are not just my own. Rather, it is the Father, living in me, who is doing his work. 11 Believe me when I say that I am in the Father and the Father is in me; or at least believe on the evidence of the miracles themselves. 12 I tell

| | | you the truth,
| | | anyone who has

faith in me will do what I have been doing. He will do even greater things than these, because I am going to the Father. 13 And I will do whatever you ask in my name, so that the Son may bring glory to the Father. 14 You may ask me for anything in my name, and I will do it.

15 "If you love me, you will obey what I command. 16 And I will ask the Father, and he will give you another Counselor to be with you forever — 17 the Spirit of truth. The world cannot accept him, because it neither sees him nor knows him. But you know him, for he lives with you and will be[e] in you. 18 I will not leave you as orphans; I will come to you. 19 Before long, the world will not see me anymore, but you will see me. Because I live, you also will live. 20 On that day you will realize that I am in my Father, and you are in me, and I am in you. 21 Whoever has my commands and obeys them, he is the one who loves me. He who loves me will be loved by my Father, and I too will love him and show myself to him."

22 Then Judas (not Judas Iscariot) said, "But, Lord, why do you intend to show yourself to us and not to the world?"

23 Jesus replied, "If anyone loves me, he will obey my teaching. My Father will love him, and we will come to him and make our home with him. 24 He who does not love me will not obey my teaching. These words you hear are not my own; they belong to the Father who sent me.

25 "All this I have spoken while still with you. 26 But the Counselor, the Holy Spirit, whom the Father will send in my name, will teach you all things and will remind you of everything I have said to you. 27 Peace I leave with you; my peace I give you. I do not give to you as the world gives. Do not let your hearts be troubled and do not be afraid.

28 "You heard me say, 'I am going away and I am coming back to you.' If you loved me, you would be glad that I am going to the Father, for the Father is greater than I. 29 I have told you now before it happens, so that when it does happen you will believe. 30 I will not speak with you much longer, for the prince of this world is coming. He has no hold on me, 31 but the world must learn that I love the Father and that I do exactly what my Father has commanded me. Come now; let us leave.

[a]The Greek is plural. [b]Some early manuscripts do not have "twice".
[c]Or "You trust in God". [d]Some early manuscripts "If you really have
known me, you will know". [e]Some early manuscripts "and is".

246

155. LEAVING THE UPPER ROOM, JESUS CONTINUES HIS FAREWELL DISCOURSE TO THE DISCIPLES ON THE WAY TO THE GARDEN OF GETHSEMANE

Jerusalem. Thursday night, April 6

Matt. 26:30	Mark 14:26	Luke 22:39	John 15-16
30 When they had sung a hymn, they went out to the Mount of Olives.	26 When they had sung a hymn, they went out to the Mount of Olives.	39 Jesus went out as usual to the Mount of Olives, and his disciples followed him.	1 [*On the way he said to them,**]*

"I am the true vine and my Father is the gardener. 2 He cuts off every branch in me that bears no fruit, while every branch that does bear fruit he trims clean so that it will be even more fruitful. 3 You are already clean because of the word I have spoken to you. 4 Remain in me, and I will remain in you. No branch can bear fruit by itself; it must remain in the vine. Neither can you bear fruit unless you remain in me.

5 "I am the vine; you are the branches. If a man remains in me and I in him, he will bear much fruit; apart from me you can do nothing. 6 If anyone does not remain in me, he is like a branch that is thrown away and withers; such branches are picked up, thrown into the fire and burned. 7 If you remain in me and my words remain in you, ask whatever you wish, and it will be given you. 8 This is to my Father's glory, that you bear much fruit, showing yourselves to be my disciples.

9 "As the Father has loved me, so have I loved you. Now remain in my love. 10 If you obey my commands, you will remain in my love, just as I have obeyed my Father's commands and remain in his love. 11 I have told you this so that my joy may be in you and that your joy may be complete. 12 My command is this: Love each other as I have loved you. 13 Greater love has no one than this, that one lay down his life for his friends. 14 You are my friends if you do what I command. 15 I no longer call you servants, because a servant does not know his master's business. Instead, I have called you friends, for everything that I learned from my Father I have made known to you. 16 You did not choose me, but I chose you to go and bear fruit — fruit that will last. Then the Father will give you whatever you ask in my name. 17 This is my command: Love each other.

18 "If the world hates you, keep in mind that it hated me first. 19 If you

*These italicized words are not in the scriptural record; they are inserted in this Harmony to provide grammatical continuity in the composite narrative.

|belonged to the world, it would love you as its own. As it is, you do not belong to the world, but I have chosen you out of the world. That is why the world hates you. 20 Remember the words I spoke to you: 'No servant is greater than his master.' If they persecuted me, they will persecute you also. If they obeyed my teaching, they will obey yours also. 21 They will treat you this way because of my name, for they do not know the One who sent me. 22 If I had not come and spoken to them, they would not be guilty of sin. Now, however, they have no excuse for their sin. 23 He who hates me hates my Father as well. 24 If I had not done among them what no one else did, they would not be guilty of sin. But now they have seen these miracles, and yet they have hated both me and my Father. 25 But this is to fulfill what is written in their Law: 'They hated me without reason.'

26 "When the Counselor comes, whom I will send to you from the Father, the Spirit of truth who goes out from the Father, he will testify about me; 27 but you also must testify, for you have been with me from the beginning.

1 "All this I have told you so that you will not go astray. 2 They will put you out of the synagogue; in fact, a time is coming when anyone who kills you will think he is offering a service to God. 3 They will do such things because they have not known the Father or me. 4 I have told you this, so that when the time comes you will remember that I warned you. I did not tell you this at first because I was with you.

5 "Now I am going to him who sent me, yet none of you asks me, 'Where are you going?' 6 Because I have said these things, you are filled with grief. 7 But I tell you the truth: It is for your good that I am going away. Unless I go away, the Counselor will not come to you; but if I go, I will send him to you. 8 When he comes, he will convict the world of guilt in regard to sin and righteousness and judgment: 9 in regard to sin, because men do not believe in me; 10 in regard to righteousness, because I am going to the Father, where you can see me no longer; 11 and in regard to judgment, because the prince of this world now stands condemned.

12 "I have much more to say to you, more than you can now bear. 13 But when he, the Spirit of truth, comes, he will guide you into all truth. He will not speak on his own; he will speak only what he hears, and he will tell you what is yet to come. 14 He will bring glory to me by taking from what is mine and making it known to you. 15 All that belongs to the Father is mine. That is why I said the Spirit will take from what is mine and make it known to you.

16 "In a little while you will see me no more, and then after a little while you will see me."

17 Some of his disciples said to one another, "What does he mean by saying, 'In a little while you will see me no more, and then after a little while you will see me,' and 'Because I am going to the Father'?" 18 They kept asking, "What does he mean by 'a little while'? We don't understand what he is saying."

19 Jesus saw that they wanted to ask him about this, so he said to them,

"Are you asking one another what I meant when I said, 'In a little while you will see me no more, and then after a little while you will see me'? 20 I tell you the truth, you will weep and mourn while the world rejoices. You will grieve, but your grief will turn to joy. 21 A woman giving birth to a child has pain because her time has come; but when her baby is born she forgets the anguish because of her joy that a child is born into the world. 22 So with you: Now is your time of grief, but I will see you again and you will rejoice, and no one will take away your joy. 23 In that day you will no longer ask me anything. I tell you the truth, my Father will give you whatever you ask in my name. 24 Until now you have not asked for anything in my name. Ask and you will receive, and your joy will be complete.

25 "Though I have been speaking figuratively, a time is coming when I will no longer use this kind of language but will tell you plainly about my Father. 26 In that day you will ask in my name. I am not saying that I will ask the Father on your behalf. 27 No, the Father himself loves you because you have loved me and have believed that I came from God. 28 I came from the Father and entered the world; now I am leaving the world and going back to the Father."

29 Then Jesus' disciples said, "Now you are speaking clearly and without figures of speech. 30 Now we can see that you know all things and that you do not even need to have anyone ask you questions. This makes us believe that you came from God."

31 "You believe at last!"[a] Jesus answered. 32 "But a time is coming, and has come, when you will be scattered, each to his own home. You will leave me all alone. Yet I am not alone, for my Father is with me.

33 "I have told you these things, so that in me you may have peace. In this world you will have trouble. But take heart! I have overcome the world."

[a] Or "Do you now believe?"

156. CHRIST'S INTERCESSORY PRAYER

Perhaps in the temple court, Jerusalem, on the way to the Garden of Gethsemane. Thursday, April 6, toward midnight.

1 After Jesus said this, he looked toward heaven and prayed:

"Father, the time has come. Glorify your Son, that your Son may glorify you. 2 For you granted him authority over all people that he might give eternal life to all those you have given him. 3 Now this is eternal life: that they may know you, the only true God, and Jesus Christ, whom you have

John 17

|sent. 4 I have
| brought you glory
on earth by completing the work you gave me to do. 5 And now, Father, glorify me in your presence with the glory I had with you before the world began.

6 "I have revealed you[a] to those whom you gave me out of the world. They were yours; you gave them to me and they have obeyed your word. 7 Now they know that everything you have given me comes from you. 8 For I gave them the words you gave me and they accepted them. They knew with certainty that I came from you, and they believed that you sent me. 9 I pray for them. I am not praying for the world, but for those you have given me, for they are yours. 10 All I have is yours, and all you have is mine. And glory has come to me through them. 11 I will remain in the world no longer, but they are still in the world, and I am coming to you. Holy Father, protect them by the power of your name — the name you gave me — so that they may be one as we are one. 12 While I was with them, I protected them and kept them safe by that name you gave me. None has been lost except the one doomed to destruction so that Scripture would be fulfilled.

13 "I am coming to you now, but I say these things while I am still in the world, so that they may have the full measure of my joy within them. 14 I have given them your word and the world has hated them, for they are not of the world any more than I am of the world. 15 My prayer is not that you take them out of the world but that you protect them from the evil one. 16 They are not of the world, even as I am not of it. 17 Sanctify[b] them by the truth; your word is truth. 18 As you sent me into the world, I have sent them into the world. 19 For them I sanctify myself, that they too may be truly sanctified.

20 "My prayer is not for them alone. I pray also for those who will believe in me through their message, 21 that all of them may be one, Father, just as you are in me and I am in you. May they also be in us so that the world may believe that you have sent me. 22 I have given them the glory that you gave me, that they may be one as we are one: 23 I in them and you in me. May they be brought to complete unity to let the world know that you sent me and have loved them even as you have loved me.

24 "Father, I want those you have given me to be with me where I am, and to see my glory, the glory you have given me because you loved me before the creation of the world.

25 "Righteous Father, though the world does not know you, I know you, and they know that you have sent me. 26 I have made you known to them, and will continue to make you known in order that the love you have for me may be in them and that I myself may be in them."

[a]Greek "your name"; also in verse 26.   [b]Greek "hagiazo" ("set apart for sacred use" or "make holy"); also in verse 19.

157. CHRIST'S AGONY IN THE GARDEN OF GETHSEMANE

Thursday, April 6, about midnight

Matt. 26:36-46	Mark 14:32-42	Luke 22:40-46	John 18:1
			1 When he had finished praying, Jesus left with his disciples and crossed the Kidron Valley. On the other side there was an olive grove,
36 Then Jesus went with his disciples to a place called Gethsemane, and he said to them, "Sit here while I go over there and pray." 37 He took Peter and the two sons of Zebedee along with him, and he	32 They went to a place called Gethsemane, and Jesus said to his disciples, "Sit here while I pray." 33 He took Peter, James and John along with him,	40 On reaching the place, he said to them,	and he and his disciples went into it.
began to be sorrowful and troubled. 38 Then he said to them, "My soul is overwhelmed with sorrow to the point of death. Stay here and keep watch with me."	and he began to be deeply distressed and troubled. 34 "My soul is overwhelmed with sorrow to the point of death," he said to them. "Stay here and keep watch."	"Pray that you will not fall into temptation."	
39 Going a little farther, he fell with his face	35 Going a little farther, he fell	41 He withdrew about a stone's throw beyond them,	

251

Matt. 26	Mark 14	Luke 22
to the ground and prayed, "My Father, if it is possible, may this cup be taken from me.	to the ground and prayed that if possible the hour might pass from him. 36 "*Abba*,[a] Father," he said, "everything is possible for you.	knelt down and prayed,
		42 "Father, if you are willing, take this cup from me; yet not my will, but yours be done."
Yet not as I will, but as you will."	Take this cup from me. Yet not what I will, but what you will."	
		43 An angel from heaven appeared

to him and strengthened him. 44 And being in anguish, he prayed more earnestly, and his sweat was like drops of blood falling to the ground.[b]

Matt. 26	Mark 14	Luke 22
		45 When he rose from prayer and went back to the
40 Then he returned to his disciples and found them sleeping.	37 Then he returned to his disciples and found them sleeping.	disciples, he found them asleep, exhausted from sorrow.
	"Simon," he said to Peter, "are you asleep?	
"Could you men not keep watch with me for	Could you not keep watch for	46 "Why are you sleeping?" he asked them. "Get up
one hour?" he asked Peter. 41 "Watch and pray so that you will not fall into temptation. The spirit is willing, but the body is weak."	one hour? 38 Watch and pray so that you will not fall into temptation. The spirit is willing, but the body is weak."	and pray so that you will not fall into temptation."
42 He went away a second time and prayed,	39 Once more he went away and prayed the same thing.	
"My Father, if it is not possible for this cup to be taken away unless I drink it, may your		

Matt. 26	Mark 14
will be done."	
43 When he came back, he again found them sleeping, because their eyes were heavy.	40 When he came back, he again found them sleeping, because their eyes were heavy. They did not know what to say to him.
44 So he left them and went away once more and prayed the third time, saying the same thing.	
45 Then he returned to the disciples	41 Returning the third time,
and	
said to them, "Are you still sleeping and resting?	he said to them, "Are you still sleeping and resting? Enough! The
Look, the hour is near, and the Son of Man is betrayed into the hands of sinners.	hour has come. Look, the Son of Man is betrayed into the hands of sinners. 42 Rise!
46 Rise, let us go! Here comes my betrayer!"	Let us go! Here comes my betrayer!"

aAramaic for "Father". bSome early manuscripts do not have verses 43 and 44.

PART XII

CHRIST'S CROWNING SACRIFICE

FRIDAY AND SATURDAY, APRIL 7-8, A.D. 30

158. JESUS IS BETRAYED, ARRESTED AND FORSAKEN

The Garden of Gethsemane, Friday, April 7,
just after Thursday midnight

Matt. 26:47-56	Mark 14:43-52	Luke 22:47-53	John 18:2-12a
47 While he was still speaking, Judas, one of the Twelve, arrived. With him was	43 Just as he was speaking, Judas, one of the Twelve, appeared. With him was a crowd armed with swords and clubs,	47 While he was still speaking a crowd came up, and the man who was called Judas, one of the Twelve, was	2 Now Judas, who betrayed him, knew the place, because Jesus had often met there with his disciples. 3 So Judas
a large crowd		leading	came to the grove, guiding a detachment of soldiers and some officials
armed with swords and clubs, sent from the chief priests and the elders of the people.	sent from the chief priests, the teachers of the law, and the elders.	them.	from the chief priests and Pharisees. They were carrying torches, lanterns and weapons.
48 Now the betrayer had arranged a signal with them: "The one I kiss is the man;	44 Now the betrayer had arranged a signal with them: "The one I kiss is the man; arrest him		

254

Matt. 26	Mark 14	Luke 22	John 18
arrest him." 49 Going at once to Jesus, Judas said,	and lead him away under guard." 45 Going at once to Jesus, Judas said,	He approached Jesus to kiss him, 48 but	
"Greetings, Rabbi!" and kissed him.	"Rabbi!" and kissed him.		
			4 Jesus, knowing all that was

going to happen to him, went out and asked them, "Who is it you want?"
5 "Jesus of Nazareth," they replied.
"I am he," Jesus said. 6 When Jesus said, "I am he," they drew back and fell to the ground.
7 Again he asked them, "Who is it you want?"
And they said, "Jesus of Nazareth."
8 "I told you that I am he," Jesus answered. "If you are looking for me, then let these men go." 9 This happened so that the words he had spoken would be fulfilled: "I have not lost one of those you gave me."[a] 5b (And

Matt. 26	Mark 14	Luke 22	John 18
			Judas the traitor was standing there with them.)
50 Jesus replied,		Jesus asked him, "Judas, are you betraying the Son of Man with a kiss?"	
"Friend, do what you came for."[b] Then the men stepped forward, seized Jesus and arrested him.	46 The men seized Jesus and arrested him.		
		49 When Jesus' followers saw what was going to happen, they said, "Lord, should we strike with our swords?" 50 And	10 Then
51 With that, one of Jesus' companions reached for his sword, drew it out and struck the servant of the high priest, cutting off his ear.	47 Then one of those standing near drew his sword and struck the servant of the high priest, cutting off his ear.	one of them struck the servant of the high priest, cutting off his right ear.	Simon Peter, who had a sword, drew it and struck the high priest's servant, cutting off his right ear. (The

Matt. 26	Mark 14	Luke 22	John 18
			servant's name was Malchus.)
		51 But Jesus answered, "No more of this!" And he touched the man's ear and healed him.	11 Jesus commanded Peter,
52 "Put your sword back in its place," Jesus said to him, "for all who draw the sword will die by the sword. 53 Do you think I cannot call on my Father, and he will at once put at my disposal more than twelve legions of angels? 54 But how then would the Scriptures be fulfilled that say it must happen in this way?"			"Put your sword away!
			Shall I not drink the cup the Father has given me?"
		52 Then Jesus said to the chief priests, the officers of the temple guard, and the elders, who had come for him, "Am I leading a rebellion, that you have come with swords	
55 At that time Jesus said to the crowd, "Am I leading a rebellion, that you have come out with swords and clubs to capture me? Every day I sat in the temple courts teaching,	48 "Am I leading a rebellion," said Jesus, "that you have come out with swords and clubs to capture me? 49 Every day I was with you, teaching in	and clubs? 53 Every day I was with you in the temple courts,	

Matt. 26	Mark 14	Luke 22	John 18
and you did not arrest me.	the temple courts, and you did not arrest me.	and you did not lay a hand on me. But this is your hour—when darkness reigns."	
56 This* has all taken place that the writings of the prophets might be fulfil-led."	But the Scriptures must be fulfilled."		
			12 Then the detachment of soldiers with its commander and the Jewish officials arrested Jesus.
Then all the disciples deserted him and fled.	50 Then everyone deserted him and fled.		
	51 A young man, wearing nothing		

but a linen garment, was following Jesus. When they seized him, 52 he fled naked, leaving his garment behind.

aJohn 6:39.   bOr "Friend, why have you come?"

159. JESUS IS FIRST EXAMINED BY ANNAS, THE FORMER HIGH PRIEST

Jerusalem. Friday, April 7, probably before 1 a.m.

Luke 22:54a	John 18:12b–14,19–23
54 Then seizing him, they led him away and took him into the house of the high priest.	
	12b They bound him

*The NIV reads "But this". To avoid an awkward connection in the composite narrative, the conjunction has been omitted.

| | | 13 and brought him |
| | | first to Annas, |

who was the father-in-law of Caiaphas, the high priest that year. 14 Caiaphas was the one who had advised the Jews that it would be good if one man died for the people.

19 Meanwhile, the high priest* questioned Jesus about his disciples and his teaching.

20 "I have spoken openly to the world," Jesus replied. "I always taught in synagogues or at the temple, where all the Jews come together. I said nothing in secret. 21 Why question me? Ask those who heard me. Surely they know what I said."

22 When Jesus said this, one of the officials nearby struck him in the face. "Is that any way to answer the high priest?" he demanded.

23 "If I said something wrong," Jesus replied, "testify as to what is wrong. But if I spoke the truth, why did you strike me?"

160. PETER AND ANOTHER DISCIPLE (PROBABLY JOHN) GAIN ADMISSION TO THE COURTYARD OF THE HIGH PRIEST'S RESIDENCE

Jerusalem. Friday, April 7, probably about 1 a.m.

Matt. 26:58	Mark 14:54	Luke 22:54b-55	John 18:15-18
			15 Simon Peter and another disciple were following Jesus.
58 But Peter followed him at a distance,	54 Peter followed him at a distance,	54b Peter followed at a distance.	
right up to the courtyard of the high priest.			Because this disciple was known to the high priest, he went with Jesus into the high priest's courtyard, 16 but Peter had to wait

outside at the door. The other disciple, who was known to the high priest, came back, spoke to the girl on duty there and brought Peter in.

17 "Surely you are not another of this man's disciples?" the girl at the door asked Peter.

---

*This is a respectful reference to the former high priest, Annas, to whom Jesus was sent first, probably while Caiaphas was hastily summoning the members of the Sanhedrin.

Matt. 26	Mark 14	Luke 22	John 18
			He replied, "I am not."
			18 It was cold, and the servants and officials
		55 But when they had kindled a fire in the middle of	
	right in-	the courtyard and had sat down	stood around a fire they had made
	to the courtyard of the high priest. There he	together, Peter	to keep warm. Peter also
He entered and sat down with the guards to see the outcome.	He sat with the guards	sat down with them.	was standing with them,
	and warm- ed himself at the fire.		warming himself.

161. JESUS IS INFORMALLY TRIED AND CONDEMNED BY THE SANHEDRIN

The high priest's council chamber, Jerusalem.
Friday, April 7, about 2-3 a.m.*

Matt. 26:57,59-68	Mark 14:53,55-65	Luke 22:63-65	John 18:24
57 Those who had arrested Jesus took him to	53 They took Jesus to the high priest, and		24 Then Annas sent him, still bound, to
Caiaphas, the high priest, where			Caiaphas the high priest.[a]
the teachers of the law and the elders had assembled.	all the chief priests, elders and teachers of the law came together.		
59 The chief priests and the whole Sanhedrin	55 The chief priests and the whole Sanhedrin		

*The mock trials and subsequent activities of the Sanhedrin were undertaken with utmost haste in the very early morning darkness and the hours of daylight on Friday, so that the execution of Jesus could be accomplished before the Sabbath began at 6 p.m. that day.

Matt. 26   Mark 14

were looking for false evidence against Jesus so that they could put him to death. 60 But they did

not find any, though many false witnesses came forward.

Finally two came forward 61 and

declared, "This fellow said, 'I am able to destroy the

temple of God and

rebuild it in three days.'"

62 Then the high priest stood up and said to Jesus, "Are you not going to answer? What is this testimony that these men are bringing against you?" 63 But Jesus remained silent.
The high priest said to him,

were looking for evidence against Jesus so that they could put him to death, but they did

not find any. 56 Many testified falsely against him, but their statements did not agree.

57 Then some stood up and gave this false testimony against him: 58 "We heard him say, 'I will destroy this man-made

temple and

in three days will build another, not made by man.'" 59 Yet even then their testimony did not agree.

60 Then the high priest stood up before them and asked Jesus, "Are you not going to answer? What is this testimony that these men are bringing against you?" 61 But Jesus remained silent and gave no answer.
Again the high priest asked him, "Are you the Christ,[b] the Son of the Blessed One?"

Matt. 26	Mark 14	Luke 22

"I charge you under oath by the living God: Tell us if you are the Christ, [b] the Son of God."

64 "Yes, it is as you say," Jesus replied. "But

62 "I am," said Jesus. "And

I say to all of you: In the future you will see the Son of Man sitting at the right hand of the Mighty One and coming on the clouds of heaven."

you will see the Son of Man sitting at the right hand of the Mighty One and coming on the clouds of heaven."

65 Then the high priest tore his clothes and said, "He has spoken blasphemy! Why do we need any more witnesses? Look, now you have heard the blasphemy.

63 The high priest tore his clothes. "Why do we need any more witnesses?" he asked. 64 "You have heard the blasphemy.

66 What do you think?"
"He is worthy of death," they answered.

What do you think?"
They all condemned him as worthy of death.

63 The men who were guarding Jesus began mocking and beating him.

65b And the guards took him and beat him.

67 Then they

65 Then some began to

spit in his face

spit at him;

they blindfolded him,

64 They blindfolded him

and struck him with their fists. Others slapped him 68 and said, "Prophesy to

struck him with their fists, and said, "Prophesy!"

and demanded, "Prophesy!

Matt. 26	Luke 22
us, Christ.[b] **Who hit you?"**	you?" Who hit
	65 And they said many other insulting things to him.

[a]Or "(Now Annas had sent him, still bound, to Caiaphas the high priest.)"
[b]Or "Messiah".

162. PETER'S TRIPLE DENIAL OF CHRIST

Courtyard of the high priest's residence, Jerusalem.
Friday, April 7, about 3—4.30 a.m.

A. THE FIRST DENIAL

Matt. 26:69-71a	Mark 14:66-68	Luke 22:56-57
69 Now Peter was sitting out in the courtyard, and a servant girl came to him.	**66 While Peter was below in the courtyard, one of the servant girls of the high priest came by. 67 When she saw Peter warming himself, she looked closely at**	
		56 A s e r v a n t
		g i r l saw
	him.	him seated there in the firelight.
"You also were with	**"You also were with that Naza- rene,**	She looked close- ly at him and said, "This man was with him."
Jesus of Galilee," she said.	Jesus," she said.	57 But he de- nied it.
70 But he denied it before them all.	68 But he de- nied it.	
		"Woman, I don't know him,"
"I don't know	**"I don't know or under- stand**	he said.

262

Matt. 26	Mark 14
what you're talk-ing about," he said. **71 Then he went** out to the gate-way,	what you're talking about," he said, and went **out into the entryway.**[a]

[a]Some early manuscripts "entryway and the rooster crowed".

B THE SECOND DENIAL

Matt. 26:71b-72	Mark 14:69-70a	Luke 22:58	John 18:25
		58 A little lat-er	
71b where an-other girl saw him and said **to the people there, "This fellow was with Jesus of Nazareth."** *	**69 When the ser-vant girl saw him there, she said again** to those standing around, "This fellow is one of them."	someone else saw him and said, "You also are one of them."	
			25 As Simon Pe-ter stood warming himself, he was asked, "Surely you are not another of his disciples?"
72 He denied it again, with an oath: "I don't know the man!"	70 Again he de-nied it.	"Man, I am not!" Peter replied.	He denied it, saying, "I am not."

---

*It is to be noted that Matthew attributes this statement, not to the maid who first recognized Peter (Mark 14:66-69), but to another (cf. Luke 22:58). Such apparent discrepancies are only to be expected when one reflects that the remark of the first maid would naturally result in Peter being recognized and chal-lenged by others also. This, indeed, is clearly indicated by all the Gospel narratives comprising this section.

C. THE THIRD DENIAL

Matt. 26:73-75	Mark 14:70b-72	Luke 22:59-62	John 18:26-27
73 After a little while, those standing there **went up to Peter and said, "Surely you are one of them, for** your **accent gives you away."**	70b After a little while, those **standing near** said to Peter, "Surely you are one of them, for **you are a Galilean."**	59 About an hour later another asserted, "Certainly this fellow was with him, for he is a Galilean."	
		60 Peter replied, "Man, I don't know what you're talking about!"	26 One of the high priest's servants, a relative of the man whose ear Peter had cut off, challenged him, "Didn't I see you with him in the olive grove?"
74 Then he began to call down curses on himself and he swore to them, "I don't know the man!"	71 He began to call down curses on himself, and he swore to them, **"I don't know this man you're talking about."**		27 Again Peter denied it, and
Immediately a rooster crowed.	72 Immediately the rooster crowed the second time.[a]	**Just as he was speaking,** the rooster crowed.	at that moment a **rooster began to crow.**
		61 The Lord turned and looked straight at Peter. Then Peter remembered the word the Lord had spoken to him: "Before the	
75 Then Peter remembered the word Jesus had spoken: "Before	Then Peter remembered the word Jesus had spoken to him: "Before the	him: "Before the	

264

Matt. 26	Mark 14	Luke 22
the rooster crows, you will disown me three times." And he went outside and wept bitterly.	rooster crows twice[b] you will disown me three times." And he broke down and wept.	rooster crows today, you will disown me three times." 62 And he went outside and wept bitterly.*

[a]Some early manuscripts do not have "the second time".   [b]Some early manuscripts do not have "twice".

163. CHRIST'S FORMAL CONDEMNATION BY THE SANHEDRIN

Jerusalem. Friday, April 7, before 5 a.m.

Matt. 27:1-2	Mark 15:1	Luke 22:66—23:1	John 18:28a
1 Early in the morning, all the chief priests and the elders of the people came to the decision to put Jesus to death. 2 They bound him,	1 Very early in the morning, the chief priests, with the elders, the teachers of the law and the whole Sanhedrin, reached a decision. They bound Jesus,	66 At daybreak the council of the elders of the people, both the chief priests and teachers of the law, met together,	and Jesus was led before

them. 67 "If you are the Christ,[a]" they said, "tell us."
Jesus answered, "If I tell you, you will not believe me, 68 and if I asked you, you would not answer. 69 But from now on, the Son of Man will

*Incidents recorded in sections 162-163 took place about the same time. Peter's third denial occurred while the Sanhedrin was concluding the final Jewish trial of Jesus (sec. 163). Following the Sanhedrin's formal condemnation of Jesus, He was being led from the council chamber out across the courtyard just after Peter had vehemently disowned him. Passing by at that moment, to appear before Pilate, the Roman governor, Jesus "turned and looked straight at Peter" (Luke 22:61, sec. 162).

Matt. 27	Mark 15	Luke 22-23	John 18

| | | be seated at the right hand of the mighty God." | |

70 They all asked, "Are you then the Son of God?"
He replied, "You are right in saying I am."
71 Then they said, "Why do we need any more testimony? We have heard it from his own lips."

		1 Then the whole assembly rose and	28 Then the Jews
led him away and handed him over to Pilate, the governor.	led him away and handed him over to Pilate.	led him off to Pilate.	led Jesus from Caiaphas to the palace of the Roman governor.

aOr "Messiah".

164. THE REMORSE AND SUICIDE OF JUDAS ISCARIOT

Jerusalem. Friday morning, April 7.

Matt. 27:3-10

3 When Judas, who had betrayed him, saw that Je-		

sus was condemned, he was seized with remorse and returned the thirty silver coins to the chief priests and the elders. 4 "I have sinned," he said, "for I have betrayed innocent blood."

"What is that to us?" they replied. "That's your responsibility."

5 So Judas threw the money into the temple and left. Then he went away and hanged himself.

6 The chief priests picked up the coins and said, "It is against the law to put this into the treasury, since it is blood money." 7 So they decided to use the money to buy the potter's field as a burial place for foreigners. 8 That is why it has been called the Field of Blood to this day. 9 Then what was spoken by Jeremiah the prophet was fulfilled: "They took the thirty silver coins, the price set on him by the people of Israel, 10 and they used them to buy the potter's field, as the Lord commanded me."a

aZech. 11:12,13; Jer. 32:6-9.

165. JESUS BEFORE PILATE THE FIRST TIME

Jerusalem. Friday, April 7, about 5 a.m.*

Matt. 27:11-14	Mark 15:2-5	Luke 23:2-7	John 18:28b-38
11 **Meanwhile** Jesus stood before the governor, and			28b By now **it was early morning, and**

to avoid ceremonial uncleanness the Jews did not enter the palace; they wanted to be able to eat the Passover. 29 So Pilate came out to them and asked, "What charges are you bringing against this man?"
30 "If he were not a criminal," they replied, "we would not have **handed him over to you."**

		2 **And they began to accuse him, saying, "We have found this man subverting our nation. He opposes payment of taxes to Caesar and claims to be Christ,[a] a king."**	
the governor asked him, "Are you the king of the Jews?" "Yes, it is as you say," Jesus replied.	2 "Are you the king of the Jews?" asked Pilate. "Yes, it is as you say," Jesus replied.	3 So Pilate asked Jesus, "Are you the king of the Jews?" "Yes, it is as you say," Jesus replied.	
12 **When he was accused by the chief priests and the elders, he gave no answer. 13 Then Pilate asked him,**	3 The chief priests accused him of many things. 4 So again Pilate asked him, "Aren't you going to answer? See how many things		
"Don't you hear how many things	how many things		

---

*Probably by sending an urgent message to Pilate that they had seized a dangerous insurrectionist, the Jewish leaders induced the Roman governor to appear at a very early morning hour.

Matt. 27	Mark 15	Luke 23	John 18

they are accusing you of?" **14 But Jesus made no reply, not even to a single charge— to the great amazement of the governor.**

they are accusing you of."

5 But Jesus still made no reply,

and Pilate was amazed.

31 Pilate said, "Take him yourselves and judge him by your own law."

"But we have no right to execute anyone," the Jews objected. **32 This happened so that the words Jesus had spoken indicating the kind of death he was going to die would be fulfilled.**

33 Pilate then went back inside the palace, summoned Jesus and asked him, "Are you the king of the Jews?"

34 "Is that your own idea," Jesus asked, "or did others talk to you about me?"

35 "Do you think I am a Jew?" Pilate replied. "It was your people and your chief priests who handed you over to me. What is it you have done?"

36 Jesus said, "My kingdom is not of this world. If it were, my servants would fight to prevent my arrest by the Jews. But now my kingdom is from another place."

37 "You are a king, then!" said Pilate.

Jesus answered, "You are right in saying I am a king. In fact, for this reason I was born, and for this I came into the world, to testify to the truth. Everyone on the side of truth listens to me."

38 "What is truth?" Pilate asked. With this he went out again to the Jews and

4 Then Pilate announced to the chief priests and the crowd, "I find no basis for a charge against this man."

said, "I find no basis for a charge against him.

5 But they insisted, "He stirs up the people all over Judea[b] by his teaching. He started in Galilee and has come all the way here."

6 On hearing this, Pilate asked if the man was a Galilean. 7 When he learned that Jesus was under Herod's jurisdiction, he sent him to Herod, who was also in Jerusalem at that time.

[a]Or "Messiah".   [b]Or "over the land of the Jews".

166. JESUS BEFORE HEROD ANTIPAS

Jerusalem. Friday, April 7, before 6 a.m.

Luke 23:8-12

8 When Herod saw Jesus, he was greatly pleased, because for a long time he had been wanting to see him. From what he had heard about him, he hoped to see him perform some miracle. 9 He plied him with many questions, but Jesus gave him no answer. 10 The chief priests and the teachers of the law were standing there, vehemently accusing him. 11 Then Herod and his soldiers ridiculed and mocked him. Dressing him in an elegant robe, they sent him back to Pilate. 12 That day Herod and Pilate became friends — before this they had been enemies.

167. JESUS BEFORE PILATE THE SECOND TIME

Jerusalem. Friday, April 7, about 6 a.m.

Matt. 27:15-31   Mark 15:6-20   Luke 23:13-25   John 18:39—19:16a

13 Pilate called together the chief priests, the rulers and the people, 14 and said to them, "You brought me this man as one who was inciting the people to rebellion. I have examined him in your presence and have found no basis for your charges against him. 15 Neither has Herod, for he sent him back to us; as you can see, he has done nothing to deserve death. 16 Therefore, I will punish him and then release him.[a]"

19 While Pilate was sitting on the judge's seat, his wife sent him this message: "Don't have anything to do with that innocent man, for I have suffered a great deal today in a dream because of him."

15 Now it was the governor's custom at the Feast to release a prisoner chosen by the crowd. 16 At that time they had a notorious prisoner, called Barabbas.	6 Now it was the custom at the Feast to release a prisoner whom the people requested. 7 A man called Barabbas was in prison		39 But it is your custom for me to release to you one prisoner at the time of the Passover.

Matt. 27	Mark 15	Luke 23	John 18
	with the insurrectionists who had committed murder in the uprising.	**19 (Barabbas had been thrown into prison for an insurrection in the city, and for murder.)**	
17 So when the crowd had gathered, Pilate asked them, **"Which one do you want me to release to you: Barabbas, or Jesus who is called Christ?"**	**8 The crowd came up and asked Pilate to do for them what he usually did.**		
18 For he knew it was out of envy that they had handed Jesus over to him.	**9 "Do you want me to release to you the king of the Jews?" asked Pilate, 10 knowing it was out of envy that the chief priests had handed Jesus over to him.**		Do you want me to release 'the king of the Jews'?"
20 But the chief priests and the elders persuaded the crowd to ask for **Barabbas and to have Jesus executed.** **21 "Which of the two do you want me to release to you?" asked the governor.**	11 But the chief priests stirred up the crowd **to have Pilate release** Barabbas instead.		
"Barabbas," they answered. 22 "What shall I do, then, with Jesus who is	**12 "What shall I do, then, with the** one you call the	**18 With one voice they cried out, "Away with this man! Release Barabbas to us!"**	40 They shouted back, "No, not him! Give us Barabbas!" Now Barabbas had taken part in a rebellion.

Matt. 27	Mark 15	Luke 23

called Christ?" Pilate asked. They all answered, "Crucify him!" 23 "Why? What crime has he committed?" asked Pilate. But they shouted all the louder, "Crucify him!" | king of the Jews?" Pilate asked them. 13 "Crucify him!" they shouted. 14 "Why? What crime has he committed?" asked Pilate. But they shouted all the louder, "Crucify him!"

20 Wanting to release Jesus, Pilate appealed to

them again. 21 But they kept shouting, "Crucify him! Crucify him!" 22 For the third time he spoke to them: "Why? What crime has this man committed? I have found in him no grounds for the death penalty. Therefore I will have him punished and then release him."

23 But with loud shouts they insistently demanded that he be crucified, and their shouts prevailed.

24 When Pilate saw that he was getting nowhere, but that instead an uproar was starting, he

24 So Pilate

decided to grant their demand. 25 He

took water and washed his hands in front of the crowd. "I am innocent of this man's blood," he said. "It is your responsibility!"

25 All the people answered, "Let his blood be on us and on our children!" 26 Then

15 Wanting to satisfy the crowd, Pilate released Barabbas

he released Barabbas to them.

to them.

released the man who had been thrown into prison for insurrection and murder,

271

Matt. 27	Mark 15	Luke 23	John 19
But he had Jesus flogged, and handed him over to be crucified.	He had Jesus flogged, and handed him over to be crucified.	the one they asked for, and	1 Then Pilate took Jesus and had him flogged.
27 Then the governor's soldiers took Jesus into the Praetorium	16 The soldiers led Jesus away into the palace (that is, the Praetorium)		
and gathered the whole company of soldiers around him. 28 They stripped him and put a scarlet robe on him, 29 and then wove a crown of thorns and set it on his head. They put a staff in his right hand and knelt in front of him and mocked him.	and called together the whole company of soldiers. 17 They put a purple robe on him, then wove a crown of thorns and set it on him. 19b Falling on their knees, they worshiped him. 18 And they		2 The soldiers twisted together a crown of thorns and put it on his head. They clothed him in a purple robe 3 and went up to him again and again, saying, "Hail, O king of the Jews!"
"Hail, King of the Jews!" they said. 30 They spit on him, and took the staff and struck him on the head again and again.	began to call out to him, "Hail, King of the Jews!" 19 Again and again they struck him on the head with a staff and spit on him.		And they struck him in the face.

4 Once more Pilate came out and said to the Jews, "Look, I am bringing him out to you to let you know that I find no basis for a charge against him." 5 When Jesus came out wearing the crown of thorns and the purple robe, Pilate said to them, "Here is the man!"

6 As soon as the chief priests and their officials saw him, they shouted, "Crucify! Crucify!"

But Pilate answered, "You take him and crucify him. As for me, I find no basis for a charge against him."

Matt. 27	Mark 15	Luke 23	John 19

7 The Jews insisted, "We have a law, and according to that law he must die, because he claimed to be the Son of God."

8 When Pilate heard this, he was even more afraid, 9 and he went back inside the palace. "Where do you come from?" he asked Jesus, but Jesus gave him no answer. 10 "Do you refuse to speak to me?" Pilate said. "Don't you realize I have power either to free you or to crucify you?"

11 Jesus answered, "You would have no power over me if it were not given to you from above. Therefore the one who handed me over to you is guilty of a greater sin."

12 From then on, Pilate tried to set Jesus free, but the Jews kept shouting, "If you let this man go, you are no friend of Caesar. Anyone who claims to be a king opposes Caesar."

13 When Pilate heard this, he brought Jesus out and sat down on the judge's seat at a place known as The Stone Pavement (which in Aramaic is Gabbatha). 14 It was the day of Preparation of Passover Week, about the sixth hour.*

"Here is your king," Pilate said to the Jews.

15 But they shouted, "Take him away! Take him away! Crucify him!"

"Shall I crucify your king?" Pilate asked.

Matt. 27	Mark 15	Luke 23	John 19
			"We have no king but Caesar," the chief priests answered.
		surrendered Jesus to their will.	16 Finally Pilate handed him over to them to be crucified.
31 After they had mocked him, they took off the robe and put his own clothes on him. Then they led **him away to crucify him.**	20 And when they had mocked him, they took off the purple robe and put his own clothes on him. Then they led him out to crucify him.		

ᵃSome manuscripts "him. 17 Now he was obliged to release one man to them at the Feast".

---

*The "sixth hour" was 6 a.m. John, who wrote in Asia Minor long after the destruction of Jerusalem, apparently used Graeco-Roman time throughout his Gospel; see the footnote on page 25.

273

168. JESUS ON THE WAY TO CALVARY

Jerusalem. Friday, April 7, about 8 a.m.

Matt. 27:32	Mark 15:21	Luke 23:26-32	John 19:16b-17a
			16b So the soldiers took charge of Jesus.
		26 As they led him away,	
32 As they were going out, they met a man from Cyrene, named Simon, and they forced him to carry the cross.	21 A certain man from Cyrene, Simon, the father of Alexander and Rufus, was passing by on his way in from the country, and they forced him to carry the cross.	they seized Simon from Cyrene, who was on his way in from the country, and put the cross on him and made him carry it behind Jesus. 27 A large number of people	17 Carrying his own cross,

followed him, including women who mourned and wailed for him. 28 Jesus turned and said to them, "Daughters of Jerusalem, do not weep for me; weep for yourselves and for your children. 29 For the time will come when you will say, 'Blessed are the barren women, the wombs that never bore and the breasts that never nursed!' 30 Then

"'they will say to the mountains, "Fall on us!"

and to the hills, "Cover us!"' '

31 For if men do these things when the tree is green, what will happen when it is dry?"

32 Two other men, both criminals, were also led out with him to be executed.

169. THE CRUCIFIXION OF JESUS

Jerusalem. Friday, April 7, from 9 a.m. to 3 p.m.

Matt. 27:33-56	Mark 15:22-41	Luke 23:33-49	John 19:17b-37
33 They came to a place called Golgotha	22 They brought Jesus to the place called Golgotha	33 When they came to the place	17b he went out to The Place of the Skull

Matt. 27	Mark 15	Luke 23	John 19
(which means The Place of the Skull).	(which **means The Place of the Skull).**	called The Skull,	**(which in Aramaic** is cal-led Golgotha).
34 There they offered him wine to drink, mixed with gall;	23 Then they of-fered him wine mixed with **myrrh,**		
but after tasting it, he re-fused to drink it.	but he did not take it.	there they	
	24 And they		
	cru-cified him. 27 They crucified	cru-**cified him, along with the criminals**	18 Here they crucified him,
38 Two robbers were crucified with him, one on his right and one on his left.	**two robbers** with him, one on his right and one on his left.a	**— one on his right,** **the other on his left.**	and with him two others — one on each side and Jesus in the middle.
	25 It was the third hour* when they crucified him.	38 There was a written notice	
	26 The written notice **of the charge against him**		**19 Pilate had a notice prepared**
			and fastened
37 Above his head they placed the written charge against him: THIS IS JESUS, THE KING OF THE JEWS.	read: THE KING OF THE JEWS.	**above him,** which read: THIS IS THE KING OF THE JEWS.	**to the cross. It read, JESUS OF NAZA-RETH, THE KING OF THE JEWS. 20 Many of the Jews read this**

sign, for the place where Jesus was crucified was near the city, and the sign was written in Aramaic, Latin and Greek. 21 The chief priests of the Jews protested to Pilate, "Do not write 'The King of the Jews,' but that this man claimed to be king of the Jews."

22 Pilate answered, "What I have written, I have written."

		34 Jesus said, "Father, forgive them, for they do not know what they	

---

*That is, 9 a.m., Jewish time, reckoned from 6 a.m.

Matt. 27	Mark 15	Luke 23	John 19
		are doing.[nb]	
35 When they had crucified him, they divided up his clothes	24b Dividing up his clothes,	And they divided up his clothes	23 When the soldiers crucified Jesus, they took his clothes, dividing them into four shares, one for each of them, with the undergarment remaining. This garment was seamless, woven in one piece from top to bottom.
	they cast lots to see what each would		24 "Let's not tear it," they said to one another. "Let's decide by
by casting lots.[c]	get.	by casting lots.	lot who will get it."

This happened that the Scripture might be fulfilled which said,
"They divided my garments among them
and cast lots for my clothing."

Matt. 27	Mark 15	Luke 23	John 19
			So this is what the soldiers did.
36 And sitting down, they kept watch over him there.			
		35 The people stood watching, and the rulers	
39 Those who passed by hurled insults at him, shaking their heads 40 and saying, "You who are going to destroy the temple and build it in three	29 Those who passed by hurled insults at him, shaking their heads and saying, "So! You who are going to destroy the temple and build it in three	even sneered at him.	
days, save yourself! Come down from the cross, if you are the Son of God!"	days, 30 come down from the cross and save yourself!"		
41 In the same way the chief	31 In the same way the chief		

276

Matt. 27	Mark 15	Luke 23
priests, the teachers of the law and the elders mocked him. 42 "He saved others," they said, "but he can't save himself!	priests and the teachers of the law mocked **him among themselves. "He saved others," they said, "but he can't save himself! 32 Let**	They said, "He saved others; let him save himself if he is the Christ[d] of God, the Chosen One."
He's the king of Israel! Let him come down now from the cross, and we will **believe in him.** 43 **He trusts in God. Let God rescue him now if he wants him, for he said, 'I am the Son of God.'"**	this Christ,[d] this King of Israel, come down now from the cross, that we may see and believe."	
		36 **The soldiers also came up and mocked him. They offered him wine vinegar** 37 **and said, "If you are the king of the Jews, save yourself."** 39 **One of the criminals who hung there**
44 In the same way the robbers who were crucified with him also heaped insults on him.	Those crucified **with him also** heaped insults on him.	**hurled insults at him:** "Aren't you the Christ[d]? Save yourself and us!"

40 But the other criminal rebuked him. "Don't you fear God," he said, "since you are under the same sentence? 41 We are punished justly, for we

Matt. 27	Mark 15	Luke 23	John 19

are getting what
our deeds deserve.

But this man has done nothing wrong."
42 Then he said, "Jesus, remember me when you come into your kingdom."
43 Jesus answered him, "I tell you the truth, today you will be
with me in para-
dise."

25 Near the cross
of Jesus stood his
mother, his mother's sister, Mary the wife of Clopas, and Mary of Magdala.
26 When Jesus saw his mother there, and the disciple whom he loved
standing nearby, he said to his mother, "Dear woman, here is your son,"
27 and to the disciple, "Here is your mother." From that time on, this
disciple took her
into his home.

45 From the
sixth hour until
the ninth hour
darkness came
over all the land.

33 At the sixth
hour darkness
came over the
whole land until
the ninth hour.

44 It was now
about the sixth
hour, and darkness
came over the whole
land until the ninth
hour,* 45 for the
sun stopped shin-
ing.

46 About the ninth
hour Jesus cried
out in a loud
voice, *"Eloi,
Eloi,*[e] *lama sa-
bachthani?"* —
which means, "My
God, my God, why
have you forsak-
en me?"
47 When some of
those standing
there heard this,
they said, "He's
calling Elijah."

34 And at the ninth
hour Jesus cried
out in a loud voice,
*"Eloi, Eloi, lama
sabachthani?"* —
which means, "My
God, my God, why
have you forsaken
me?"
35 When some of
those standing near
heard this, they
said, "Listen, he's
calling Elijah."

28 Later, know-
ing that all was
now completed,
and so that the
Scripture would
be fulfilled, Je-

---

*That is, 12 o'clock noon to 3 p.m., Jewish time, reckoned
from 6 a.m.

Matt. 27	Mark 15	Luke 23	John 19
			sus said, "I am thirsty." 29 A jar of wine vinegar was there, so
48 Immediately one of them ran and			they
got a sponge. He filled it with wine vinegar, put it on a stick, and offered it to Jesus to drink.	36 One man ran, filled a sponge with wine vinegar, put it on a stick, **and offered it to Jesus to drink.**		soaked a sponge in it, put the sponge on a stalk of the hyssop plant, and lifted it to Jesus' lips.
49 But the rest said, "Leave him alone. Let's see if Elijah comes to save him."	"Leave him alone now. Let's see if Elijah comes to take him down," he said.		
			30 When he had received the drink, Jesus
50 And when Jesus had cried out again in a loud voice,	37 With a loud cry,	46 Jesus **called out with a loud voice,**	said, "It is finished."
		"Father, into your hands I commit my spirit." When he had said this, he	With that, he
he gave up his spirit.	Jesus breathed his last.	breathed his last.	bowed his head and gave up his spirit.
51 At that moment the curtain of the temple was torn in two from top to bottom. The earth shook and the rocks split.	38 The curtain of the temple was torn in two from top to bottom.	45b And the curtain of the temple was torn in two.	

52 The tombs broke open and the bodies of many holy people who had died were raised to life. 53 They came out of the tombs, and after Jesus' resurrection they went into the holy city and

Matt. 27	Mark 15	Luke 23
appeared to many people. **54 When the centurion and those with him who were** guarding Jesus saw the earthquake and a l l that h a d happened, **they were terrified, and** exclaimed, "Sure-ly h e was the Son[g] of God!"	39 And when the centurion, who stood there **in front** of Jesus, **heard his cry and**[f] **saw how he died,** he said, **"Surely this man was the Son**[g] **of God!"**	47 The centuri-on, seeing what h a d happened, praised God and said, "Surely this was a righteous man."
		48 When all the people who had gathered to wit-ness this sight saw what took place, they beat their breasts and went away. 49 But all those who knew him, including the women who had followed him from Galilee, stood at a dis-tance, watching these things.
55 Many women w e r e t h e r e, watching from a distance. 56 Among them were Mary Magdalene, Mary the mother of James and Joseph, and **the mother of Zebedee's sons. 55b They had fol-lowed Jesus from Galilee to care for his needs.**	40 Some women w e r e watching from a distance. **Among them were Mary Magdalene, Mary the mother of James the younger and of Joses, and Salome.** 41 In Galilee t h e s e women had fol-lowed him and cared for his needs.	

Mark 15	John 19
Many other women who had come up with him to Jerusalem were also there.	

31 Now it was the day of Prep-aration, and the next day was to be a special Sabbath. Because the Jews did not want the bodies left on the crosses during the Sabbath, they asked Pilate to have the legs broken and the bodies taken down. **32** The soldiers therefore came and broke the legs of the first man who had been crucified with Jesus, and then those of the other. **33** But when they came to Jesus and found that he was already dead, they did not break his legs. **34** Instead, one of the soldiers pierced Jesus' side with a spear, bringing a sudden flow of blood and water. **35** The man who saw it has given testimony, and his testimony is true. He knows that he tells the truth, and he testifies so that you also may believe. **36** These things happened so that the Scripture would be fulfilled: "Not one of his bones will be broken," **37** and, as another Scripture says, "They will look on the one they have pierced."

aSome manuscripts "left 28 and the scripture was fulfilled which says, 'He was counted with the lawless ones'. bSome early manuscripts do not have this sentence. cA few late manuscripts "lots that the word spoken by the prophet might be fulfilled: 'They divided my garments among themselves and cast lots for my clothing'." dOr "Messiah". eSome manuscripts "Eli, Eli". fSome manuscripts do not have "heard his cry and". gOr "a son".

170. THE BURIAL OF JESUS

Jerusalem. Friday, April 7, before 6 p.m.

Matt. 27:57-61	Mark 15:42-47	Luke 23:50-56a	John 19:38-42
	42 It was Prep-aration Day (that is, the day before the Sabbath). So as evening ap-proached,		
57 As evening approached,			
there came a rich man	**43** Joseph of Arima-	50 Now there was a man	
from Arimathea, named Joseph,	thea,	named Joseph,	
	a prominent member of the Council,	a member of the Council,	

281

Matt. 27	Mark 15	Luke 23	John 19
		a good and upright man, 51 who had not consented to their decision and action. He came from the Judean town of Arimathea and he was waiting for the kingdom of God.	38 Later, Joseph of Arimathea asked Pilate for the body of Jesus.
	who was himself waiting for the kingdom of God,		
who had himself become a disciple of Jesus. 58 Going	went		Now Joseph was a disciple of Jesus, but secretly because he feared the Jews.
	boldly	52 Going	
to Pilate, he asked for Jesus' body,	and asked for Jesus' body. 44 Pilate was surprised to hear that he was already dead. Summoning the centurion, he asked him if Jesus had already died. 45 When he learned from the	to Pilate, he asked for Jesus' body.	
and	centurion that it was so,		
Pilate ordered that it be given to	he gave the body		With Pilate's permission, he came
him.	to Joseph. 46 So Joseph bought some linen cloth,		
59 Joseph took the body,	took down the body,	53 Then he took it down,	and took the body. 39 He was accompanied by Nicodemus, the man who earlier had visited Jesus at night. Nicodemus brought a mixture of myrrh and aloes, about seventy-five pounds.[a]

282

Matt. 27	Mark 15	Luke 23	John 19
			40 Taking Jesus' body, the two of them wrapped it, with the spices,
wrapped it in a	wrapped it in	wrapped	
clean linen cloth,	the linen,	it in linen cloth	**in strips of linen. This was in accordance with Jewish burial customs.**
60 and placed it	and	and placed it in	
in his own new	placed it in a	a tomb	**41 At the place where Jesus was crucified, there was a garden, and**
tomb that he had	tomb		
cut out of the	cut out of		**in the garden a new tomb,***
rock.	rock.	**cut in the rock, one in which no one had yet been laid.**	in which no one had ever been laid.
		54 It was Preparation Day,	**42 Because it was the Jewish day of Preparation**
		and the Sabbath was about to begin.	
			and since the tomb was nearby, they laid Jesus there.
He **rolled a big stone in front of the entrance to the tomb and went away.**	**Then Joseph**** **rolled a** stone against the entrance of the tomb.		
61 Mary Magdalene and the other Mary	**47 Mary Magdalene and Mary the mother of Joses**	55 The women **who had come with Jesus from Galilee**	

---

*Note the additional information given by Matthew (27:60) that it was Joseph's "own new tomb that he had cut out of the rock".

**The NIV reads "he". By specifying "Joseph", the composite narrative is clarified.

Matt. 27	Mark 15	Luke 23
were		followed Joseph and
sitting there across from the tomb.		
	saw where he was laid.	saw the tomb and how his body was laid in it. 56 Then they went home . . .

aGreek "a hundred litrai" (about 34 kilograms).

171. ON THE SABBATH DAY, WHILE THE SANHEDRIN, WITH PILATE'S PERMISSION, SEAL CHRIST'S TOMB AND PLACE A GUARD THERE, THE WOMEN REST

Jerusalem. Saturday, April 8.

Matt. 27:62-66   Luke 23:56c

62 The next day, the one after Preparation Day, the chief priests and the Pharisees went to Pilate. 63 "Sir," they said, "we remember that while he was still alive that deceiver said, 'After three days I will rise again.' 64 So give the order for the tomb to be made secure until the third day. Otherwise, his disciples may come and steal the body and tell the people that he has been raised from the dead. This last deception will be worse than the first."

65 "Take a guard," Pilate answered. "Go, make the tomb as secure as you know how." 66 So they went and made the tomb secure by putting a seal on the stone and posting the guard.

56c But the women* rested on the Sabbath in obedience to the commandment.

*The NIV reads "they". By specifying "the women", the composite narrative is clarified.

172. AT THE CLOSE OF THE SABBATH, THE WOMEN PREPARE SPICES TO ANOINT THE BODY OF JESUS

Jerusalem. Saturday, April 8, after 6 p.m.

Mark 16:1	Luke 23:56b
1 When the Sabbath was over, Mary Magdalene, Mary the mother of James, and Salome bought	
spices	56b and prepared spices and perfumes.
so that they might go to anoint Jesus' body.	

PART XIII

THE RESURRECTION, APPEARANCES
AND ASCENSION OF JESUS

FORTY DAYS — PROBABLY APRIL 9 TO MAY 18, A.D. 30

173. THE EARTHQUAKE, THE ROLLING AWAY OF THE STONE AT THE TOMB, AND THE TERROR OF THE GUARD

Jerusalem. Sunday, April 9, before dawn.

Matt. 28:2-4

2 There was a violent earthquake, for an angel of the Lord came down from heaven and, going to the tomb, rolled back the stone and sat on it. 3 His appearance was like lightning, and his clothes were white as snow. 4 The guards were so afraid of him that they shook and became like dead men.

174. ARRIVING AT THE TOMB EARLY SUNDAY MORNING, MARY MAGDALENE SEES THAT THE STONE HAS BEEN REMOVED FROM THE ENTRANCE, AND SHE HURRIES AWAY TO PETER AND JOHN, REPORTING A GRAVE ROBBERY

Jerusalem. Sunday, April 9, before dawn.

Matt. 28:1		John 20:1-2
1 After the Sabbath, at dawn on the first day of the week, Mary Magdalene and the other Mary* went to look at the tomb.		1 Early on the first day of the week, while it was still dark, Mary of Magdala went to the tomb and

---

*Mary Magdalene evidently arrived at the tomb first (see John 20:1), ahead of "the other Mary", who arrived with Salome (Mark 16:1) and other women (Luke 24:10); see section 175.

John 20

	saw that the stone had been removed

from the entrance. 2 So she came running to Simon Peter and the other disciple, the one Jesus loved, and said, "They have taken the Lord out of the tomb, and we don't know where they have put him!"

175. THE OTHER WOMEN ARRIVE AT THE TOMB, AND AFTER RECEIVING AN ANGELIC MESSAGE OF CHRIST'S RESURRECTION, THEY DEPART QUICKLY TO REPORT THE GOOD NEWS TO HIS DISCIPLES

Jerusalem. Early Sunday morning, April 9.

Matt. 28:5-8	Mark 16:2-8	Luke 24:1-8
	2 Very early on the first day of the week,	1 On the first day of the week, very early in the morning,
	just after s u n r i s e,	
	they were	the wo-men took the spices they had prepared and went
	on their way to the tomb 3 and they asked each other, "Who will roll the stone away from the entrance of the tomb?"	to the tomb.
	4 But when they looked up, they saw that the stone, which was very large, had been rolled away. 5 As they entered the tomb,	2 They found the stone rolled away from the tomb, 3 but when they entered,
		they did not find the body of the Lord Jesus. 4 While they were wondering about this, suddenly

287

Matt. 28	Mark 16	Luke 24
	they saw a young man dressed in a white robe sitting on the right side, and they were alarmed.	two men in clothes that gleamed like lightning stood beside them.* 5 In their fright the women bowed down with their faces to the ground, but the men said to them,
5 The angel said to the women,	6 "Don't be alarmed," he said.	
"Do not be afraid,		
for I know that you are looking for Jesus, who was crucified.	"You are looking for Jesus the Nazarene, who was crucified.	
6 He is not here; he has risen, just as he said.	He has risen! He is not here. See	"Why do you look for the living among the dead? 6 He is not here; he has risen! Remember how he

told you, while he was still with you in Galilee: 7 'The Son of Man must be delivered into the hands of sinful men, be crucified and on the third day be raised again.'"

Matt. 28	Mark 16	Luke 24
Come and see the place where he lay.	the place where they laid him.	
7 Then go quickly and tell his disciples:	7 But go, tell his disciples and Peter,	
'He has risen from the dead and is	'He is	
going ahead of you into Galilee. There you will see him.'	going ahead of you into Galilee. There you will see him, just as he told you.'"	
Now I have told you."		
		8 Then they remembered his words.

*Matthew and Mark mention only one angel.

Matt. 28	Mark 16		
8 So the women hurried away from the tomb, afraid yet filled with joy, and ran to tell his disciples.	**8 Trembling and bewildered, the women went out and** fled from the tomb. **They said nothing to anyone, because they were afraid.**		

176. MEANWHILE, PETER AND JOHN (LEAVING MARY MAGDALENE TO FOLLOW) RUN TO THE TOMB TO VERIFY HER GRAVE ROBBERY REPORT, AND THEY DEPART FROM THE EMPTY TOMB BEWILDERED

Jerusalem. Sunday morning, April 9.

	Luke 24:12	John 20:3-10
	12 Peter, however, got up and ran to the tomb.	**3 So Peter and the other disciple started for the tomb. 4 Both were running,**

but the other disciple outran Peter and reached the tomb first. 5 He bent over and looked in at the strips of linen lying there but did not go in. 6 Then Simon Peter, who was behind him, arrived and went

		into the tomb. He saw the strips of linen lying
	Bending over, he saw the strips of linen lying	**there, 7 as well as the burial cloth that had been around Jesus' head. The cloth was folded up by it-**
	by themselves,	**self, separate from the linen. 8 Finally the other disciple, who had**

reached the tomb first, also went inside. He saw and believed. 9 (They still did not understand from Scripture that Jesus had to rise from the dead.)

	Luke 24	John 20
	and he went away,	10 Then the disciples went back to their homes,
	wondering* what had happened.	

177. WHEN MARY MAGDALENE REACHES THE TOMB SOON AFTER THE DEPARTURE OF PETER AND JOHN, JESUS APPEARS TO HER

Jerusalem. Sunday morning, April 9.

Mark 16:9   John 20:11-17

11 but Mary stood outside the tomb crying. As she wept, she bent over to look into the tomb 12 and saw two angels in white, seated where Jesus' body had been, one at the head and the other at the foot.
13 They asked her, "Woman, why are you crying?"
"They have taken my Lord away," she said, "and I don't know where they have put him." 14 At this, she turned around and saw Jesus standing there, but she did not realize that it was Jesus.
15 "Woman," he said, "why are you crying? Who is it you are looking for?"
Thinking he was the gardener, she said, "Sir, if you have carried him away, tell me where you have put him, and I will get him."

Mark 16:9 — 9 When Jesus rose early on the first day of the week, he appeared first to Mary Magdalene, out of whom he had driven seven demons.

John 20:16-17 — 16 Jesus said to her, "Mary."
She turned toward him and cried out in Aramaic, "Rabboni!" (which means Teacher).
17 Jesus said, "Do not hold on to me, for I have not yet returned to the Father. Go instead to my brothers and tell them, 'I am returning to my Father and your Father, to my God and your God.'"

---

*The NIV reading, "wondering to himself", has been abbreviated for the sake of proper grammatical sequence in the composite narrative.

178. WHILE THE OTHER WOMEN ARE ON THEIR WAY TO TELL THE DISCIPLES ABOUT THE ANGELS' MESSAGE OF CHRIST'S RESURRECTION, HE APPEARS TO THOSE WOMEN ALSO

Near Jerusalem. Sunday morning, April 9.

Matt. 28:9-10

9 Suddenly Jesus met them. "Greetings," he said. They came to him, clasped his feet and worshiped him. 10 Then Jesus said to them, "Do not be afraid. Go and tell my brothers to go to Galilee; there they will see me."

179. THE WOMEN ALL REPORT TO THE DISBELIEVING DISCIPLES THAT JESUS HAS APPEARED TO THEM

Jerusalem or Bethany. Sunday morning, April 9.

Mark 16:10-11	Luke 24:9-11	John 20:18
	9 When they came back from the tomb,	
10 She went and told those		18 Mary of Magdala went to the disciples with the news: "I have seen the Lord!" And she told them that he had said these things to her.
	they told all these things to the Eleven and to all the others.	
who had been with him and who were mourning and weeping.		
	10 It was Mary Magdalene, Joanna, Mary the mother of James, and the others with them who told this to the apostles.	
11 When they heard that Jesus was alive and that she had seen him, they did	11 But they did	

291

Mark 16   Luke 24

| not believe it. | not believe the women, because their words seemed to them like non-sense. |

180. SOME OF THE GUARDS REPORT TO THE SANHEDRIN, WHO BRIBE THEM TO SPREAD A FALSE STORY

Jerusalem. Sunday morning, April 9.

Matt. 28:11-15

11 While the women were on their way, some of the guards went into the city and reported to the chief priests everything that had happened. 12 When the chief priests had met with the elders and devised a plan, they gave the soldiers a large sum of money, 13 telling them, "You are to say, 'His disciples came during the night and stole him away while we were asleep.' 14 If this report gets to the governor, we will satisfy him and keep you out of trouble." 15 So the soldiers took the money and did as they were instructed. And this story has been widely circulated among the Jews to this very day.

181. JESUS APPEARS TO CLEOPAS AND HIS COMPANION ON THE WAY TO EMMAUS

Sunday afternoon, April 9.

Mark 16:12   Luke 24:13-32

13 Now that same day two of them were going to a village called Emmaus, about seven miles[a] from Jerusalem. 14 They were talking with each other about everything that had happened. 15 As they talked and discussed these 12 Afterward things with each Jesus appeared other, Jesus him-

Mark 16	Luke 24
in a different form to two of them while they were walking in the country.	self came up and walked along with them; 16 but they were kept from recognizing him.

17 He asked them, "What are you discussing together as you walk along?" They stood still, their faces downcast. 18 One of them, named Cleopas, asked him, "Are you the only one living in Jerusalem who doesn't know the things that have happened there in these days?"

19 "What things?" he asked.

"About Jesus of Nazareth," they replied. "He was a prophet, powerful in word and deed before God and all the people. 20 The chief priests and our rulers handed him over to be sentenced to death, and they crucified him; 21 but we had hoped that he was the one who was going to redeem Israel. And what is more, it is the third day since all this took place. 22 In addition, some of our women amazed us. They went to the tomb early this morning 23 but didn't find his body. They came and told us that they had seen a vision of angels, who said he was alive. 24 Then some of our companions went to the tomb and found it just as the women had said, but him they did not see."

25 He said to them, "How foolish you are, and how slow of heart to believe all that the prophets have spoken! 26 Did not the Christ[b] have to suffer these things and then enter his glory?" 27 And beginning with Moses and all the Prophets, he explained to them what was said in all the Scriptures concerning himself.

28 As they approached the village to which they were going, Jesus acted as if he were going farther. 29 But they urged him strongly, "Stay with us, for it is nearly evening; the day is almost over." So he went in to stay with them.

30 When he was at the table with them, he took bread, gave thanks, broke it and began to give it to them. 31 Then their eyes were opened and they recognized him, and he disappeared from their sight. 32 They asked each other, "Were not our hearts burning within us while he talked with us on the road and opened the Scriptures to us?"

[a]Greek "sixty stadia" (about 11 kilometers).   [b]Or "Messiah".

182. RETURNING TO JERUSALEM TO REPORT TO THE DISCIPLES, CLEOPAS AND HIS COMPANION ARE INFORMED THAT CHRIST HAS APPEARED TO PETER

Sunday evening, April 9.

Mark 16:13	Luke 24:33-35
13 These returned	33 They got up and returned at once to Jerusalem.

Mark 16	Luke 24
and reported it to the rest; but they did not believe them either.	There they found the Eleven* and those with them, assembled together 34 and saying, "It is true! The Lord has risen and has appeared to Simon." 35 Then the two told what had happened on the way, and how Jesus was recognized by them when he broke the bread.

183. JESUS APPEARS TO THE DISCIPLES WHILE THOMAS IS ABSENT, AND GIVES THEM A COMMISSION — THEY FAIL TO CONVINCE THOMAS

Jerusalem. Sunday evening, April 9.

Mark 16:14	Luke 24:36-43	John 20:19-25
	36 While they were	19 On the evening of that first day of the week, when the disciples were
	still talking about this,	together,
		with the doors locked for fear
14 Later Jesus appeared to the Eleven	Jesus	of the Jews, Jesus
	himself stood among them	came and
as they were eating;		stood among them
	and said to them,	and said, "Peace

*To be exact, there were only ten of the apostles present, for John states (20:24) that Thomas was absent on this occasion. After the suicidal death of Judas, the expression "the Eleven" was evidently used with reference to the apostles as a group, even though all the members of the group might not always be present.

Mark 16	Luke 24	John 20
	"Peace be with you." 37 They were	be with you!"

startled and frightened, thinking they saw a ghost. 38 He said to them,
"Why are you troubled, and why do doubts rise in your minds? 39 Look
at my hands and my feet. It is I myself! Touch me and see; a ghost
does not have flesh and bones, as you see I have."

		40 When he had said this,
he rebuked them for their lack of faith and their stubborn refusal to believe those who had seen him after he had risen.	h e	
	showed them his hands	20 After he said this, he showed them his hands
	and feet.	and side.
	41 And while they still did not be-	

lieve it because of joy and amazement, he asked them, "Do you have
anything here to eat?" 42 They gave him a piece of broiled fish, 43 and he

|||took it and ate it
in their presence.|
|||The dis-
ciples were over-
joyed when they
saw the Lord.|

21 Again Jesus said, "Peace be with you! As the Father has sent me, I am
sending you." 22 And with that he breathed on them and said, "Receive
the Holy Spirit. 23 If you forgive anyone his sins, they are forgiven; if you
do not forgive them, they are not forgiven."

24 Now Thomas (called Didymus), one of the Twelve, was not with the
disciples when Jesus came. 25 When the other disciples told him that they
had seen the Lord, he declared, "Unless I see the nail marks in his hands
and put my finger where the nails were, and put my hand into his side, I
will not believe it."

184. A WEEK LATER, JESUS APPEARS AGAIN TO HIS DISCIPLES, WITH THOMAS PRESENT, AND HE IS CONVINCED THAT JESUS IS ALIVE

Jerusalem. Sunday, April 16.

John 20:26-29

26 A week later his disciples were in the house again, and Thomas was with them. Though the doors were locked, Jesus came and stood among them and said, "Peace be with you!" 27 Then he said to Thomas, "Put your finger here; see my hands. Reach out your hand and put it into my side. Stop doubting and believe."

28 Thomas said to him, "My Lord and my God!"

29 Then Jesus told him, "Because you have seen me, you have believed; blessed are those who have not seen and yet have believed."

185. JESUS APPEARS TO SEVEN OF HIS DISCIPLES AT THE SEA OF GALILEE, AND AFTER A MIRACULOUS CATCH OF FISH, PETER IS TESTED

Probably in early May

John 21:1-23

1 Afterward Jesus appeared again to his disciples by the Sea of Tiberias.[a] It happened this way: 2 Simon Peter, Thomas (called Didymus), Nathanael from Cana in Galilee, the sons of Zebedee, and two other disciples were together. 3 "I'm going out to fish," Simon Peter told them, and they said, "We'll go with you." So they went out and got into the boat, but that night they caught nothing.

4 Early in the morning, Jesus stood on the shore, but the disciples did not realize that it was Jesus.

5 He called out to them, "Friends, haven't you any fish?"

"No," they answered.

6 He said, "Throw your net on the right side of the boat and you will find some." When they did, they were unable to haul the net in because of the large number of fish.

7 Then the disciple whom Jesus loved said to Peter, "It is the Lord!" As soon as Simon Peter heard him say, "It is the Lord," he wrapped his outer garment around him (for he had taken it off) and jumped into the water. 8 The other disciples followed in the boat, towing the net full of fish, for they were not far from shore, about a hundred yards.[b] 9 When they landed, they saw a fire of burning coals there with fish on it, and some bread.

10 Jesus said to them, "Bring some of the fish you have just caught."

John 21

| | | 11 Simon Peter climbed aboard

and dragged the net ashore. It was full of large fish, 153, but even with so many the net was not torn. 12 Jesus said to them, "Come and have breakfast." None of the disciples dared ask him, "Who are you?" They knew it was the Lord. 13 Jesus came, took the bread and gave it to them, and did the same with the fish. 14 This was now the third time Jesus appeared to his disciples after he was raised from the dead.

15 When they had finished eating, Jesus said to Simon Peter, "Simon son of John, do you truly love me more than these?"

"Yes, Lord," he said, "you know that I love* you."

Jesus said, "Feed my lambs."

16 Again Jesus said, "Simon son of John, do you truly love me?"

He answered, "Yes, Lord, you know that I love you."

Jesus said, "Take care of my sheep."

17 The third time he said to him, "Simon son of John, do you love me?" Peter was hurt because Jesus asked him the third time, "Do you love me?" He said, "Lord, you know all things; you know that I love you."

Jesus said, "Feed my sheep. 18 I tell you the truth, when you were younger you dressed yourself and went where you wanted; but when you are old you will stretch out your hands, and someone else will dress you and lead you where you do not want to go." 19 Jesus said this to indicate the kind of death by which Peter would glorify God. Then he said to him, "Follow me!"

20 Peter turned and saw that the disciple whom Jesus loved was following them. (This was the one who had leaned back against Jesus at the supper and had said, "Lord, who is going to betray you?") 21 When Peter saw him, he asked, "Lord, what about him?"

22 Jesus answered, "If I want him to remain alive until I return, what is that to you? You must follow me." 23 Because of this, the rumor spread among the brothers that this disciple would not die. But Jesus did not say that he would not die; he only said, "If I want him to remain alive until I return, what is that to you?"**

ᵃThat is, Sea of Galilee.   ᵇGreek "about two hundred cubits" (about 90 meters).

---

*It should be noted that in this dialogue between Jesus and Peter, two different Greek words are translated "love". The previously boastful Peter (Matt. 26:33), deeply ashamed of his denial of Christ (Matt. 26:69-75), now shrinks from using the same strong word for "love" that Jesus used in testing him.

**Other appearances of Jesus, not recorded in the Gospels, are mentioned in I Corinthians 15:6-7.

186. JESUS AND HIS ELEVEN DISCIPLES MEET BY APPOINTMENT AT A MOUNTAIN IN GALILEE, AND THERE HE GIVES THEM A GREAT COMMISSION

About the middle of May

Matt. 28:16-20   Mark 16:15-18   Luke 24:44-49

16 Then the eleven disciples went to Galilee, to the mountain where Jesus had told them to go. 17 When they saw him, they worshiped him; but some doubted. 18 Then Jesus came to them and said,

15 He said to them,

44 He said to them,

"This is what I told you while I was still with you: Everything must be fulfilled that is written about me in the Law of Moses, the Prophets and the Psalms."

45 Then he opened their minds so they could understand the Scriptures. 46 He told them, "This is what is written: The Christ[a] will suffer and rise from the dead on the third day, 47 and repentance and forgiveness of sins will be preached in his name to all nations, beginning at Jerusalem.

"All authority in heaven and on earth has been given to me.

"Go

48 You are witnesses of these things.

19 Therefore go

into all the world and preach the good news to all creation.

and make disciples of all nations, baptizing them in[b] the name of the Father and of the Son and of the Holy

298

Matt. 28	Mark 16	Luke 24

Spirit, 20 and teaching them to obey everything I have commanded you. And surely I will be with you always, to the very end of the age."

16 Whoever believes and is baptized will be saved, but whoever does not believe will be condemned. 17 And these signs will accompany those who believe: In my name they will drive out demons; they will speak in new tongues; 18 they will pick up snakes with their hands; and when they drink deadly poison, it will not hurt them at all; they will place their hands on sick people, and they will get well."

49 I am going to send you what my Father has promised; but stay in the city until you have been clothed with power from on high."

aOr "Messiah".   bOr "into"; see Acts 8:16; 19:5; Romans 6:3; I Corinthians 1:13; 10:2 and Galatians 3:27.

187. THE ASCENSION OF JESUS

The Mount of Olives, near Jerusalem. About May 18.

Mark 16:19-20	Luke 24:50-53

19 After the Lord Jesus had

50 When he had led them out to the vicinity of Bethany, he lifted up his hands and

spoken to them, he

blessed them. 51 While he was blessing them, he left them and

was taken up into heaven and he sat at the right hand of God.

was taken up into heaven.

Mark 16	Luke 24
	52 Then they wor- shiped him and returned to Jeru- salem with great joy. 53 And they stayed continually at the temple, praising God.*
20 Then the disci- ples went out and	

preached everywhere, and the Lord worked with them and confirmed his word by the signs that accompanied it.[a]

[a]The two most reliable manuscripts do not have Mark 16:9-20.

*A fuller account of Christ's ascension is recorded in Acts 1:6-12.

PART XIV

CONCLUSION

188. THE PURPOSE OF JOHN'S GOSPEL, AND THE PERSONAL TESTIMONY OF THE APOSTLE

John 20:30-31;
1:14b; 16-18;
21:24-25

20:30 Jesus did many other miraculous signs in the presence of his disciples, which are not recorded in this book. **31 But these are written that you may**[a] **believe that Jesus is the Christ, the Son of God, and that by believing you may have life in his name.** **1:14b We have seen his glory, the glory of the one and only Son,**[b] **who came from the Father, full of grace and truth. 16 From the fullness of his grace we have all received one blessing after another. 17 For the law was given through Moses; grace and truth came through Jesus Christ. 18 No one has ever seen God, but God the only**[c] **Son,**[d] **who is at the Father's side, has made him known.**

21:25 Jesus did many other things as well. If every one of them were written down, I suppose that even the whole world would not have room for the books that would be written.

21:24 This is the disciple who testifies to these things and who wrote them down. We know that his testimony is true.

[a]Some manuscripts "may continue to".   [b]Or "the Only Begotten".
[c]Or "but God the only begotten".   [d]Some manuscripts "but the only Son" (or "but the only begotten Son").